P-0766-11
3-2-87
1N

COMPUTER-LITERACY NEEDS ASSESSMENT

COMPUTER-LITERACY NEEDS ASSESSMENT:
A TRAINER'S GUIDE

Ron Zemke
President,
Performance Research Associates

Addison-Wesley Publishing Company, Inc.
Reading, Massachusetts • Menlo Park, California
Don Mills, Ontario • Wokingham, England • Amsterdam
Sydney • Singapore • Tokyo • Mexico City • Bogotá
Santiago • San Juan

Library of Congress Cataloging in Publication Data

Zemke, Ron.
  Computer-literacy needs assessment.

  Bibliography: p.
  Includes index.
  1. Management—Data processing.   2. Computer literacy.
I. Title.
HD30.2.Z46   1985   658'.054   84-15687
ISBN 0-201-09122-4

HD
30
.2
Z44
1985

Cover design by Marshall Henrichs

Set in 11 point Souvenir by Techna Type, Inc.

ISBN 0-201-09122-4

ABCDEFGHIJ-AL-8765   06-10213446

Acknowledgments

I get embarrassed when I read the heartfelt acknowledgments in most books. You know the kind: "Thanks, Mom; thanks, Dad; thanks, Miss Grundy from the third grade at P.S. 106 in Toma, Iowa; thanks, Coach Thompson; thanks, Sargeant Friday; and thanks also to Old Paint for being the best and most patient friend a fella could have had during the forty-seven years it has taken me to write this my humble offering for the salvation of mankind."

I wince, but, faced with the same task, acknowledge the simple fact that writing a book, far from being a solitary activity, is a collaborative effort; at least it is for me. In the end there really are a lot of people you want to formally thank for all the direct and indirect help they gave. And no matter how sure you are that your prose will be pale, your expression of thanks inadequate, or how sure you are that those not involved will think the whole thing silly, a writer's gotta do what a writer's gotta do, Joey . . . so here goes.

Thanks are due Jerry Peloquin and Karl Albrecht for looking at the early models of the process described in this book and for putting them down hard enough that they cracked where they were thin, but not so hard that I cracked where I am thin. Thank you, Marie Swanson and Barb Spannus, for helping me see the data pro's perspective. Thank you, Phil Jones, Jack Gordon, and Chris Lee, for helping get the trial balloon up and flying. Thank you, tolerant TRAINING conference attendees, who listened to the ideas in this book in their early and unleavened form and responded to them with tolerance and favor despite the flaws. Thank you, Ann Dilworth, for believing that a six-page magazine article could actually be the backbone of a book. Thank you, Bill Kane and Scott Shershow, for turning a ton of typing into a for-real book. And last but never least, thank you, Mrs. Murphy, for being friend, colleague, confidante, critic, healer, and sweetheart. Thank you one and all.

CONTENTS

PREFACE: THE COMPUTER, WORK, AND YOU

There is a computer in your future. There is a computer in everyone's future. You didn't need to pick up this book to find that out. Had you spent the last three years sealed in a cave in the Himalayas, you *might* not have come to that conclusion on your own, but I doubt it: not in a three-year period when the United States Congress debated the pros and cons of allowing Apple Computer Company to donate a free microcomputer to every high school in the country; when *Business Week* decreed a million Americans in need of computer literacy training and *Time* magazine named the personal computer "Machine of the Year." Though by no means the only player in the high-stakes, high-tension game of technological revolution, the personal computer is the star and more. It is the symbol of the transformation going on in the American marketplace and mentality. The image of youthful wizards heroically stirring micromagic of blended sand and plastic, saving the economy and restoring lost face for the nation, comforts us—as it does *The Wall Street Journal,* the Dow Jones ticker, the editors at *Fortune,* and politicos of every water. The air is electric with promise. Each announcement of a new circuit boarded, a new gene spliced, and another gidget or widget marketed successfully, reinforces our collective affirmation that Daniel Bell's post-industrial society is now, that John Nesbitt is right, that old America is dead, that the information era has arrived and, by golly, Alvin Toffler's electronic cottage is just around the corner. But you and I both know that between here and there, between image and actualization, lie a myriad ways the future can go amok, and more than enough heroic acts to go around. And on the front lines, congratulations, is you.

THE COMPUTER-LITERACY CRUNCH

Organizational America is, by most knowledgeable accounts, headed for a computer-literacy crisis. The development of relatively inexpensive desktop computers, combined with a crushing demand for data-processing services, makes inevitable the necessity for managers and professionals to learn what microcomputers can do and how personal computing power can be applied to their jobs. A recent study by IBM and the Sloan School of MIT concluded that the demand for data-processing services will increase at an annual rate of 18 percent per year for the rest of this decade, while response capacity will increase at about 6 percent. Managers and professionals are simply going to have to learn to do their own data manipulation if it is going to get done at all. The problem is that for years professional data-processing people have stood squarely between the management core of most organizations and the computer room. "Leave the driving to us" may be a great slogan for a bus company, but it is turning out to be a bad policy for a data-processing operation. The upshot is that most managers and professionals are about as ready for desktop computing as a Neanderthal would be prepared to fly a 747. The magnitude of the training problem thus created is only now beginning to seep into our awareness.

The computer-literacy problem has at least two parts. The first and most obvious is the "Welcome to the black box" problem. Call it a management workstation if you like, but the desktop computer is still a foreign and sometimes unwelcome addition to a manager's work life. There is not only a basic ignorance of how, when, or why a manager would want to turn one on, but a rather hostile attitude toward anything remotely resembling typing to be overcome. "I didn't get an MBA to become a secretary!" is an often-voiced objection to desktop computing and personal work-processing activities.

The second part of the computer-literacy training problem is more subtle and less easily addressed than the "This is a computer, when you get to know it a little better it will be your good friend" problem. It is, rather, a problem of conceptual basics. The much-touted computer software that is supposed to make managing fun, such as Lotus 1-2-3 and dBase II, assumes quite a bit about the way managers manage. Before a computerized spreadsheet is of much use to a manager, the manager has to know what a spreadsheet is and why he or she might ever want to use one in the first place. And despite the cute "computer awareness" articles in the in-flights, a database is not really just computerized filing any more than word processing is simply electronic typing. There are, in short, some fundamental assumptions about work at work in desktop computing. Helping managers to become conversant and comfortable with such concepts may prove to be a more difficult training task than overcoming the minor problem of executive resistance to keyboarding.

WHERE HIDETH
THE TRAINER?

It would seem logical and inevitable that it would fall to the trainers of organizational America to address the computer-literacy problem. That doesn't seem to be happening. Arthur Luehrmann, founder of Computer Literacy, a computer education firm based in Berkeley, California, says bluntly, "It's hard to find someone who knows about computers and can explain his way out of a paper bag." Luehrmann suspects that the reason is simply one of economics, reasoning that "the same process that creates the demand for training is using up the supply of people who could teach." David Brinkerhoff, president of Abbott Smith Associates, a training and HRD search firm based in Millbrook, New York, thinks that the average trainer may be going out of his or her way to avoid computer-related things. "You would expect that trainers would be among the most computer-literate people in the organization. But they're not. They are among the most illiterate." Explaining that there seems to be an 80/20 split among working trainers, he observes that "the old-school trainers, the eighty percent, seem to be trying to tough it out and hope that computers will either just go away or that their retirement date will arrive before the box with the PC in it." Brinkerhoff sees this as rather destructive behavior in that "over half of the new openings we have booked this year specify some sort of computer familiarity. Many require an even higher level of mastery."

This means, of course, that trainers in a good many organizations are passing up an opportunity to build organizational and personal credibility. Far worse organizationally, is the specter of computer-literacy training becoming, by default, the province of the data-processing professional alone? In *most* organizations, data-processing people are not only uninterested in such a prospect, they are also the least suited for the job. "They don't know how to speak to earthlings" says Dr. Karl Albrecht, publisher of the *Computers in Training* newsletter, adding that what is really needed isn't a computer expert but someone who can "translate the propeller heads for the pinstripers," terms he uses to signify those who live and love computers and those for whom the computer is simply another office machine.

YOU CAN RUN BUT
YOU CAN'T HIDE

In the final analysis, trainer as-technology-translator is a fundamental piece of the action. It doesn't just "go-with" the territory, it *is* the territory. But you needn't start planning early retirement or pricing Chicken Licken franchises just because you don't speak bits and bytes fluently or can't tell a disk from a DOS. In fact, you are probably much better off starting from square one.

The computer hacker, the computer-loving hobbyist, has never faced a CRT palms awash with perspiration and wouldn't have the slightest empathy for any one who did. You, on the other hand, are going to be a model of understanding with the market manager who asks for yet a third explanation of why a floppy disk has to be initialized. It's the patience only those who have been there can show.

How do you begin this personal transformation from computer illiterate to literacy leader? Start with a good book. The test of a good computer-literacy book is simple. If you can pull it off the shelf, turn to page 99, and understand most of what it says, it's a good book for you, "user-friendly" in the computer-literacy parlance. There are good overview films and videos beginning to show up on the market as well. Best of all, find another illiterate who is willing to jump in the water with you. The buddy system is as useful here as it is at the shore. And finally, go to your organization's data-processing people and start a dialogue about the computer literacy needs of the organization. They will be more than pleased to see you, and relieved to know that someone else is concerned about the organization's information and data problems. Working with these people, who are used to systems thinking, you can be an integral part of the long-range planning for the organization's computer future. And the reality of your own experiences in becoming computer-literate will give you an understanding of the human side.

In short, if you are one of the computer reluctants, one of those hiding from the computer revolution, it is time to stop. The fact that you weren't weaned on RAMs and ROMs isn't a liability, it's an asset. Your willingness to stand up, admit to your temporary ignorance, and then do something about it will be a valuable and important model for your organization.

ABOUT THIS BOOK

That said, we push on to the purpose of this book. As more and more of the people in organizations who need to learn about computers look less and less like computer hobbyists and closet hackers, the more important it becomes that the training they receive does *not* look like a school-of-engineering course in microchip circuit design. A lot of what is passing for computer-literacy training these days reminds me of that old shaggy dog story: Little Johnny is assigned a book to report on by teacher. The book is titled *Our Friend the Penguin*. The first line of Johnny's report reads, "This book told me more about penguins than I ever wanted to know." A lot of current computer-literacy training strikes the nonhobbyist, new computer user just that way. A significant slice of this new audience for computer training has a low, low tolerance for tech talk as an end in itself. These folks are apt to meet a stunning lecture on mail merge technology with "Excuse me, Professor Squackenbush, but do I really need to know all that to put the PTA mailing list on the kid's Coleco?" They are a new and completely different audience looking for computer-skills training. *The purpose of this book is to help you sift and sort this undistinguished mass of soon-to-be computer users and put them into little piles so that you can provide them, not with computer training, but with training that will help them quickly and successfully integrate computers into their workaday world!*

The key to doing that sorting and sifting successfully is the needs assessment. It is only through some sort of needs assessment that you can hope to isolate the techies from the fearful, the zealots from the uninterested, and successfully provide the training that each of these diverse groups needs to succeed. It is only through needs assessment that you can hope to provide the training best suited to the sub-populations in your organization in a cost-effective and effective manner. And it is only through needs assessment that you can gain the perspective to evaluate, accept, and reject the onslaught of commercially available computer-literacy training resources that face you today in the marketplace.

The approach presented here is one that works—for me, at least. It has been tested and used successfully in parts and in toto. It represents the end product of a lot of effort on the part of a lot of people. And it probably isn't even close to perfect. Why? Well, for one thing, it is a model designed for working with today's adult who works in an organization that was no more interested in that individual's computer-literacy quotient when he or she was hired than it was in his or her shoe size, but who must make up for that hole in his or her background *now* if he or she is going to continue to be an asset in the organization. Ten years from now, when every new hire has been LOGOed and BASICed and RAMed and ROMed from cradle through college, we will be looking at a different population and will undoubtedly have to analyze their needs in a different way. Whereas we and our peers are computer-conscious, they will be computer-competent; whereas many of our trainees wonder whether there is any way they will ever master computers at all, they will be wondering how different the things they learned in school will be from the way things operate in the "real world." And they will need training too. But that is tomorrow's agenda, and problem. By then we'll be old-timers and there will be lots of tales of the old days to tell around campfires. For now we've got some pioneering to do, with only today's tools to use. And the point of the digression is that these, as far as we can tell, are the best tools currently available.

A CAVEAT

The concept of personal computing is tossed around quite a bit in this book. It is used to represent not only a microcomputer sitting on someone's desk, but the whole gamut of "remote," user-driven, user-performed computer operations. It covers any application that an "end user" can be involved in that doesn't require help from a data-processing professional or department on a day-to-day basis. It covers organizational people using mainframes, minis, and micros for the purpose of solving an organizational problem or providing an organizational service. That I speak frequently of the microcomputer in my examples and illustrations in no way means that this approach is limited in usefulness only to those situations where an organization has chosen to use microcomputers as workstations. The process covers remote, mainframe and minicomputer applications as well.

CHAPTER 1 AN OVERVIEW OF THE COMPUTER-LITERACY NEEDS-ASSESSMENT PROCESS

NEEDS ASSESSMENT: THE CONCEPT

The *concept* of training needs assessment is pretty straightforward:

> Before people can perform their tasks properly, they must master the special technology used by their organizations. This means acquisition of knowledge and skill. Sometimes this acquisition is needed when the employee is new to the organization; sometimes it is needed because the organization changes its technology; sometimes it is necessary if an individual is to change places within the organization. . . .
>
> A training need exists when an employee lacks the knowledge or skill to perform an assigned task satisfactorily.[1]

But the practice of figuring out what is "needed" to fill the gap between "existing" knowledge and skill and "desired" knowledge and skill is an increasingly tricky affair. In a very simple work world, one where jobs and procedures are completely and accurately defined and described, where they remain stable for long periods of time, and where job performance is carefully and frequently measured, the assessment of training needs may be a simple and clear process. For most trainers, however, reality is jobs so undefined or ill-defined that only a personnel rep could love them. Trainers face a world in which job details and procedures, indeed whole jobs, change overnight; where job performance is evaluated, if at all, in terms so behaviorally coarse as to shed scarce light on the idealized kinds of data called for in the classic definitions of needs assessment. The increasingly rapid introduction of computers to the workplace has only served to compound the problem. Ironically, as the world of jobs becomes more and more fluid, the concept of training needs assessment becomes *more,* not less, relevant. As more people need retraining and updating more and more often, it becomes increasingly

---

[1]Dugan Laird, *Approaches to Training and Development* (Reading, Mass.: Addison-Wesley, 1978).

important that the training being provided is timely, *effective,* and *efficient;* that it is the "right stuff," if you'll excuse the pun. That means, of course, that the upfront work, the performance analysis, the needs assessment, must be right.

BUT WHY COMPUTER-LITERACY NEEDS ASSESSMENT? Since personal computing *is* so new and advancing so rapidly, isn't it superfluous to talk about a needs assessment? Isn't it sufficient to assume that everyone in the organization is at square one and they all need basic training?

In fact, the answer may be yes. If you work in a small organization—under fifty employees, say—and this big crateful of new Polar Bear 77 microcomputers represents your organization's first significant contact with computer equipment, then it may make perfect sense, as a start, to send everyone to Maude and Phil's one-day Computer Boot Camp Seminar at $29.95 a head. Allowing that Maude and Phil are really familiar with the Polar Bear and that their approach is applications-oriented, their seminar, and an in-house user's group (for support and self-help), might stand you in good stead.

But if you are manager of data-processing education and training for a worldwide corporation of several thousand employees, you face quite a different level of challenge. When your computer-literacy training has to address the needs of so many people, "effective" and "efficient" become critical criteria; and matching specific learning needs to specific training options becomes an important part of your strategy. In such a milieu, "computer literacy" can mean something very different at each and every level and tier in the organization. That means determining the functional, operational, and conceptual meaning of computer literacy for each of these many different audiences in order to prescribe training intelligently.

To define computer literacy this way, as a *variable* instead of a *constant,* the computer-literacy training you will eventually provide must have many facets.

I recently interviewed Raymond Hass, manager of data-processing training for the 3M Company of St. Paul, Minnesota, who constantly faces the problem of hitting this multitude of moving targets. Hass's approach to computer literacy training for 3M's 88,000 employees worldwide is to take care of the needs assessment and specificity of training objectives in-house, and to mix homegrown and vendor-supplied training to meet the identified needs.

"We have an in-house program to educate executives on modern data processing," says Hass; "the analysts in our PC [personal computing] department hold awareness seminars for managers and professionals interested in sizing up personal computing as an option; and we use a variety of resources—from computer-based training to outside computer schools—for skills training.

"We could never build a staff large enough to meet all our computer-literacy training needs," he concludes. "But we can define them accurately and manage the way they are met."

After talking with Hass and other training and data-processing people in small, medium, and large organizations, as well as with a variety of computer-literacy training purveyors, I am comfortable concluding that many small organizations may be able to slide into the modern computing era without a lot of pondering and study—which is fortunate, because pondering and study can get expensive. But those 200,000 or so American organizations with more than fifty employees will be better served with a clearly focused and articulated approach to computer-literacy training.

That means you have some questions to answer:

▶ What roles will computers play in your organization?
▶ How do you want your people to work with computers?
▶ Who, if anyone, needs "general" knowledge about how computers work?
▶ Who, if anyone, needs to be trained only to perform specific tasks on specific machines?
▶ Who, if anyone, ought to receive enough advanced training to enable them to use computers to expand or modify their contributions to the organization in ways you can only guess at?

Having pieced together the views of a variety of experts on both computer literacy and needs assessment, we recommend a five-step proactive approach for determining an organization's computer-literacy training needs. It begins, as Ray Hass and others suggest, with understanding what computer literacy is—and is not—for your organization.

BUT FIRST . . .
STEP ZERO

If defining computer literacy is where your needs assessment begins, step zero of the process is to take the data-processing director to lunch. Two reasons:

First, it is valuable to get to know the one person in your organization who can be considered computer-literate in any man's army, who is least likely to be either computerholic or computerphobic, and who can, by virtue of his or her position, play a vital role in your effort to bring computer literacy to yourself and others. (Surprised that DP directors are unlikely to be computerholics? We find that they tend to be overworked people who are too busy trying to get computers to perform practical tasks to wax poetic about the magnificence of the information age.)

Second, it is critical that you identify your organization's attitude and policy toward remote computing and computer literacy for the masses. Your company's policymakers—particularly its DP policymakers—will have certain feelings about the notion of "a computer on every manager's desk," and about general access to computer power. Those feelings will have a powerful influence on what computer literacy means in your organization and ultimately, on the content and conduct of any training you undertake.

Even if you work in one of those organizations with a mandate from the CEO to "Get thee hence and bring my people computation!", you will need the support, goodwill, and help of your data-processing pros.

When you corner the DP chief—and you must keep after this appointment for however long it takes—you need the answers to three questions before you can carry out your quest for the functional definition (or, more likely, several definitions) of computer literacy upon which the rest of your efforts will hang.

1. *Does your organization take an "institutional" or a "personal" view of desktop computing?* This distinction is one that gets a lot of ink in *Personal Computing* magazine, whose editors consider it a key issue in the transition from industrial-age to information-age work. *Personal Computing's* managing editor, Ernest Baxter, defines the institutional approach to desktop computing as one in which "computers are brought into a complex and hooked up one to another in production-line fashion. . . . Limits of use are imposed. . . . The product of each machine [is] assembled at the end of the line into one whole unit. . . . The machine's functions are . . . tightly proscribed until . . . the machine will only do that portion of the job it has been limited to do. . . . A person is brought in and instructions are given on the way in which to operate the tool."

    The "personal" approach, according to Baxter, is the polar opposite of institutional computing. It involves "an exploration productivity . . . unencumbered by . . . constraints imposed before the individual appears on the scene. . . . Individuals are offered an opportunity [to use] the computer to accomplish their jobs . . . limited only by their own initiative, creativity . . . [and] will to succeed. No limitations are imposed on the tools. . . . The tool becomes an extension of the mind of the user."

    It's not difficult to guess which approach Baxter prefers. But quite a few good-sized organizations seem to lean toward the "personal" computing concept. If yours is one of them, there is a broader range of possible answers to the next two questions than if your company takes the "institutional" view.

2. *Does your organization have an "open" or "closed" policy toward the implementation of desktop computing?* You need to know how desktop and remote computing will be introduced—or are being introduced—to the organization. Will the company provide counsel and advice to individuals and departments that want to look into desktop computing applications? Or will the organization—and in particular the DP people—be satisfied with a laissez-faire approach, merely blessing the endeavor from afar?

   As you might guess, the "open" policy makes for nervousness in the controller's office, and gives internal auditors fits. On the other hand, rigid control seems counterproductive and may not be a real option. Small computers have become inexpensive enough that managers who really have the hots for computing can simply dig into their own pockets if the organization is exerting too much control.

   As one DP trainer we interviewed said, "Microcomputers are like mushrooms: they pop up overnight. Every morning there's another computing machine on another desk. I think the cobbler's elves have gone high tech." The point, of course, is that "control" should simply mean making expert help available and desirable.

   That said, however, there still are levels of openness and control that must be explored and understood if your computer-literacy training efforts are to be on target. The implementation policy will affect not only training content, but also the way you position the availability of training, and your method of delivery.

3. *Has your organization established a policy regarding makes and models of hardware and/or software? If not, will it establish such a policy?* If your organization already has mainframes or mini-computers, data-processing people will have some strong opinions and recommendations about the makes of micros and types of peripherals and software that will be most compatible with existing systems.

   If those recommendations are already being heard, you have an indication that your organization is taking the computer revolution seriously and that the topic of computer-literacy training is about to become an important issue.

STEP 1. LOOK AT THE LITERATURE . . . AND LIVE TO TELL OF IT

Once you've come to grips with your organization's philosophy about desktop or remote computing, you are ready to tackle the task of building a functional definition of computer literacy. We will spend the next chapter on the problem of defining computer literacy for your organization. I've interviewed quite a number of experts on their approach to defining computer literacy, and I've spent some time sifting the moving sands of the literature on the topic. I hope some of this will shortcut your work. But just the same, it would be a good idea to spend a day in a bookstore and a day on the phone pumping experts for their views and opinions.

How will you know when you've done enough work and it is time to move to the next step? Simple. When you find that skimming two books in a row or talking to two experts in a row fails to give you a single idea you haven't heard before, you're ready for step 2. It shouldn't take more than a day or two.

STEP 2. BRING THE SEARCH BACK HOME

Armed with a clear conception of your organization's philosophy, policy, and attitude toward computers, and a fistful of computer-literacy definitions from the experts, you can begin to paste together a definition—or several definitions—of what the term means in your situation. The starting point is to find out what computer literacy "looks like" when it is embodied by people in your organization.

In classic needs-assessment parlance, you have to determine what "competent performers" in your organization know and are able to do. In this case, competent performers are people who already are computer-literate—by anybody's definition. With any luck at all, your organization will contain at least a few.

Where do you look? The key, again, most likely is the data-processing department. The same people who understand and probably have shaped the organization's data-processing and remote-computing policies are going to have equally strong opinions about what ought to constitute computer literacy at the nonprofessional level.

Your DP experts also are very likely to be able to point you to people in other departments (sales, production, accounting, engineering, etc.) who already are using microcomputers successfully. These "early innovators," as market researchers call them, probably have made themselves known to DP pros. After all, what hacker can resist the temptation to "interface" with real "computer jocks"?

Ask the DP people to finger anyone they can think of who falls into one of two categories: "competent computer user" or "frustrated computer struggler." You will want to interview individuals from both groups.

Each group, including the DP experts themselves, has a special viewpoint to add to your understanding and planning. DP people have the "should knows" and "ought to be able tos," as well as knowledge of the organization's information and data-handling needs.

Successful computer users outside of the data-processing department represent your "competency models." From these people you will find out how computers are used and what they can do in various branches of the organization, and the type of skills and knowledge required to make them do it. You will want to find at least one competent computer user in every department for which you suspect you may need a specific definition of "computer literacy." If the potential role of computers in the production department is clearly going to be different from their role in engineering, and nobody in the production department is using a computer successfully, you may have to go outside the company for competency models relevant to your situation.

The successful computer users also have important personal learning histories you will find useful. "If you were to start over again . . ." is an excellent preface for questions to this group. Ask how they use desktop computing. Ask them to react to your accumulated definitions of computer literacy. Find out what their best and worst learning experiences were and why.

The unsuccessful users will be good sources of information about how things go wrong. Why did they find computers disappointing? Where was needed support lacking? What were they unable to master? This is vital information for the lower limits of your definition of computer literacy—and for the structure of your training.

STEP 3. DEFINE COMPUTER LITERACY . . . YOUR WAY

By now you should have enough information to build a working draft of what computer literacy means in your organization—and, more important, what it will mean in your training effort. So write something.

The computer literacy definitions in chapter 2 will help. But most of all, you need something for people to react to; to say, "Yes, that's it" or "No, there is more to it than that" or "Good, but shouldn't we add . . . ?"

Statements such as " . . . should be able to use a published spreadsheet to . . ." are preferable to ". . . should be able to use VisiCalc [or Lotus 1-2-3, or dBase II, or DataWriter] to . . . ." Your statements, in other words, should be relatively general. At this point, you are *not* trying to come up with a list of specific training objectives for people at various levels in the organization: you'd wind up with a book, not a definition. At the same time, your definitions must be specific enough to serve as meaningful standards against which to evaluate training designs, products, and services for specific levels in the organization. For example:

> Worldwide Widget sales personnel should be able to use the Polar Bear 77 personal computer to manage an array of activities, using published and specially designed software programming. Account analysis, time and route planning, order processing, and correspondence are key areas in which personal computing can improve productivity, and for which procedures have been worked out. It is WW's view, however, that the possibilities for productivity improvement inherent in personal computing are limited only by the imagination of our employees.

Or:

> Smorg Foundries believes that microcomputers can be of significant use to superintendents and supervisors for scheduling, planning, and costing purposes. Specially designed programs have been developed for these applications, and instruction in their use with our new Polar Bear 77 hardware will soon be available. The automation of these processes is another step in Smorg's dedication to the principle of providing you with the most advanced tools and techniques in the industry.

Notice that Worldwide Widget's statement is clearly a credo for personal computing, while Smorg's is unmistakably institutional in intent. Both reflect the philosophies, policies, and personal computer-literacy levels required in those organizations.

STEP 4.
QUANTIFYING
THE NEED
The final information-gathering step involves testing your definition against what people in the organization already know about computers and computing. Finding out where people "are" compared and contrasted with where they "should be" is the heart of the needs-assessment process; everything else is make-ready work.

You could, of course, stop the process once you have developed an accepted set of definitions, and start building and buying training. In modest-sized organizations, those of 100 to 200 employees, that may even be advisable. The worst outcome of this approach would be that some people would need a second turn at the training if it is geared too high—that is, if it assumes too much—while other people might go unchallenged if it is geared too low.

There are, however, at least four circumstances under which you definitely should continue your needs assessment to step 4:

> ▶ *Multiple levels of definition:* You are, in fact, faced with multiple definitions of computer literacy, striated by organization level, rather than with a single definition.

▶ *Heterogeneous functions:* Your organization, although small, performs several very dissimilar functions.

▶ *Lots of employees:* The more people you have, the more any small savings you achieve through efficient training will add up.

▶ *Many desktop computer users on staff:* When you already have a lot of people doing personal computing, it is important to identify beginning, intermediate, and advanced users, and to treat each group according to its needs.

Under any of these four circumstances, failing to classify your trainees correctly can be very expensive. It becomes prudent, then, to test individuals in the organization against your functional definition of computer literacy.

1. *Structured one-to-one interview.* Interviewers using a structured questioning guide ask a sample of employees what they know and how they feel about remote or desktop computing. What are the reservations? How do they feel computers might affect their jobs?

   Karl Albrecht, a San Diego–based psychologist and consultant who has begun to concentrate on computer-literacy training, recommends that you tap into more at this stage than just the skills and knowledge of employees. "I believe we are doing a great disservice to people," he says, "if we don't recognize first that some of them are very reluctant to be involved with computers. We call those people 'technophobes,' though that is probably too strong a term—no normal person is phobically afraid of computers.

   "This computer fear has a range of causes. Some simply fear they will cause the thing to explode if they press the wrong keys. Others fear for their jobs; they aren't sure the computer won't eventually replace or at least 'robotize' them. Still others are panicked that they will never master the computer and will 'flunk out' organizationally."

   Albrecht observes that something as simple as a lack of typing skills can create panic. "People who don't type sometimes fear the keyboard; others associate keyboards with typewriters and secretaries, and will be damned if they're going to start doing secretarial work."

   One-to-one interviews tend to be most useful with senior managers and executives, who need the protection of anonymity. The technique is less useful with lower-level employees who might interpret the interview as a threat to their jobs.

2.   *Small-group discussions.* Focus groups, deep-sensing groups, even nominal (technique) groups can be used to get past the insecurity of individuals who are reluctant to discuss their attitudes toward computing one to one. Small interview groups also have the advantage of "idea building." One member of a group says, "I don't understand what all this floppy-disk stuff is about and I don't think I need to." Encouraged by that admission, another adds, "I know one when I see one, but what the heck does it mean to 'boot' one?"

Small groups are very effective for first-line supervisors, line operators, and the like. Some of the structuring techniques of the nominal group method can be helpful in organizing the information you gather.

3   **and 4.** *Surveying and testing.* Computer-literacy experts differ sharply over the value of surveys and tests in determining what trainees know and what they need to know. David O. Olson, founder and president of Computer Workshops and Seminars, Inc., of Philadelphia, sees surveys as very useful, and considers them "helpful in determining the scope of user needs."

Edward B. Yarrish of Executive Technology Associates in Allentown, Pennsylvania, has quite the opposite view. "The technology changes so quickly that survey results are meaningless," he asserts.

I am of the view that both knowledge and attitude surveys are useful for answering "How much?" and "How many?"

Karl Albrecht brings up an issue that points to a need for some specialized testing as well. "A thing that seems least considered in planning computer-literacy training is learning style," he says, adding that the result is a plethora of computer-literacy training designed *by* "techies" *for* techies and frequently taught by techies.

The problem with this, according to Albrecht, is that large numbers of people are accidentally being discriminated against when it comes to the availability of computer training. "People who don't learn well the way the technophiles do are self-selecting away from computer-literacy training," he says. "This keeps quite a bit of high-quality organizational talent away from computer training. We're seeing a two-class computing society develop in some companies. No organization can afford that situation for long."

Reviewing Albrecht's data and pursuing a parallel exploration of the learning style issue has brought me to a very similar conclusion. Matching training methodology and trainee learning style can be of considerable value in easing the learning burden for at least one specific class of trainees—those with little or no previous exposure to computer functions and concepts.

STEP 5.
RECOMMENDATIONS
TO MANAGEMENT

Your needs-assessment work isn't done until you recommend action—or inaction, as the case sometimes may be. Assuming you have decided that training is needed, you have a variety of options to recommend to management. Learning-style research and adult-learning theory suggest that classroom seminars, hands-on workshops, multimedia-training techniques, and computer-based training all have appropriate roles in the computer-literacy milieu. But some special resources are available as well.

Computer clubs and user groups are very popular with microcomputer hobbyists. The same vehicles can be useful within an organization. John Hunter, a management development specialist at Perpetual American Federal Savings in Alexandria, Virginia, sees the computer club as extremely important to his company's computer-literacy push. "We have a mandate to become computer-literate here," he says. "The user's group is the only way we can guarantee that help is available for everyone who needs it, when they need it."

Also coming along fast is the concept of the microcomputer information center. Here, DP professionals and training types come together to provide consulting, counseling, and one-on-one tutoring as needed.

The mix you choose to present to management should be well thought out, costed carefully, and supported by the organization's data-processing pros.

SUMMING UP AND
MOVING ON

To sum up, the goal of a computer-literacy needs assessment is to provide the quantity and quality of information necessary to design an *effective* and *efficient* computer-literacy training program. As I have suggested, it would be advisable early on to take a DP professional to lunch. Make sure it is one from your own organization since the goal is to have your dining partner give you a briefing on the organization's attitude toward remote computing. Also take some time to get a feel for what it means when people bandy about the term "computer literacy." Check out the bookstores, call on some consultants, and check out chapter 2 of this book. There is also a list of basic computer literacy books in Appendix E. Pick one or two of the ones that seem to fit your needs and style. I said earlier that this activity will probably take you a day or two, but don't rush it. If you are starting from a position of little or no personal computer knowledge, the "get smart" dictum could take two or three weeks, perhaps a month or two. The goal is to get comfortable with the computer-literacy concept. Throughout this process you should find—and learn from—the successful. Seek out and study the people in your organization who are already computer-literate—who are using computers the way you want everyone else to. What do they know? How did they learn it? How long did it take? What did they learn or study that they found of no value on the job? The point of the exercise is to find the currently successful, find out how they became successful, and compare them with the currently unsuccessful. Naming and debriefing the organization's currently literate and not so literate is a powerful step in developing a functional—as opposed to theoretical—definition of computer literacy for your organization.

Finally, you should attempt to define computer literacy as it applies to your organization and situation. As I have already said, this may require defining computer literacy differently for different levels of the organization. For some levels a "keystroke" or operator's level of definition will dominate; at other levels the definition will be much more conceptual and abstract. *Every* definition will have cognitive and keystroke elements, but the balance of each of these elements will depend upon the specific job or job level for which computer literacy is being defined. We will look closely at the problem of defining computer literacy in more detail in chapter 2.

CHOICE POINT

If you are defining computer literacy and designing and developing computer literacy training for 250 or fewer employees, it is time to stop analyzing and be about the job of developing or finding the training that will best bring people to the desired level of computer literacy for your organization.

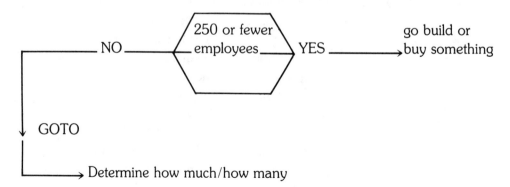

Quantify the need for your organization. *If:*

  ▶ Multiple definitions of computer literacy seem necessary
  ▶ The organization is characterized by heterogeneous job func-
     tions—is highly specialized and compartmentalized
  ▶ The employee population (potential trainee population) is large
  ▶ There is a good sized computer using "base" already

Then:

Consider a very formal information-gathering approach, consisting of:

  ▶ Interviews (one-to-one and small-group)
  ▶ Surveys
  ▶ Knowledge tests
  ▶ Attitude and style instruments

The last step is to recommend a course of action to management. This step supposes that you are in a large organization and that there is a need to sell an individual or a decision-making group on a course of action. If you work in an environment that requires such formal presentations to gain permission to do what you were hired to do in the first place (when you say it that way, it *does* seem a little silly, doesn't it?), know that there is a fine art to such presentations. This step requires tact, guile, and panache.

NEXT

The remainder of this book fleshes out the details and elaborates on the basic ideas sketched in this chapter. The last third of the book is a Computer-Literacy Learning Resources Guide: a set of five appendices that will help you find the training materials necessary to fill the computer-literacy learning needs you uncover with your computer-literacy needs assessment.

As discussed in this chapter, your organization's specific learning needs will depend on the size and heterogeneity of your organization. That means not every chapter in the remainder of the book will be of interest to you. To help you decide what to read next, here is a thumbnail sketch of each of the remaining chapters.

  ▶ *Chapter 2: Computer Literacy Is . . .* This chapter summarizes the problem of defining or giving meaning to the concept of *computer literacy.* Common definition, the parameters of the concept, and some thoughts on what your computer literacy definition(s) should contain are explored.

► *Chapter 3: Interviewing for Computer-Literacy Learning Needs.* How to use one-to-one and small-group interviews to distinguish between the computer-literate and -illiterate; to learn about people's fears and reservations; and to determine the differences in computer-literacy learning needs by level.

► *Chapter 4: Using Tests, Instruments, and Surveys.* How to survey and *test* for computer-literacy knowledge levels.

► *Chapter 5: Computer phobia: Measuring and Dealing with Reluctance.* This chapter examines the concept of computer phobia and explains an approach to designing a computer reluctance survey.

► *Chapter 6: Computer-Literacy Training and Learning Style.* Ways of tapping into trainee learning style and using it to prescribe training media.

► *Chapter 7: Presenting Recommendations to Management.* Some tips and tricks for making an effective presentation of results and recommendations to management.

► *Chapter 8: Designing Your Computer Literacy Training Program.* A few—very few—words on designing effective computer literacy training programs.

► *Appendices: Learning Resources for Computer Literacy Training.* An annotated catalogue of films, videos, books, audiotapes, and CAI that can help you meet your organization's computer literacy learning needs. More than a listing.

A BIAS

I have one more bias to expose to you. I have a favorite strategy, a pet approach to computer-literacy learning. It is simply a strategy I have seen work for many trainers in many organizations. It has three steps:

Step 1: General Orientation Seminar

Step 2: Individual Assessment

Step 3: Individual Prescription

As obvious as these steps are, I will belabor them a tiny bit more.

GENERAL
ORIENTATION
SEMINAR
This is simply an overview, "welcome to the computer," small-group presentation. The content depends on the level of individuals in the group—if grouping by job level is appropriate and desirable in your organization. The content is generally how computers work, some "Look at this; it's a computer," a bit of hands-on, and a pitch or sales talk from the session leader on available resources for learning to *use* computers on the job.

INDIVIDUAL
ASSESSMENT
The tests and surveys used for the general needs assessment are useful for "*gating*" or *assessing* individual trainee skill/knowledge level, reluctance, and learning style so that the most appropriate learning materials and forms of instruction can be prescribed.

INDIVIDUAL
PRESCRIPTION
My bias is to see as many different resources and ways of learning to use computers made available as possible. Some trainees are more comfortable and learn better in small groups. Others need to do it alone. Trainees differ in their ability to learn from, and be comfortable with, audio lessons, video lessons, hands-on lessons, or simply written lessons.

It is useful to understand this bias since it permeates the way the following chapters are shaped.

COMPUTER LITERACY: THE GOSPEL ACCORDING TO EVERYBODY

It is probably fair to define basic computer literacy as some familiarity with what computers do, and your ability to make them do what you want. Doing all that with pleasure, originality, and style might better be called computer fluency.

> Trudy E. Bell
> Associate Editor
> *Personal Computing*

"Computer literacy" is the term most frequently used to describe the basics that "noncomputer" people need to know about computers. . . . It consists of at least five components: (1) knowledge about computers, (2) knowledge of computer applications, (3) experience in computer use, (4) skills in computer programming, and (5) awareness of the issues involved when personal computer technology is implemented in an organization

> David O. Olson
> President
> Computer Workshops and Seminars
> Philadelphia, Pennsylvania

To the business and professional person, computer literacy really means skills. "How do I use this computer?" "How do I use this software?" That's what they want to know. Learning about computers and having to use computers are very different. In my mind, I separate computer literacy from computer skills and both from software literacy and software skills.

> Joel Rakow
> Executive Vice-President and Co-Founder
> American Training International
> Manhattan Beach, California

A person is considered "literate" if he or she is educated or has knowledge or experience in certain areas. To be computer literate, you need to know about computers and have some experience in using them.

> Ellen Richman
> *The Random House Book of Computer Literacy*
> (New York: Vintage Books, Random House, 1983)

For a manager, it means knowing what a computer can do and being able to effectively define the information they need from a computer.

> Alan Freedman
> The Computer Language Co.
> New York, New York

One who is truly computer-literate must be able to "do computing," to conceptualize problems algorithmically, to represent them in the syntax of a computer language, to identify conceptual "bugs," and to express computational ideas clearly, concisely, and with a high degree of organization and readability.

> Arthur Luehrmann
> Consultant
> Berkeley, California

Computer literacy is simply the fundamental knowledge of how computers work and the ability to read, write and analyze simple programs.

> Leon Starr
> "A Programming Primer"
> *Personal Computing*, 1982

Computer Literacy is: knowing the capabilities of microcomputers and knowing how to make the microcomputer work to your best advantage.

> *Computer Literacy is not:* knowing how to program, and knowing the mechanics of computer operation.

> Ralph Granger
> President
> Compulearning
> CES Training Corp.
> River Edge, New Jersey

In general, people need to know as much about computers as they do about their refrigerators, ranges and telephones. You don't need to be a nuclear engineer to live in the nuclear age and understand the issues surrounding nuclear power plants.

> Franklynn Peterson
> Editor/Publisher
> *Computer Newsletter*
> to Nicholas Johnson on *New Tech Times*
> March 1984

CHAPTER **2** COMPUTER LITERACY IS . . .

"When I use a word," Humpty Dumpty said, in rather a scornful tone, "it means just what I choose it to mean neither more nor less."

"The question is," said Alice, "whether you *can* make words mean so many different things."

"The question is," said Humpty Dumpty, "which is to be master— that's all."

From *Alice through the Looking Glass*

"Computer literacy" is a Humpty Dumpty phrase if there ever was one. It means exactly, and neither more nor less than, what the definer wants it to mean. That shouldn't surprise anyone. Literacy in the traditional sense is an equally elusive concept. Is someone literate who can read a restaurant menu and the evening newspaper? Or must one be facile with the works of Shakespeare and Thomas Mann to be deemed literate? The problem of definition is the same for computer literacy. Is a person who operates a word processor computer-literate, or is being able to write a checkbook reconcilement program in BASIC the minimum criterion?

Out of curiosity, I spent several weeks, on and off, finding and comparing definitions of computer literacy. I did a literature search—which means I went to the library at a local university and read a lot—and I polled a number of experts—which means that I found a quiet cubicle with a WATS line and phoned a dozen or so computer-literacy training vendors and asked two questions:

- ▶ What is computer literacy?
- ▶ What do people in an organization need to know or be able to do to be considered computer-literate?

The disparity in, and variety of, answers that my little project uncovered was quite a surprise. The quotations at the beginning of this chapter make the point rather well. What can we deduce from this definitional smorgasbord? There are three or four useful conclusions we can draw. First, there are at least two very distinct schools of thought. Robert Newton Barger, an Eastern Illinois University professor of education who conducted a similar but decidedly more systematic study, calls them the "to program" or "not to program" views. "There does not seem to be any room for compromise between these two views," he writes. "Either one needs to know how to program to be considered computer literate or one does not." As an intellectual exercise, taking and defending either view can be stimulating. The best pro-programming arguments go like this: "One would not say that a person who knew *about* reading and writing (in the sense of what they were, how they worked, and what their applications and limitations were, how they worked, and what their applications and limitations were) was 'literate' unless he could actually read and write." This is, in fact, the analogy Barger draws on his way to concluding, "It would seem imprecise to say that a person who knew about computer structure and function and computer applications and limitations but who could not program at a minimal level, was computer literate." A companion argument we often hear is, "Learning to program makes you a more logical, structured thinker." That somehow reminds me of advice once given by high school counselors: "Take Latin. It's awful, but it's good for you."

The anti-programming argument is also straightforward: "Programming is impractical for anyone but professional software developers and engineers. In a few years computers won't need to be programmed anyway. They will speak straight English."

For what it's worth, I come down on the side of the "not to program" arguments. My reasoning is dead simple: I've been through BASIC, preceded by FORTRAN, and before that by a couple of machine languages, and none of that has made mastering WordStar, StatPac, or dBase II one bit easier. Nor has the "discipline" raised my I.Q. or kept me from misplacing my car keys at least once a week.

A second observation is that all definitions of computer literacy are usually independent of the kind of computer—in the mini, micro, or mainframe sense—one is expected to use. That said, it is also clear that our dozen or so experts were using the microcomputer for a frame of reference in their concept of computer literacy.

David O. Olson, president of Computer Workshops and Seminars, Philadelphia, faced that anomaly directly. "It is users of personal computers [who] are requesting assistance in getting started," Olson observes. "It is their requests that can be broadly stated as [defining] computer literacy." This makes considerable sense, in the same practical way that leads us to accept being able to read the want ads in a newspaper and fill out a job application as minimal criteria for functional reading and writing literacy in the workplace. Needs tend to define themselves very practically. Gary D. Brown, of CRWTH Computer Coursewares, Santa Monica, California, also sees no problem with a definition of computer literacy that takes its lead from micro or personal computers. "It is the commonality of function in using computers that helps us define computer literacy. A text editor is a text editor in a micro or a mainframe. And a file is not a work space regardless of the computer you're talking about. The thing anyone's approach to computer literacy training should emphasize is that the computer is a tool and the way that tool works and can be of help in a given environment."

The third lesson we can take away from looking at so many definitions of computer literacy, and talking to so many experts, is that the functional or operational specification of your definition is the most critical feature. Our experts frequently emphasized that they needed to know more about the given organization or job level before their definitions could be more than an approximation or generality. These distinctions may be the most important thing I learned over several weeks of trying to nail down a useful definition of computer literacy. Conceptual and operational definitions can, and probably should, be quite different and dependent upon circumstance.

The key to moving from a general definition and concept of computer literacy to doing training—the operationalizing of computer literacy in your organization—is to understand and work with the variables that change from job to job and level to level. In other words, talk job-specific objectives as well as general concepts.

SO WHERE ARE WE?

We are at the point where it's useful to summarize a bit. As we have seen, the first step in determining your organization's computer-literacy learning needs is to define computer literacy for your organization. But, as we have also seen, defining computer literacy for your organization means more than just adopting one of the definitions found in the literature or throwing one together in the back room of the training department. Defining computer literacy for your organization really means determining how computers are now being used or will soon be used in your organization. In our approach to determining computer-literacy learning needs, it is important to know how specific people will be using computers in your organization. An engineer's use of a microcomputer and a clerk/typist's use will, and should, vary significantly. Our bias is that the learning objectives of your training should be significantly shaped by the kinds of applications different trainee populations make of computers. It makes sense to assume that computer-literacy training designed for managers or technicians or doctors or clerks won't contain the exact same information or teach the exact same skills. Having an organizationally acceptable *generic* definition of computer literacy will most certainly give you guidance and, more important, will be a comforting touchstone for your trainees. But when the rubber hits the road, having objectives and criteria for each population you must instruct, or find instruction for, is an important outcome at which your needs assessment should be aimed.

IDENTIFYING CORPORATE COMPUTING POLICY

I have suggested several times that corporate policy regarding personal computing must be taken into account early on in the computer-literacy needs assessment process. My experience working with organizations that were trying to establish an organization-wide computer literacy program convinced me of the importance of this step. Such programs were always more successful in organizations with a considered personal computing policy. Where no uniform organizational policy existed, our needs assessment efforts continually bogged down in issues not related to training but directly related to those organizations' indecision about the whole issue of personal computing. In one organization we worked with, individual department managers determined what, if anything, personal computing meant for their departments; which, if any, personal computing equipment and software would be used in the department; and who, if anyone, would be allowed access to the computing equipment. We witnessed the personal computing opportunity in this organization deteriorate to a nearly primordial state. The little bits of computing equipment that department managers were able to sneak through their miscellaneous-expenditures budgets were jealously guarded behind locked conference-room doors and parceled out like black magic only to the truly deserving at the whim of the Keeper of the System Magic. In other situations we have seen people of good faith in different parts of an organization find themselves unable to communicate on any number of interpersonal and technical levels because of a basic incompatibility, not just of equipment and programs, but of analysis techniques and results as well.

Until not too many weeks ago, my conviction that a uniform corporate personal computing policy is a greater good, was backed primarily by the handful of personal anecdotes I had assembled. But the scope of my argument, and the conviction with which it is held, increased tenfold when I stumbled across the March 1984 issue of *Computer Decisions* magazine. All 152 pages of that issue were devoted to—you guessed it—the importance of corporate personal computing policy. As special-issue editor Susan Foster

Bryant expressed it, "Personal computing has caused organizations to re-think, and sometimes re-structure, their information resources. Moreover, it has hastened the demise of some traditional work habits and accelerated demands for systems that provide the best information and provide it yesterday." There seem to be two levels of policy decision clearly discussed in this fine set of articles. The first is the same set of issues I described in chapter 1; when an organization is willing to accept personal computing as a viable means of handling organizational information, system-specific questions arise. Will the organization accept the microcomputer as the standard for personal computing, or is there a reason to argue in favor of such other alternatives as remote terminals, dedicated word processors, or minicomputers? Though the personal or freestanding microcomputer is the most popular approach to personal computing, it is not necessarily the most cost-effective or even most efficient one in every organizational situation.

If the microcomputer *is* to be a standard for personal computing, what hardware, software, and operating systems will the computer professionals support? (The word "support" is organizationese for "help people learn to use and keep in good repair.") Will the organization's computer experts actively encourage people in the organization to experiment with the sanctioned systems, or will the policy position be reactive rather than proactive? Will application procedures be rigidly defined from above, or will end users be on their own to make it up as they go?

The next level of issues discussed in that March issue of *Computer Decisions* consist of basic, raw questions of organizational power and control. As Bryant explains it, "Personal computing brings the classic conflict between managerial authority and individual autonomy into sharp focus. On the one side are professionals and executives who want to use personal computing tools any way they see fit. On the other side is the sometimes heavy hand of corporate management. . . . The mission is to help corporate executives who plan, implement, and manage personal computing find a productive solution to the fundamental conflict between authority and autonomy."

How tightly drawn is the conflict Bryant sketches? In the ensuing articles in the issue we see data-processing managers such as Norman Epstein of E. F. Hutton promising, "I'd expire before allowing personal computers to tap our databases." In what is probably the best article in the issue, David Kull, the magazine's management-issues editor, gives voice to the opposing view when he describes such heavy-handed views as akin to "telling employees how to arrange their desks."

Kull's article also introduces a third issue, one we suggest you be much on the alert for in your interviews: the issue of how the organization uses information and data regardless of whether it is computerized or not.

Kull cites University of Southern California business policy professor Ian Mitroff as observing that "if one of the unwritten rules of the organization is 'don't share information; keep it close to the vest because it's power,' throwing in personal computers will only accentuate secrecy." In my own work, I have witnessed instances where the introduction of personal computing capacity has had a very disruptive effect on organizational harmony. In one of the cases I am familiar with, the West Coast office of a large federal agency is in great turmoil because managers are taking charge of all matters related to certain databases, working out their own "what if" questions and answers, and leaving the legitimate department data analysts with little beyond clerical work. You can cut the tension with a knife. It seems to me that as the advanced computerization of the workplace becomes more and more common, there are going to be many organizational issues to be dealt with. We've only seen the surface of the scratching. You owe it to yourself to get your hands on that March 15, 1984, issue of *Computer Decisions* and read it cover to cover as part of your personal education. A back issue of the magazine costs $4 plus $1 handling. It is available from Computer Decisions, P.O. Box 1417, Riverton, NJ 08077. You will also find David Kull's article from the same said issue of the magazine reprinted in Appendix F.

WHAT DOES A GOOD PERSONAL COMPUTING POLICY LOOK LIKE?

Good question. And another reason why you need to get a copy of that issue of *Computer Decisions* I keep shoving at you; it has a good sample of policies and procedures others have found workable.

At the Irving Trust Company in New York City, a chatty, instructional document serves to transmit organizational policy about personal computing to the troops. The following is an excerpt:

> GETTING A MICROCOMPUTER: The most important thing you have to do is demonstrate that you need it and can justify the cost. Microcomputers can be justified if they increase productivity, reduce staff, take the place of existing or planned equipment, or provide a service that no other department in the bank can provide.
>
> The Administrative Automation Services Group is available to help you make these determinations, as well as offer limited use of its own microcomputers. This will help you determine exact applications and software requirements before you decide to make a request for a specific configuration.

This policy statement goes on to address software, communications, data security, documentation, and so on, but note that it is above all else very consultative in approach and friendly in tone.

Based on the admittedly small sample of policies I have seen, there seem to be five specific elements your organization's personal computing policy should contain if it is to be helpful to people in the organization investigating personal computing, as well as to those who have to support that effort (that's you):

1. A general statement of how the organization views personal computing.

2. A specification of hardware and software the organization is supporting and, where appropriate, a specification of exactly which equipment and systems the computer professionals in the organization are *not* willing to support. (Avoid "thou shalt nots" if at all possible. They aren't usually necessary, and have a tendency to give a paternalistic tone to the policy statement.)

3. An itemization of the ways the organizational computer professionals will be able to help (support) the new computer users in the organization.

4. The special issues the would-be user should think about or be made aware of, such as security, programming, cost controls, data integrity, communications, and so on.

5. The step-by-step procedures the user must follow in order to obtain a computer or terminal, programming, equipment, and advice, and the details of establishing a cost/use justification if appropriate. (The goal is to make the process of getting started as simple and unencumbered of red tape as possible.)

Note: This information is as useful for understanding the parameters—and some of the content—of the training you are trying to describe as it is for managers attempting to understand the place of personal computing in their departments.

SOME AFTERTHOUGHTS

In the end, just what does it mean to say someone is computer-literate? It is a specific case of the general question of how we know when and if anyone is competent at anything. Philosopher Eric Hoffer observes in *The True Believer* that it is easy to tell a journeyman carpenter from a novice by the sweat on the brow. "The two may accomplish the same quantity of work but the experienced worker does so with less sweat and strain, less expenditure of energy on the whole," he writes. By the same token, a colleague tells of having worked for several months as part of a team developing a physics curriculum at one of the military academies. Their final step, as for all good Instructional Systems Design (ISD) people, was to ask a panel of experienced physicists to review the boxcar full of instructional objectives that defined the curriculum. One of the experts patiently sifted the objectives and criterion measures and graciously complimented the team for their diligence and thoroughness. But then he added, "If I really wanted to know if a young person who graduated from this curriculum was able to do physics, if he was on the way to being a physicist, then I would simply talk to him for fifteen minutes. I would know for sure then." This dilemma, the tension between competence and criterion passing, has become much more problematic for trainers in recent years, and is yet to be solved. It comes down to understanding in some reliable way what it means to be literate or competent—with any body of knowledge. I have no solution to offer, but an example of competence in action may be instructive.

PERSONAL PERSPECTIVE
I like to sit alone in my office on Saturdays and write. When I have the opportunity to enjoy this wonderful luxury, I like to turn my radio to the local all-talk radio station. Saturday is when the "ask the expert" shows are on. There is an "Ask the Mechanic" show and "Ask the Lawyer" show, a gardening show in the summer, and, recently, a computer talk show. The computer call-in show follows the automobile repair show. To hear the automotive expert question callers about symptoms and situations is to listen to a master in action:

Caller: I have a 1978 Chevrolet, it runs fine, it's excellent, but sometimes when I start it up and go awhile, shut her down and start it up, five or ten minutes later it's flooded. That leads me to believe it's a needle and seat or a float that is sticking. What do you think?

Auto Expert: Those are good possibilities. Some other possibilities that come to mind are an internal freeze plug leak in the carburetor body itself. Most GM carburetors like the hydrojets protect themselves from moisture freezing in the float well by putting aluminum plugs in the bottom of the well. Over the years, these tend to work loose and allow a little leakage from the carburetor to the engine, and this tends to flood it if the engine is hot and sits there.

Also, think about heat buildup causing fuel vaporization that forces the throat open.

Caller: Why that now and not at fifty thousand miles?

Auto Expert:	You might have a thermostat starting to stick and makes the engine warmer than usual.
Caller:	Would you suggest a rebuilt carburetor or just replacing a needle and float and seat?
Auto Expert:	It's practical to buy a carburetor repair kit as well as a new float–that might be getting porous and not working quite right—forcing fuel out. That's only about fifteen dollars. You can't get a rebuilt for that.

Compare that with a slice of dialogue from the computer talk show:

Caller:	I'm kind of boggled when it comes to buying diskettes. I don't know what to buy in floppy disks; what should you look for in buying decent disks?
Computer Expert:	You have an Apple Computer, you said?
Caller:	Yeah, an Apple IIe.
Computer Expert:	I would recommend you buy a diskette that has a hub ring.
Caller:	A hub ring?
Computer Expert:	Yes, a hub ring. A little reinforcing ring that goes in the center of the diskette. Apple disk drives are notorious for chewing up this little support area, so you want to have something real firm there.
Caller:	Would that be for both single- and double-sided disks?
Computer Expert:	The Apple only uses single-sided disks.
Caller:	Can't you just turn them over?
Computer Expert:	If you turn a double-sided disk over, you would have a problem because the Apple disk has an envelope with a liner that traps dirt and dust. If you turn the disk over, then it runs backwards and you risk breaking that dirt free and impairing your recording head and causing problems recording data.
Caller:	You *can't* use double-sided disks on an Apple?
Computer Expert:	No—you can use them on the IBM and some other computers with disk drives that

have double recording heads—but not the Apple.

Caller: Oh, I don't want to know about that—only about the Apple.

The point here is *not* that the people who work the computer call-in show are illiterate while the auto-advice guy is literate. It is simply to remind us that being computer-literate as we are talking about it in this book—and in your organization—is a very different matter from being automobile- or mathematics-literate in the same broad, general sense. It is important that we do not sell ourselves and our trainees on the mistaken notion that to be able to type on a computer keyboard is to be computer-literate. By the same token, we don't want to suggest to ourselves or others that there is so much to know about computers that none of us can ever really become literate or competent in the sense we are literate in other areas. At the same time, we have to recognize that developing competence, becoming literate and facile with a body of knowledge, really means being able to think and solve problems in an effective and efficient way. That level of functioning takes time and practice to develop. If you are literate in "autotalk" the way the people on the auto call-in show demonstrated themselves to be, you know it didn't happen overnight. It was a product of a lot of driving, a lot of shade-tree tinkering, a lot of learning, and a lot of being curious and asking questions.

In my case, there are wrenches in my automobile emergency road repair kit that are older than the first microcomputer. I have worked around computers for a long time, but have owned a microcomputer for a relatively short time. I am making rapid progress in my facility to think and solve problems in microcomputerese. Training others has helped a lot. So has writing articles and books. Just the same, I keep a list of phone numbers of my *really* competent friends at hand whenever I am attempting something new, like making two different printers work from the same computer at the same time, communicating with a computer across town, or simply tinkering with a piece of software to make it run faster. It is going to be a while before I am as computer-literate as I am automobile-literate. It will take even longer for our society in general to achieve a computer-literacy level comparable to that of our other shared literacy levels.

The message in all this is *patience.* Be patient with yourself, with your learning, and with other people's learning. Becoming literate, in anything, in the sense we've been talking about here, is a lifelong process.

CHAPTER 3 INTERVIEWING FOR COMPUTER-LITERACY LEARNING NEEDS

THE ONE-ON-ONE INTERVIEW

The personal interview is the most common information-gathering technique. Face-to-face interviewing is the primary source of information for dozens of occupations. Reporters do it, recruiters do it, trainers do it, managers and market researchers do it. But few do it well.

Dr. Gary Latham of Washington State University contends that even though the face-to-face interview is the least reliable hiring technique, it continues to be the number-one way people are hired. "Despite the data, the face-to-face interview feels right," says Latham. "When you think of it, how many people do you know who would hire someone without interviewing them? It really wouldn't feel right, would it?"

For two reasons, we continue to use face-to-face interviews for gathering information. First of all, as Latham suggests, they are expected. What senior manager would accept a report from a consultant—internal or external—if the consultant hadn't interviewed him or her and demonstrated that his or her views were being duly noted and recorded? No one in management is going to accept a critical research report he or she hasn't contributed to. But, more important, certain pieces of critical information, things that shape, make, or break a study, can be garnered only face to face.

Social scientists and market researchers, well aware that the interview has much potential for error, have proposed and tested numerous "solutions" to the error problem. Extensive interviewer training has been shown to help increase both the reliability and validity of data gathered from interviews, as have random selection of people to be interviewed, selective assignment or "matching" of interviewers and interviewees, and mathematical treatment of interview data.

My tactic is to use the face-to-face interview as a primary information-gathering tool only when I must, and then to control as many troublesome factors as I can. When I work in this mode, I refer to what I am doing as a structured interview. When I use the interview process as only part of the information source—for instance, when I am observing someone or having someone show how he or she does such and so with a computer and we are chatting about "things," I refer to what we are doing as either a conversational or informational interview. Let's take a quick look at the two.

STRUCTURED INTERVIEWS

Four features characterize the structured interview. First, the interview is the only contact we will probably have with the informant. Second, the interviewee is in a unique position and is privy to information we can only obtain from him or her. Third, the interview is positioned as a formal, fact-finding affair; it is scheduled, is planned, has rules of conduct, and has a defined focus. Fourth, the results are formally analyzed in some fashion. By the way, because the information gathered in many structured-interview situations is so important, I will frequently give the respondent an opportunity to review a summary of key points from the interview.

I undertake the structured interview for specific reasons. I interview the senior management of an organization to determine the nature and implications of the problem under consideration; in this way, I try to obtain the information I need to make a succinct statement about what management wants. In short, I use the structured-interview technique when I am trying to find the perceived problem and determine why people are in an uproar over it—for example, why they think computer-literacy training is needed, and what exactly the operational definition of computer literacy is in their minds. The formal, structured interview is the process I use when I am trying to state the organization's meaning of computer literacy in fifty words or less. (Toward the end of this chapter, we will take up the issues you need to probe with your management if you are going to develop a functional definition of computer literacy for the organization.)

INFORMAL INTERVIEWS

The informal, or conversational, interview is characterized by its much more spontaneous nature and lack of structure. We use the informal approach to add depth of understanding to things observed or learned in other ways. It taps the opinions of a broad range of performers and provides us with quotes and thoughts for enriching data gathered other ways. For example, during a site visit we were having a highly-skilled personal computer user explain a data management system she was working on. Between lecturettes, she took a sip of her coffee and mused that "this project would go a lot faster if I had a computer I could take home." This offhand comment became the basis of a standard interview and survey question, and helped us recommend using and buying portable computers for the department under study.

In an informal interview, we are listening for certain kinds of verbal behavior from the respondents. There are some general probes or questions we will be sure to ask *every* member of the class of employee we are dealing with. At the same time, I keep the interview agenda open to change so I can be surprised by the discovery of attitudes, opinions, issues, and facts not anticipated beforehand.

ANATOMY OF THE STRUCTURED INTERVIEW

The structured interview consists of five steps:

1. Preparing for the interview
2. Starting the interview
3. Conducting the interview
4. Concluding the interview
5. Compiling and analyzing results

1. PREPARING FOR THE INTERVIEW

▶ *Learn the local language.* As a consultant, I am forever a stranger in a strange land, struggling with the language. So is the in-house trainer who bounces from marketing to data processing to service. If you can speak—or at least understand—the local jargon, your credibility is immeasurably increased. DP handbooks, banking dictionaries, and even organizational glossaries are readily available. Find one. You at least should be able to nod intelligently when the VP of DP says, "Our biggest problem to date is convincing our users that real-time interface has a better mini/max than remote processing or current micro/mini capacities for ROMI in this configuration."

▶ *Hold an introductory meeting.* If you are going to work in a central location, hold a brief, informational, introductory meeting with the people you will be interviewing in depth. At that meeting, you *and* the supervisor of the people you will be interviewing can clarify the objectives for the interviews and make a pitch for candor and guarantee anonymity.

▶ *Make an interview schedule outline.* The first top-management interview is the toughest to set an outline for, but even a sketchy one is better than none. We approach that initial interview with three inputs: (1) the general issues surrounding the use of computers (2) some idea of the problem parameters, based on phone contacts and whatever else precipitated the need for this informational meeting, and (3) the upshot of at least one discussion with the company, division, or department liaison person. After the first management interview, the questions and topics to cover become more apparent. But even in a structured interview, you have to leave room for the informant to shape the agenda.

▶ *Don't structure your interview around yes or no questions, even if you think you need yes or no answers.* Asking open-ended, problem-solving questions—just as in a performance-improvement interview—gets more information and commitment than asking yes or no questions.

▶ *It is more appropriate to let the informant ramble than to try to force your personal outline on him or her.* Often you will be the first person who has asked the interviewee to explain the job or problem in standard English. That means he or she will be generating information on the spot and will be as interested in the resulting remarks as you are. Give interviewees room to roam in their heads. You get longer answers but better information.

▶ *Be aware that you can't get away with as many vague or naive questions or "tell me about it" queries as you can in a focus group.* (I will discuss later the ways in which these two kinds of interviews differ.) It is better to be overprepared with questions and not need them than to be caught short with a recalcitrant interviewee.

▶ *Bounce your questions off some neutral and knowledgeable source before the interview.* You need to know that you are asking the right questions of the right person and that the questions make sense. Having to explain a pointless question to a safe source may save you time and face when you encounter a key management person.

▶ *Cluster your questions topically.* By organizing your questioning, you keep the interviewee focused where you want him or her, and you increase the likelihood that he or she will elaborate on the topic at hand.

▶ *If your questions pertain to reports, published data, production charts, and the like, gather these sources together and have them with you.* The other person may not have those things at hand or may never even have seen the data.

▶ *Always conclude with an open-ended question.* "What haven't I asked about that I should have?" is pretty good. So is "You know quite a bit about the problem of ____. What aspect might I be overlooking?"

▶ *If the interviews are to be at a midlevel in the organization, you might want to prepare a list of items for an interviewee to rank from most to least important, a questionnaire to work through aloud with you, or a card-sorting task, wherein items of interest are sorted into categories of examples or nonexamples of problems, ideas, and so on.* Not long ago, during a problem-clarification meeting with the president of a bank with eighteen branches, we were able to persuade the interviewee to rank his branches from "best" to "worst" by arranging on a long table three-by-five cards on which had been typed each branch name and performance statistics. We had him arrange the cards so that those branches that performed similarly were close to each other on the table and those that differed were placed farther apart. Later in the interview, we pinpointed key characteristics of "successful branch management" by using the visual scale he had built as a frame of reference.

▶ *The meeting should be scheduled at the interviewee's convenience.* The more you push to have the meeting at your convenience, the less credible you become.

A TRUE STORY A line manager of my acquaintance, a man with responsibility over several hundred equipment installers, truck drivers, and repair people for the installation and repair division of a computer company, related the following exchange between himself and a would-be in-house HRD helper:

Mr. Process:	Mr. Big Shot, I'm Mr. Process Consultant. I have a commission from internal OD to meet with all key managers to set a schedule of meetings with you and your direct reports.
Mr. Big Shot:	My calendar is pretty full. It will have to be later this month.
Mr. Process:	Oh, that won't do. Mr. Top Dog insists that we meet with all key managers by the fifteenth.
Mr. Big Shot:	Let's see. I have a Wednesday sunrise prayer-group meeting, but if Mr. T.D. is going to be on your neck, I'll skip the meeting and see you here in my office at 5:45 this Wednesday morning.
Mr. Process:	(Silence)
Mr. Big Shot:	Hello?

| *Mr. Process:* | Gee, I come in on the bus. I'd have to leave home at . . . oh, gosh, I don't think so. |
| *Mr. Big Shot:* | Okay, pal. Let's put 'em on the table. You don't want to see me any more than I want to see you. Doesn't sound like you're as convinced as T.D. that this deal is necessary. So you come here, ask me your questions on Friday from 3:30 to 4:15, and we're done. Got it? |

The point? Simple. The consultant went out on a limb to create a sense of urgency and importance about his assignment. When the line manager rose to the bait and called his bluff, the consultant's credibility went up in smoke.

SOME SCHEDULING TIPS

- ▶ Schedule a specific time.
- ▶ Leave at least forty-five minutes between interviews.
- ▶ Try not to schedule interviews late in the day or just before lunch.
- ▶ Avoid meet-and-eat interviews if possible, but be flexible.
- ▶ Leaving messages is fine, but keep calling. Many people throw away phone messages from callers they don't know.
- ▶ Arrive five minutes early.
- ▶ Don't interrupt a person while he or she is occupied with another person or agenda.

2. STARTING THE INTERVIEW

One-to-one interviews differ from group interviews in both content and process. In focus-group work, the presence of peers usually gives the group members a sense of power and protection. If the group members don't like or are bored with what you're doing, they'll tell you—usually by moving the group away from your topic and toward theirs.

In face-to-face interviewing, there's neither protection nor autonomy. To say that interviewees are often "tensed up" about the interview is an understatement.

So Rule 1 for face-to-face interviewing has to be: Don't touch content until you've built a trusting relationship with the interviewee. Before an interview can address specific content, the interviewee must be put at ease. That requires answering the *interviewee's* questions about the interview. Interviewees tend to ask three sorts of questions about an interview:

▶ *Intent questions.* "What is this person's reason for interviewing me?" "What is he or she going to do to me?" "How will talking to this person affect me and my job?" Notice the *me* focus. Real "bottom of the pyramid" stuff, in Maslow's terms.

▶ *Competency questions.* "Is this person qualified to talk with me on this subject?" "Does he or she understand our business well enough not to misunderstand what I'm saying?" "Can this person be trusted to interpret and convey my opinions and ideas correctly?" Here the focus is less defensive because it's on *you.*

▶ *Propriety or commonality questions.* "Can this person understand where I'm coming from?" "Are we—the interviewer and I—enough alike to have real communication?" "Is this a peer-to-peer, person-to-person interview, or is it a one-up, one-down thing?" *Us* and *we* questions are the least emotional and are fairly easy to handle. Dress, body language, and the peripherals make a big impact on propriety.

Rule 2 is: Be prepared, but admit to knowing a lot less than the interviewee. The interviewee is often the only subject-matter expert in the area of your concern. Attempting to treat an interviewee as a testee—someone who knows less than you, someone you're testing—blocks content communication and shuts off the information-gathering process.

After relationship matters are taken care of, position yourself relative to the interviewee and clarify your expectations of the interview. I do that by reviewing the purpose of the meeting. After all, I asked to see the interviewee, so I must make clear why I need the time and then restate and clarify the purpose. Here is an example of one opening statement we used for a series of face-to-face interviews with regional sales managers:

> Ms. _____, I work for _____, a consulting company that has been retained by Mr. _____ of the national training center. We are looking at the possibility of conducting some introduction to computer training. To do that, we need to talk to people like yourself who are using computers already. So the purpose of this discussion is to get your feelings about training programs and to tap your insights into problems that can affect new computer users.

3. CONDUCTING THE INTERVIEW

Now it's time to let the interviewee focus on the topic. Don't jump right into the interview; move in slowly and calmly so the interviewee has a chance to get his or her bearings. Here are some tips, tricks, and topics to keep in mind when doing the actual interview.

A. FOCUS YOUR It takes considerable energy to be focused on the interviewee 100 per-
ATTENTION cent of the time. A full day of interviewing is more tiring than a full
day of hod hauling. But when you've done your homework and scheduled
the interview for a time when you won't be too tired or hungry to hear, you
will have the necessary energy. Some helpful focusing hints are:

> ▶ Use "extra" mind time to evaluate what the speaker is saying.
> People hear faster than they speak, so a wandering mind is a
> continual danger.
> ▶ Form more than one conclusion. As you listen, write "possible
> hypothesis" statements and reminder questions next to your
> interview notes.
> ▶ Ask for concrete examples when the theory, concept, and jar-
> gon jungle gets especially thick.
> ▶ Ask key questions more than once and in more than one way.
> ▶ If your mind does wander or if you don't understand, ask the
> person to repeat what was said. "Could you say that another
> way? I'm not sure I followed you" works for us.

B. SEQUENCE THE When asking questions, sequence from general to specific. Keep your
QUESTIONING questioning upbeat, and maintain your interest, genuine or otherwise,
in the answer. Sometimes people need time to think about a question. Give
it to them in the form of respectful silence. Summarizing the answer or ideas
in a long statement gives you a double-check on what you heard and encourages elaboration. Above all, be flexible. Follow the twists and turns the
interviewee wants to take. What looks like blind alleys are sometimes shortcuts to new, unexplored avenues.

C. ASK FOR While emphasizing that names and blames aren't of interest to you, be
CONSTRUCTIVE CRITICISM sure your interviewee understands the realities of the problem you are
being paid to explore. If you are chasing after a supposed training need but
there is resistance to it—for instance, an antitraining value in the field that
nobody in the home office wants to acknowledge—you need the information. However, criticism or "ain't it awfuling" can run on forever if encouraged and reinforced. Ask for it and note it, but don't agree with it, amplify it,
or even repeat or rephrase it. Simply ask, "Are there political or other issues
around the topic of computers that I should know about? I'm not asking you
to criticize the company, name villains, or point the finger, but are there any
special factors about this problem that I should understand?"

D. PUT ANSWERS IN
PERSPECTIVE
While you want mostly to gather opinions and ideas in a face-to-face interview, you do need a context for those opinions. Ask for specific examples. Ask what opinion others might hold; try to determine if other managers would agree with the interviewee's assessment of the situation. Ask for definitions or at least the intent of such loaded words as *disaster, impact, urgent, important, hard-headed, vital, critical, uncooperative.*

Be careful not to misinterpret opinion as fact. If someone says, "Hell, half our people are scared to death of computers," ask later if literally half the staff is afraid. Be as wary of an absence of criticism as you are of an excess. Asking about a person's *experience* with computing gets him or her off the hook a bit. Six types of answers should raise a caution flag in your mind and on your notepad:

- ▶ Sweeping generalizations
- ▶ Convoluted answers peppered with complex terms you scarcely understand
- ▶ Answers that fit your preconceived notions too well or that line up too well with head-office or the guy-next-door's view of the issues
- ▶ Confidential just-between-us replies
- ▶ Sentences beginning with "It stands to reason," "As you well know," "We can all agree," and other assumptive openers

E. AVOIDING
DISAGREEMENT
When someone demands, "What do you think we should be doing?" or "How do they view it in head office?" you could be in for trouble. Toss the monkey back with, "I guess if they thought they knew better than you, I wouldn't be here." By admitting that you aren't an expert and clarifying that you need confidential input, you usually can win people over to your side. Keep them there by:

- ▶ Avoiding sarcasm
- ▶ Playing "Can you top this?"
- ▶ Correcting facts or dates
- ▶ Contradicting an opinion
- ▶ Admitting an error if you make one
- ▶ Effecting reconciliation if you somehow offend or step out of line

When you find yourself in one of those uncomfortable and occasionally unavoidable personality conflicts, terminate the interview and look for another route of information gathering. Above all, remember you are working with a human being who has a right to good treatment from you and who can do you good or bad later.

F. MANAGING THE INTERVIEW TIME
Meeting time costs money, yours and theirs. So maximize it by doing the following:

- ▶ Avoid arguments over facts, opinions, and trivialities.
- ▶ Change the focus when the interviewee lapses into a monologue about how it was done in the old days.
- ▶ Shift the topic if the interviewee starts selling you his or her opinion or pressing you for agreement.
- ▶ Above all, keep the small talk in balance. Some people need small talk to establish trust. Some abhor it. Some hide behind it. Keep your antennae sharp for what's going on in the exchange of small talk.

G. NOTE TAKING
How do you capture the data from a face-to-face? The most common approach is to take notes. Tape recording and questionnaire completion can also bring order to the interview process, but note taking seems to be the most flexible and usable approach to capturing the data.

Too much note taking, however, can get in the way of the interview. Edward Price Bell, a 1920s reporter who was as famous as the heads of state, captains of industry, and stars he interviewed, never took a note, preferring to reconstruct "a piece at a time from memory"; of course, he often took a fortnight to reconstruct a 5,000-word interview. Truman Capote trained himself to remember long passages of conversation with the help of a tape recorder; his spellbinding *In Cold Blood* was largely researched that way. Many a hard-bitten newspaper reporter takes pride in the ability to write up a news conference from memory, using notes to confirm facts and references.

Since note taking is the province and paycheck skill of the professional reporter, consider the following ten tips from Ken Metzler, a reporter and author of *Creative Interviewing: The Writer's Guide to Gathering Information.*

▶ *Record names, dates, spellings, ages, percentages, and figures.* Quotes, quips, and anecdotes might lodge in your memory, but figures are elusive.

▶ *Note major conceptual points, and follow up with a facts-and-figures probe.* Some reporters split their notebooks down the center, using one side for ideas and the other for data. For instance:

Part of fear problem	20%–30%
related to fear of	
losing job.	50 jobs lost
	last year
Supervisors are primarily males	
and females operate computers.	Sups.
Females w/ambition turn over	25% ♀
quickly	75% ♂

▶ Develop a personal shorthand. Getting a direct quote verbatim is a major note-taking problem. One solution is to train your mind to hold a quote in memory until you can write it down. Another is to take a speed-writing or shorthand course or to develop your own system. One simple trick is to drop the vowels and use symbols for common words: "ths hlps u gt ur inf wrd 4 wrd."

▶ *Slow the pace.* Asking clarifying questions lets you catch up. So does saying, "That's a good way to say that. Let me get that verbatim." Or "Just a moment. That's an important idea. I want to get it down right."

▶ *Discipline the conversation.* If the interviewee tells you that there are three reasons for something, scribble down "3 rsns" and number each point. If he or she only mentions two, ask for the third point.

▶ *Use nonverbal reinforcement.* Note taking encourages talk in the direction of the most pencil movement. So do head-nodding and non-committal verbal clucking and "uh-huh-ing." *Caution:* Some people panic when you takes notes in a flurry; to reduce tension, explain what you're writing.

▶ *Memory training.* With a bit of practice, you can learn to in-clude in your notes "recall cues," those simple sentences or phrases that bring back longer strings of conversation and ideas. A colorful phrase or un-usual incident can be a good cue.

▶ *Type up your notes.* Regardless of how good your notes and memory are, both fade. Typing your notes for file gives you a chance to flesh out what you have while it's fresh and to add impressions and suspicions. If you are working on a hypothesis, put relevant confirmation or negative instances in the typed notes. Note time, date, and names of those interviewed. If you are security-conscious or just a bit paranoid, code the notes you might use—for example, LMl for "first manager of low-performing unit interviewed." Just remember to write the code down somewhere.

4. CONCLUDING THE INTERVIEW

Don't bring the interview to a sudden halt. Ease it to a stop. Summarize what you learned, but emphasize that you need time to pull everything together. Tell the person what you intend to do with the information and what actions it may precipitate. Don't promise, but do explain what you will be doing with the data.

Be sure to thank the person graciously for his or her time and for the open way you were treated. It doesn't hurt to lay it on a bit. If the person seems to be prolonging the meeting, be aware that he or she may want to tell you something of a sensitive nature. Probe gently.

If the interview is a high-level, preliminary problem identification, promise a follow-up action. A memo or letter reiterating the explanation of the problem, a second meeting, and proposal for action are typical ways to follow-up this sort of meeting. If you are doing field management interviews, do not promise a report of findings or a specific follow-up action. If a follow-up seems needed, simply write a "bread-and-butter" memo that once again thanks the interviewee for the time and candor. Do *not* review key points in your letter; doing so might cause a case of "cold feet."

5. COMPILING AND ANALYZING RESULTS

One approach to compiling and analyzing interview results is simply to sum key opinions across interviews. In some instances, we've simply gone back over our typed notes, looking for common complaints and speculations about the problem under review.

There are still other ways to analyze interviews. You could develop a questionnaire over certain performance areas afterward, and use your interview notes to "answer" the survey as the interviewee probably would (or could) have done, based on your interview. It is even easier to send the survey back to the people you interviewed as well as to others ranked the same way your interviewees are ranked. This technique (1) verifies the key differences that seemed to separate high- and low-ranked interviewees in the review of interview notes, and (2) verifies the extent to which those same factors discriminate between others who were high or low-ranked in the same population but not interviewed.

While this sequence of interviewing, analyzing interviews, developing a questionnaire, sending a questionnaire, and analyzing a questionnaire takes *time* and *money*, it is one of the safest and surest approaches to capturing the key cognitive factors and behaviors that distinguish high and low performers and performance units.

LIMITS OF FACE-TO-FACE INTERVIEWS

The personal face-to-face interview is one of the most used and abused techniques for gathering data. When the interview process is highly structured beforehand and is systematically implemented, it can be one of the best ways to gather information. But as with *every* data-gathering technique, there are pluses and minuses.

The personal interview has a number of pluses:

▶ If the interviewer and interviewee can establish a congenial relationship, a lot of information can be shared in confidence within a short time.

▶ The interviewer can use rating scales, questionnaires, and card-sorting techniques to shape the interview and to relax and stimulate the interviewee.

▶ If the interview is especially fruitful, the length can be adjusted without having to consider other participants.

▶ The interviewer can shift and change interview style and question types to meet the style and comfort needs of the interviewee.

There are, however, at least four drawbacks to the personal interview:

▶ The one-on-one interview is definitely the most expensive, and slowest way to gather information.

▶ Because interviewees may doubt that the interview will be held in confidence—especially if a tape recorder is used—they may not answer the interviewer's questions candidly or fully.

▶ Often the people selected for interview purposes within an organization are chosen because of their verbal skills or a reputation for candor rather than because they are representative.

► It is difficult to control the one-on-one interview to the extent that the structured questions get answered. An interviewer might get carried away with some tangential lead in the interview, and the interviewee may need more time than the interview allows to consider one or more of the interview questions.

THE FOCUS-GROUP TECHNIQUE

Market researchers use the focus group to find out what consumers like and dislike about a specific product or service and why they buy certain products instead of others. I use focus groups to compare the attitudes, cognitive processes, experiences, and on-the-job applications of successful and unsuccessful computer users.

To be completely technically accurate, the objective of a focus group is to acquire a set of responses from a group of people familiar with a topic, service, experience, or product being discussed. It is a qualitative rather than a quantitative study. It gives you a feel for important issues but doesn't give you any numbers for judging how widespread a concern or idea might be or how strongly an opinion is held. The value lies in the richness of the data the focus group discussion generates and the leads it provides in looking for patterns of experience. For example, we found an interesting difference in one organization between people who had learned computing ''on their own'' and others who had failed. The big difference was that the successful ''self-teachers'' either had a computer at home, had joined a local users' group, or had paid for and taken classes on their own. The unsuccessful had simply tried to learn the craft from the documentation on the job.

Another frequent goal of the focus group is to develop hypotheses to be tested via subsequent surveys or observational techniques. Specific turns of phrase or word pictures that focus-group participants generate can often aid in the development of questionnaire items. And, of course, the greenest training rookie can see that a spinoff of the focus group is a wealth of case-study and critical-incident material for use as training content.

A FOCUS GROUP IS A GROUP FOCUSED

An actual focus group usually consists of eight to twelve people working with a moderator to express opinions and attitudes and to discuss a specific topic with which all group participants are familiar. They may qualify because they sell chocolate ice cream or drink Old Swamp Water; they are, in other words, peers who share some important criteria. Our most frequent use of the focus group in CLNA is to compare successful computer users to unsuccessful (or less successful) computer users to find out what experiences, learnings, backgrounds, and so on, separate the two. A second use is to compare users and nonusers on the same sorts of background factors and experiences. In both cases we also explore the attitude toward computers and computing.

A typical focus-group session runs from one to two hours. A group that meets longer has usually stopped being a focus group—a group discussing a specific topic—and has turned into either group therapy or a seance. A focus group's discussion differs from the organizational development consultant's "deep sensing group" in the focus and depth of its treatment of material. A sensing group is a much more broadly aimed device that concentrates on employee attitudes toward the organization. A focus group may focus on job satisfaction and attitude issues, but it is just as likely to uncover differences in cold call strategy between high- and low-sales performers or find why some supervisors use less overtime or have teams that make parts with fewer defects.

PHASES OF THE FOCUS-GROUP STUDY

Al Anderson, president of Anderson Research in Minneapolis, says that a focus-group study has eight specific stages:

1. Initial client meeting

2. Development of the interview guide

3. Second client meeting

4. Conduct of the groups

5. Transcription of the proceedings

6. Internalization

7. Organization and writing

8. Presentation of the findings

If you don't care for all those stages, just think of these three phases:

I   Planning the study

II   Running the groups

III Compiling and analyzing results

PHASE I—PLANNING THE STUDY Focus groups are highly susceptible to the "garbage in, garbage out" phenomenon. A concise definition of the problem under investigation and the kinds of input needed for understanding the nature of the problem is critical. The culmination of the planning process should be:

1. A statement of the problem

2. Identification of a specific population of people who should have valuable input and insight into the problem

3. An interview outline for conducting the actual focus-group discussion

STEP 1. INITIAL CLIENT MEETING The purpose of the initial client meeting is to scope out the problem and the parameters. This is where you learn which people are involved with the problem, what management thinks the causes of the problem might be, and what the value of solving the problem is.

This is also the time to discuss high and low performers. Part of the clients' homework at this meeting is finding the highs and lows for you to talk with. They own the criteria, so they have to identify the bodies. This is that critical point in the CLNA wherein someone in the organization is going to have to tell you (a) who is currently using desktop computers and (b) who is using them *successfully.*

STEP 2. DEVELOPMENT OF THE INTERVIEW GUIDE The interview guide is an outline of what you want to know and some things you want to remember to say. Among the important things to make clear to the group are the purposes of the meeting and the kinds of information you are seeking. Actually the outline, besides stating the focus you want to specify and providing a nicely worded promise of anonymity, is mostly a backup tool. The act of thinking your way through the development of the outline is enough to focus *you* on the issues.

The outline also reassures management that you aren't going on a fishing party or aren't going to pry into forbidden closets. Furthermore, the discussion outline provides a stick-to-it framework for the moderator. Of course, the moderator has to know—sense, really—when the group is more concerned about topics not on the outline. In that case, he or she must just "go with the flow." Sometimes the best moderator is the one who knows when it's time to shut up and listen.

STEP 3. SECOND CLIENT MEETING At the second client meeting, you go over the outline to verify what will be covered. This is the clients' last shot at providing input, so listen to them. It is especially important to find out if there are any organizational taboos. For example, in one electronics manufacturing organization, we were told to avoid the topic of compensation in our groups. Naturally, compensation came up without our asking, which doubly reinforced our report that employees were still "hot" on the subject.

This is also where you cross-check that you are getting the groups you wanted. It is best to remind the client liaison person that you *need* groups of peers *only*—no bosses and subordinates—and that high and low performers aren't mixed in the same group. We have, unfortunately, seen both these common sense rules broken. One client thought it would be good if bosses and employees could hold an honest dialogue; we replied that we weren't interested in refereeing a cat fight. Another client thought that *we* would be able to sort out high and low performers later, since we were taping the session. The lows might learn something from the highs at the same time. Nice try, but no cigar.

At this meeting, you should also solidify the "whens," "wheres," and "how manys." We have worked with Al Anderson on about a dozen sales needs-analysis studies, using focus groups as one of the techniques. Al has convinced us that it takes a maximum of *five* focus groups to cover the turf—*if*, as he says, we do a "diamond." Anderson's focus group diamond is illustrated in the accompanying diagram.

Anderson feels that the five groups in the diagram will yield all the important information a focus group can provide. The members of Group 1,

Anderson's Needs-Analysis Focus-Group Diamond

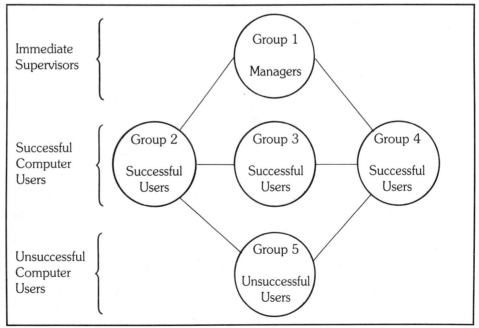

the immediate supervisors of the users, usually have some good instincts about the differences between high and low performers, as well as some ideas about what they themselves and their fellow managers might be doing to impede the performance of their charges. The least you get from this group is a description of current management practices, which forms a useful counterpoint to the users' perceptions and interpretations of how they are actually being managed. A description of what one group is trying to do to help another succeed, and a complementary description of how successful or unsuccessful those efforts are, can be valuable. Management practices that are thought to be helping with the implementation of computers, but which are in fact perceived as inhibiting computerization, often surface in the focus group process.

Group 5, the single low-performers group, generally generates all the low-performer opinions and experience we need to form a significant counterpart to the ideas, impressions, and thoughts of the high performers. Yet we seem to need two to three high-performer groups (Groups 2, 3, and 4 in the diamond) to tap completely the good ideas and tips and tricks of the high performers. High performers also seem to generate more ideas about the management support they feel they need to perform even better. Management learns more about what they are doing *right* from the high performers, so this input is doubly valuable.

PHASE II—RUNNING
THE GROUPS

If well planned, the actual group discussions can be fun.

STEP 4. CONDUCT OF
THE GROUP

The following suggestions should go a long way toward keeping you out of trouble.

> ▶ *Conduct the discussions on neutral turf.* A conference room at a convenient company facility or even an off-site hotel or motel would be appropriate.
> ▶ *Give the chosen attendees (no fewer than five, no more than twelve) plenty of lead time.* Send each of those selected for the group a letter specifying the general purpose of the meeting and its time, location, and length (preferably two to two and a half hours).
> ▶ *Have lots of coffee and goodies available in the meeting room.* These and the time spent talking, listening, and doing general relationship building can break the ice before you turn on the recorder and start the session.

► *When you're ready to begin, have everyone sit around the table.* Explain the purpose of the study, how and why the participants were chosen, and how the results of the session content will be used. Do *not* mention the high/low selection criteria. During this introduction, stress the confidentiality of the information. When all questions have been answered, ask permission to turn on your taping equipment. (We have never had a group ask us not to tape a session. Occasionally, there is a bit of "talking to the tape" behavior, but it doesn't last long.)

Anderson cautions not to scrimp on the quality of recording equipment used. "You'll regret it later if you do," he insists. Use a high-quality recorder, with two good microphones—one for each end of the table—and use new, high-quality tape. Put a heavy tablecloth or felt pad on the table because recorders pick up lots of table noise.

► *Begin the session by asking the group members to identify themselves and to tell where they work and how long they have been with the organization.* This approach (a) loosens up the group, (b) gives you feedback on how well the participants meet the selecting profile, (c) gives the participants a chance to get used to the recording equipment, and (d) gives your typist or transcriptionist a chance to become familiar with participants' voices.

► *Move from general to specific questions.* "How did you approach the task of learning to use the Orchard XBF?" is a nebulous but useful starter. Later, you can ask more detailed questions such as, "Exactly what do you mean when you say that you haven't ever needed more than a fraction of the features of dBase II? What have you used? What have you found to be useless for your job?" The group members will usually volunteer the specifics once they have warmed up on the general questions.

► *Keep your comments nonjudgmental and your probe questions focused on information.* Always ask for clarification of technical terms, local jargon, and complex ideas.

► *When a group member makes a strong statement or has an interesting but novel idea, find out how others feel about it.* In so doing, be sure to "protect" the original speaker.

► *Give everyone in the group an opportunity to contribute to every topic or question in your outline.* This entails encouraging some people to talk and tactfully diverting attention away from those who like to talk a lot about a little.

► *When you're sure the participants have covered everything on your outline and have gotten all the "hot topics" off their chests, conclude by saying, "We seem to have covered quite a bit of territory. Is there anything I should have asked or we should have discussed but didn't?"* Usually someone has been holding back or waiting for the right question before telling you something important.

One quick coda: If you are running groups from Bangor to Phoenix and back again, as is usually the case, take care to take care of yourself. Burn-out, which is a real danger for the facilitator, can destroy the energy of the group and diminish your results.

PHASE III—COMPILING AND ANALYZING RESULTS

Once all the groups have been conducted, you'll tackle the difficult part of the study. At this point, you could opt for the easy way out and simply listen through the groups' tapes again, make some notes, and write up some general findings. But I recommend a more rigorous approach. Experience has proved that enduring the tedium of the following process pays off in more precise, usable findings and a more persuasive, finely tuned report.

STEP 5. TRANSCRIPTION OF THE PROCEEDINGS

To work effectively with the data from even one group, you need a transcription of the tape. This requires an expert typist and a lot of time: one hour of focus-group discussion can easily require five hours of transcribing.

As the transcripts become available, the moderator should simultaneously listen to the tapes and edit the transcription for meaning. Often the typist will mishear local jargon as legitimate *Webster's* English. Some typists get quite good at typing what they thought they heard as opposed to what was actually said. Some even editorialize from their subconscious or out of general boredom.

STEP 6. INTERNALIZING THE DATA

When you are running the groups, running for the plane, and getting just plain run down in the process, you don't really have the time and energy to understand what the people in the groups are actually telling you. Although nervous management, usually the people who authorized your work, will want instant analysis, never decide the results in the hallway. You will hear things on the tape and read things in the transcript that you won't remember hearing or saying during the group. When you are busy keeping the group moving and on focus, you can't be effectively processing and analyzing content.

This is when you should put your feet up and let yourself be puzzled. Of course, this is also a good way to get fired. So we've devised a bit of semi-busywork that keeps the client and the boss happy and helps you process the information on the transcripts.

▶ Read through the transcripts and make notes about possible key ideas.
▶ When you think you have an exhaustive list of the key ideas contained in the transcripts, grab your scissors. Go through a photocopy of each transcript, cut out sections of dialogue and monologue that refer to entries on your initial key-ideas list, and put them in labeled envelopes—one for each key idea.
▶ Once you've separated the wheat from the chaff, so to speak, it's time to sort and cull the kernels. Go through the contents of each envelope, looking for subtopics, usable quotes (you'll want lots of these for the final report), and substantiation of the key idea.[1]

Don't be afraid to change your mind about entries on your key-ideas list. You may have thought that the idea of a computer-learning quiz show was great when the person from the Keeakuck office brought it up, but now it doesn't sound so good, especially when your review reminded you that his group thought it was a pretty dubious idea at best.

STEP 7. ORGANIZING AND WRITING This is the creative part, where you have to make flour out of the grain and bake some bread. You need to write a narrative to explain the key idea and its subparts and to hold the supporting quotes together. And you must create this without any fictionalizing or subtle editorializing. For example, if someone in each of four groups casually mentions a disparity between union and nonunion people on the role of computers, a summary statement such as "Some union employees voiced at least a little concern that they are jeopardizing their own jobs by going along with computerization without a specific contract clause" would probably convey the tone of the comments more accurately than "All groups of union employees expressed some hostility over the wholesale introduction of automation to the workplace."

No matter how you do it, bringing order from the chaos of a set of focus-group transcriptions is like unraveling spaghetti. Once we have a set of envelopes that relate to specific topics, we try to cluster those envelopes into themes—a sort of loose, by-hand factor analysis, if you will. What we end

---

[1]Some prefer a computer to our modest envelope routine. Janet E. Freeman, at Stop and Shop stores, utilizes a computer program for compiling focus-group and interview data. We've been trying this for a few months now and are just getting comfortable with it. Old habits die hard.

up with are piles of envelopes, each of which provides a major heading for our written outline.

A very brief description of what was done, a listing and explanation of the main factors differentiating high and low performers, and a summation of your recommendations should form a three- or four-page management overview section of the report and give you the structure of the rest of the report. The accompanying table gives a visual relationship between the management overview and a regular report section. An important inclusion at all levels of the report and especially in the management overview section is the direct quote. Saying, "We found that three factors discriminated high and low performing computer users: pay, training, and nose size," isn't very dramatic. Compare that with the following:

> We found that promotional opportunities—or a lack of them—distinguished between successful and unsuccessful users. As one low performer put it: "Sure, I could bust my hump. But without that golden MBA, you don't get on in this organization. That's what really counts, computer skills or no computer skills."

That seems to nail down both the concept and the import of the issue for a lot of senior managers.

The final writing task is to condense all your findings into a one- or two-page executive summary. This helps you continue the process of distilling the information you have gathered. And it gives you a summary of the study to show to others as support for the recommendations you'll eventually make. Besides, only you, other trainers, and a few corporate masochists will ever read the entire report. The executive summary will satisfy manage-

The Relationship between Management Overview Entries and Actual Report Units or Modules

Management Overview	Section II: Perceived Promotional Opportunities as a Discriminator
x x x x x x x x x x x x x x x x x x x x x x x x x x x x x x x x x x x x x x x x x x x x x	x x x x x x x x x x x x x x x x x x x x x x x x x x x x x x x x x x x x x x x x x x x x x

1. Learning strategies
2. Promotional opportunities
3. Nose size
4. Recommendations and opportunities
	o "x x x x x x x x x x x x x
	  x x x x x x x x x x x x x x"
	o "x x x x x x x x x x x x x
	  x x x x x x x x x x x x x x"
	o "x x x x x x x x x x x x x
	  x x x x x x x x x x x x x x
	  x x x x x x x x x x x x x x"

ment people who say they want to read the report but who really only want a brief idea of what you found.

STEP 8. REPORTING THE FINDINGS Chapter 7 of this book is devoted to reporting findings. That's how important the topic is. I won't go into it here except to say that at the last dance you find out who goes home with whom. The staging is crucially important.

STEP 9. THE OPTIONAL DOUBLE-CHECK STEP One researcher I know suggests that it is sometimes prudent to test the findings of the focus-group study in one-on-one interviews. Specifically, he recommends finding and interviewing four or five additional members of the population from which the focus-group members were chosen. If the individual interviews yield information similar to the focus-group information, you can be quite confident in your findings. If the one-on-one interviews don't confirm the focus-group findings, you should consider doing additional work, perhaps conducting a survey study based on the key ideas from the focus-group study.

FOCUS-GROUP TIPS AND TRICKS

Over the years, those of us who have been using focus-group discussions to gather information for the HRD effort have developed both a thick skin and a passel of useful guidelines. Here, in no particular order, are some of our hard-won lessons.

1. *Keep the group size manageable.* We are most comfortable with eight to ten people; twelve is our absolute maximum.

2. *Set up the groups about a week in advance.* You need to give people enough warning but not so much lead time that they forget to attend.

3. *Don't reveal too much of the content of the group discussion.* We overfocused a group once, and eight people arrived with prepared statements to be read into the record. We ended up with something more akin to an Iranian militants' press conference than a focus group.

4. *Management will sometimes offer to send along an observer to "help out" with content clarification, finding the offices to be visited, and the like.* We learned to say "no, thanks" after an observer from the head office decided to "defend the company" against "the awful things those people were saying about us." No

shotgun riders, no one-way mirrors, no showing of tapes and names.

It is okay to have a trainee along, someone you are teaching to run groups. But only one person moderates, and the trainee's role must be made perfectly clear.

5. *Use normal-size chairs and a square or round table.* Keep people closed in around the table—jammed in a bit, if you can—both to develop an intimate atmosphere and to give your tape recorder the best possible shot at picking up voices.

6. *Keep the microphones and tape machine visible.* Reduce the threat by being upfront about recording and then ignoring the machine as best you can.

7. *Have food and coffee in the room, but don't offer any breaks.* You want the group to form, function, and disband. Any interruption in the flow costs you information.

8. *Keep your interview outline in plain sight and refer to it.* Even though the real outline may be in your head, you want to keep the meeting focused.

9. *As the meeting starts, check to see that there are no bosses and subordinates in the same group.* Likewise, do anything you can to ensure homogeneity of the group.

10. *The moderator has some specific functions, and there are "dos" and "don'ts" in abundance.* Among the more critical are these seven:

    ▶ *Don't be threatening.* Better they see you as a bumbler than as the inspector general.
    ▶ *The first few minutes are critical.* You must start the talk flowing and stroke every contribution. "You really have some good ideas on the subject" sounds a bit corny but works. Show you appreciate what is being said, but *don't* suggest that you agree.
    ▶ *Assume a passive, gentle, guiding manner.* Let the participants carry the ball whenever you can.
    ▶ *Orchestrate the flow so that ideas piggyback but voices don't.* If you don't understand a point, don't worry about it; you can go over the tape later.
    ▶ *Use questions and statements that elicit discussion and give people a chance to express divergent ideas.*

> ▶ *It's probably impossible for the moderator to shut up too much.* Pauses aren't hazardous to your health.
> ▶ *The interview guide isn't carved in stone.* You and some other people sat down and wrote it, remember? Don't be surprised if the participants want to wander from it. If the guide isn't stimulating discussion, don't force it. Go with what the participants are hot about.

Some people worry that the focus group is too free-form and doesn't produce more than impressions. Even if that criticism were justified—which it isn't—getting out of your office and gathering some real information beats the heck out of sitting around guessing.

PROS AND CONS OF FOCUS GROUPS

We tend to use focus groups to balance out the quantitative aspects of a needs assessment. They add depth and some "blood and guts" to what we learn and confirm using other techniques. But there are some who don't share our enthusiasm for focus groups. So, to be fair, let's look at both the pluses and minuses of using this group-centered, talking-to-people technique. First, the pluses:

▶ Focus groups give you easy, fairly reliable access to the ideas and attitudes of a work group. Be they salespeople, secretaries, or division managers, focus-group participants tend to relax and interact well verbally.

▶ The group makeup can be carefully controlled and double-checked simply by having the participants introduce themselves and speak about their background for a few minutes.

▶ Video- and audio-taping of the sessions make the extra dimensions of nonverbal behavior and vocal information available to the analyst. Groups rarely object to recording, and the transcripts of the session are invaluable for purposes of recollection, analysis, and comparison.

The minuses are pretty obvious:

▶ The results of a focus-group study are qualitative, not quantitative: there's no way to tell how widespread the group's attitudes and skills are in the populations from which the participants were drawn. And, as Al Anderson cautions, "Many times a client forgoes follow-up quantitative study because of the cost and delay. That can lead to overemphasis of some relatively minor problem or idea."

▶ Considering the cost of getting interviewees together, focus groups are fairly expensive.

▶ Just gathering representatives from some populations can be a problem. One researcher, who was conducting a management-skills study with district managers of an oil company, relates that a busy manager sent his secretary halfway across the country to attend the focus group for him. Though he certainly demonstrated his delegating skills, his creative solution for being in two places at once didn't add much to the research effort.

A FINAL NOTE ON THE ROI OF FOCUS GROUPS

Focus-group research is a lot of work. A focus-group study with four group discussions, each lasting one hour, can require 120 to 150 man-hours of typing, analyzing, writing, cutting and pasting, and hair-pulling to produce a first-class finished study. Is it worth the return on investment? It depends.

If it is important to specify thoroughly the minimum knowledge, attitude, and skill needed to master *personal computing,* and if making your training as lean and mean as possible is an important goal, the focus-group technique can be very helpful.

THE NOMINAL-GROUP TECHNIQUE

The nominal-group technique (NGT), as developed by Andre Delbecq and Andrew Van de Ven in the late 1960s, is a four-step process, used with groups of five to eight participants. The process uses a trained leader and requires two and a half to four hours to complete.

The nominal group isn't a group at all, not in the sense of people getting together discussing things. The nominal-group technique was, in fact, invented to overcome some of the shortcomings of small-group discussion and decision making. The "groupiest" thing about nominal groups is that a number of people sit around in the same room responding, in writing, to the same stimulus questions, and eventually voting on possible solutions. In the context of your CLNA, it can be a very useful technique, in that it allows you to ask detailed questions you can't ask in a focus group, and allows your experienced experts to give a full measure of their understanding and knowledge to the effort. In other words, the nominal-group technique is designed so no one can monopolize the process. Everyone contributes, and no one puts anyone else's ideas down.

PROCEDURE OVERVIEW

There are several prework steps required to make the actual nominal-group meeting a success.

1. Qualified informants are nominated to participate on the basis of their experience with the problem or problems under consideration.

    In the case of the computer-literacy needs assessment there are several useful groups that may be queried using this method.

    ▶ *Successful dumb terminal/personal computer users.* Whether you are involved in a dumb terminal or desktop personal computing situation, those who have mastered use of the system make good correspondents in a nominal group.

    ▶ *Data processing/office automation professionals.* The professionals can be good contributors to establishing basic requirements of skill and knowledge, when working in this noncompetitive, semiparticipative technique.

    ▶ *Managers of successful/unsuccessful computer users.* Computer literate managers who have employees who do personal computing can be helpful in identifying important reasons that some employees succeed and others are less successful.

2. Participants are informed ahead of time what the purpose of the meeting will be, and preliminary data-gathering suggestions are made. Before the meeting, it is useful to have participants from management describe the current utilization of computers and plans for future installations. A presession survey is useful for this purpose.

CONDUCTING THE NOMINAL GROUP MEETING

1. SILENT IDEA GENERATION

▶ A general meeting is held to discuss the goals and focus of the meeting and the task to be accomplished. It is made clear at this time that the concern is for the organization as opposed to highly individual problems. The nominal-group process is sketched for participants.

▶ The large group is divided into subgroups of four to nine members each.

a.   These groups must be homogeneous.

b.   Each group has a facilitator.

c.   Each group meets in a separate physical location and at a round table.

d.   Facilitator explains the process in detail.

▶ Each group member is given a set of problem cards and instructed to write responses to the questions on the cards. Group members work on the listing of problems/ideas/suggestions related to the questions on the card *silently,* for twenty to forty minutes, depending on the type of problem and number of questions developed.

Typical nominal-group card questions are:

▶ What factors could keep your employees from *learning to use* individual computers on their jobs?

▶ What factors could keep you from learning to use computers on your job?

▶ What causes some people to be *unsuccessful* in their efforts to master individual computers?

▶ What did you find most difficult in learning to master desktop computing?

▶ What could the organization have done to make your learning easier?

▶ What did the organization do that impeded your learning?

▶ What one thing did you do that helped you most in your own learning?

2.   ROUND-ROBIN Group members read their ideas one at a time, while the facilitator REPORTING OF IDEAS lists the ideas on chart pad paper.

▶ Specifically, one member starts; reads his or her first response to the first question.

▶ The facilitator lists the answer/idea; makes no comment save requesting any clarification necessary for writing a meaningful item.

▶ A next number takes a turn, reads one item from one card, and the focus moves on.

This procedure continues around the table until all the ideas/answers from all the cards have been transferred to chart pad paper. The group takes a fifteen-minute break for coffee and personal needs.

3. DISCUSSION FOR CLARIFICATION When the group re-forms, they discuss the items listed on the chart. The facilitator's job is to find agreements and disagreements with the ideas, to facilitate clarification of the ideas, and generally to precipitate an in-depth discussion of the ideas, issues, and suggestions on the chart pads.

4. RANKING OF PROBLEMS/IDEAS/ SUGGESTIONS After the discussion is completed, the group members rank the top five problems/possible problem causes/potential problem solutions/ suggestions—depending on the focus—on a preliminary voting form.

PRELIMINARY VOTING Choose the five items from the flip chart that you think will make *learning to use a desktop computer easier* for others. List these five items from most to least importance—as you see them:

Number from Flip Chart	Description	Most Important
1.		
2.		
3.		
4.		
5.		

During lunch, the lucky facilitators list the highly ranked items from the preliminary voting forms onto the chart pads. To do this, the facilitators must first sum the rankings so that the final list can be posted on the pad from most to least favored idea.

After lunch, the subgroups reconvene as one large group. (Remember, the preceding steps have been done in subgroups, so there is one chart pad page of top ideas/answers per question from each subgroup.)

The facilitator from each subgroup explains the answers from his or her subgroup; the group discusses any items that are not clear.

When the group members are satisfied that they understand all answers to question 1, the group members vote silently, using a final ballot form, identical except in title to the preliminary voting form, listing the five best ideas from *all* the subgroups.

The discussion moves on to question 2, and the process is repeated.

This continues until all questions and answers have been explained and a final ballot taken for each.

Once the group has completed the nominal-group tasks, the facilitators have to make sense of the results. Happily, this isn't as big a job as you might think. The information from the nominal-group process can be analyzed much as I described earlier for focus group data. This process is greatly enhanced by using *all* the information generated in the NGP. That means keeping the cards, chart pad papers, and voting forms for later reference.

CHAPTER 4 USING TESTS, INSTRUMENTS, AND SURVEYS

Nothing is more threatening than a test, especially a test covering material you think you should know, and know you don't. A lot of people think they *should* know a lot about computers and computing, and know they don't. Remember the SATs? The GREs? Facing a test over computers and computing can be as awful as that. Just the same, knowledge tests, along with instruments and surveys, are an important part of the computer-literacy needs-assessment tool kit. Though the three words *test, instrument,* and *survey* are often used interchangeably in common speech, they are, in fact, three distinct and different information-gathering tools that frequently share the same presentational media: paper and pencil. Let's look at the role each plays in the process.

SURVEYS

The most widely used and roundly abused information-gathering technique around is the survey. When carefully conceived and conducted, a survey or questionnaire study can expedite your needs-assessment work. Ideally, a survey will yield highly useful information about the background of your trainees, their past experiences with computers and computing, their perceptions of their current skill levels, their feelings about the whole issue of computers in the workplace, and any organizational obstacles that may be likely to keep them from utilizing the training you are trying to design and deliver.

Too often, however, the survey or questionnaire study is used to "avoid the responsibility of in-depth confrontation of the issues being addressed," says survey critic Dr. Harry Levinson of the Levinson Institute. Levinson further believes that "no single fill-in-the-blank or multiple-choice question or group of questions can adequately plumb human insight and opinion." In addition to Levinson's and others' complaints, the fact is that it is harder to get people to respond to surveys than ever before. Shortly after

World War II, survey and polling people talked about return rates of 80 and 90 percent as average. Today, a through-the-mail survey is more likely to garner a 15 to 35 percent response rate. And people don't simply ignore surveys these days. Some are downright hostile to them. The following is a choice example of the kind of thing one occasionally receives from a hostile respondent with very little faith in the survey process:

> My boss handed out these questionnaires to all of us at our staff meeting and told us to fill them in and send them to you. He thinks I am following orders, but I'm not. First of all, I don't think the things you are asking about are any of your business. And how nuts do you think I am? Do you really think I am going to rat on myself to a computer that will screw it all up anyhow? Brother! I hope nobody answers these stupid questions and you get fired instead.

SO WHY BOTHER? Despite the skepticism and occasional hostility expressed toward surveys and polls, the opinion research business is a growth industry. This year, by one estimate, $3 billion will be spent on candidate preference studies. Why?

▶ *Cost.* Surveys are the cheapest form of information gathering yet devised. A medium-sized focus-group study (four to six groups) will cost anywhere from $11,000 to $18,000. Face-to-face interviews tally up to $30 to $75 per head, depending on the complexity of the study. Telephone polls are slightly cheaper: $5 to $30 per head. Questionnaire studies, with follow-up and contingency plans and multiple mailings, seldom exceed $10 per head.

▶ *Ease.* Questionnaires are easy to administer and easy to take. People you could never reach by phone are likely to answer questionnaires. Compilation and analysis are also relatively painless. Computers and good pocket calculators have taken most of the drudgery out of survey work and turned a whole generation into poll takers.

▶ *Standard Conditions.* All respondents are asked the same questions in the same way, at about the same time. And their answers aren't susceptible to any of the face-to-face interview biases.

▶ *Familiarity.* People are familiar with questionnaires, and they usually know how to respond candidly.

▶ *Number.* Many more people can be contacted by paper-and-pencil questionnaires than by any other currently used surveying method.

Surveys can be especially effective when you understand and can accommodate the drawbacks or limitations of survey research. There are, on the main, four down-side cautions to recognize when using surveys:

1. *GIGO* (garbage in, garbage out). Surveys are extremely vulnerable to the charge of untranslatable results. Ambiguous and even unanswerable questions confound the surveyed. Computers make this situation even worse in at least three ways:

> ▶ They hide poor questioning under impressive numbers, percentages, and correlation statistics.
> ▶ Questions are forced into computer-scorable formats such as true/false, yes/no, and multiple guess.
> ▶ Easy analysis encourages "fishing-expedition"-type questions.

2. *Hostility and misinformation.* Questionnaires are cold and impersonal. People can react unfavorably to the medium and skew their responses accordingly. Anonymity cloaks such deceit and misinformation and, of course, gives no opportunity for clarifying questions the reader can't understand. One disturbing study found that 10 percent of all mail questionnaires are answered by someone other than the person intended. A sales manager's survey that is filled out by the sales manager's secretary, spouse, or three-year-old kid may have some curiosity interest, but that's hardly what we're after.

3. *Low response rate.* A small-percentage return makes one doubt the validity and representativeness of the information received. We never really can answer the question "What do the nonrespondents look like?" After all, they didn't respond. It is feasible to argue that twelve angry truckers can seriously bias a questionnaire on speed limits and ICC regulations if only twenty or thirty out of two thousand take the time to respond.

4. *Survey results lack meaning.* Surveys are subject to overinterpretation unless they are anchored in reliable baseline or comparison data. And such is unlikely to be the case for an in-house survey. A finding that "20 percent of our sales managers say they need time-management training" could lead to erroneous training activity if you don't know that time management is, and always has been, the number-one expressed training need of sales managers. In fact, 20 percent is much lower than the figure found in a recent national survey of sales managers.

All things considered, the survey can be very helpful in your CLNA. Most of the problems common to survey studies can be contained by keeping three principles in mind:

1. BEGIN WITH LEG WORK AND BRAIN WORK

The best surveys begin with a good assessment of what you really want and need to know. You can easily spot a survey with too little front-end work by its length. The longer they are, the less likely they are to be well thought out.

The remedy is plain, old-fashioned homework. One-to-one interviews and focus groups help clarify and define the goal of your survey and give you a context for explaining the obtained results. Survey experts Douglas R. Berdie and John F. Anderson, principals in Anderson & Berdie Research and authors of *Questionnaires: Design and Use,* suggest the following four questions as a sort of quick litmus test of preparedness:

     a.   Can you state the purpose of your proposed study in twenty-five words or less? What do you want to know? Why do you want to know it? What will happen as a result of answering the research question (both plus and minus information)?
                 Question: When you have described the goal of the study, ask yourself, "Is this study *really* worth doing?"

     b.   Are *you* familiar enough with the topic and the people you will be surveying to keep subject matter experts in line when they start carping about your survey?

     c.   Do you have a sponsor who will push the project? Fund it? Utilize the results? Stand behind you when things foul up?

     d.   Are you sure you can reach the necessary population? Have you anticipated their reasons for possibly *not* responding? Can you follow up with them? Assure them anonymity?

If you can't pass this test, you're certainly not ready to begin building a survey study of your organization's computer literacy needs.

2. FOLLOW KISS GUIDELINES[1]

Keep it short and sweet. Every one of us has looked at a sophisticated attitude survey or Census Bureau beauty and marveled at its complexity. And we amateurs are frequently tempted to emulate these productions when we design our own questionnaires. Consequently, we often err by developing survey items that are "tricky" and thus open to misinterpretation and over-analysis; by developing clever response scales when they're not needed; and by going for a larger sample of the population than is necessary.

     We try to follow three KISS guidelines when designing questionnaires that will provide easy-to-analyze responses and useful results.

---

[1]"Keep it short and sweet" or, in a less friendly mood, "keep it simple, stupid."

USE YES/NO AND DATA-REPORTING ITEMS RATHER THAN SCALED ITEMS WHENEVER POSSIBLE. We're all addicted to Likert-like scales. Writing and interpreting questions answered on scales from "strongly agree" to "strongly disagree," and then sitting around asking each other, "What do these results really mean?" may be fun. But making tea-leaf explanations to management about the hidden meanings in a set of responses shrouds our work in a cloud of expertise and mystery. Unfortunately, we often end up writing items like this one just for fun and power.

I am a good supervisor.

Strongly Agree	Agree	Neither Agree Nor Disagree	Disagree	Strongly Disagree
1	2	3	4	5

Another reason for avoiding scaled items is the temptation to average the results. These 1-through-5 scales look as though they measure something in an orderly, rulerlike fashion. But the semantic distance between a 1 and a 2 response is not necessarily the same as the "distance" between a 4 and a 5 response. So computing a mean of the four responses (2, 3, 5, and 8) and concluding that 4.5 is the average answer, the mean opinion, is a dubious practice.

How, you ask, do the "big guys," the climate survey people, get away with averaging? Easy: they don't necessarily assume that their scales have equal intervals. They make their interpretations, instead, by comparing XYZ Company's answers to the answers given by hundreds or thousands of previous respondents. Our homemade surveys don't have that normed baseline data for comparison purposes.

USE THE SMALLEST SAMPLE POSSIBLE. We all tend to oversurvey. But the more surveys we send out, the more we are obliged to get back or account for as "missing in action." For example, suppose we send out a hundred surveys and receive seventy-five back. Seventy-five percent is a fair-to-middling rate, but we can only guarantee our results are accurate plus or minus 25 percent. As we mentioned earlier, a small-percentage return makes one doubt the validity and representativeness of the returned information. We never really can answer the question "What do the nonrespondents look like?," and a minority of especially sensitized respondents can throw the results in a cocked hat. Better to send out thirty surveys and work like heck to get them all back.

That said, there is a large qualification to add. In this case—the computer-literacy needs-assessment case—you are quite possibly going to be prescribing training for individuals based on their responses to the computer-literacy survey, so you will want to survey everyone in the department, division, or whatever size unit you are going to be training. You may want to forgo both sampling and anonymity so that you can properly place people in your training.

An alternative would be to allow people to select the training *they* want to attend based on very clear descriptions of the content, objectives, and advisable prerequisites. If you choose not to be in the business of assigning specific people to specific training, then you *can* go with anonymous surveys and a statistically appropriate sample size.

If you decide to do a 100 percent sample of the population(s) you will be training, your big problem is response rate. You must ensure that you get all the surveys back—or enough of them to rule out unrepresentativeness. If you decide that a sample of thirty people will suffice, you must ensure that the thirty people are randomly selected and don't just represent a specific subgroup of people who can be depended on to fill out and send in the questionnaires. They must truly be a random sample.

To avoid getting distorted and unreliable results, sample small and randomly and work hard at getting a good return rate.

USE THE SIMPLEST
STATISTIC POSSIBLE.
By and large, you won't be needing very complex statistics for the computer literacy survey. And that's good, for most of us tend to overanalyze survey information. Dr. Michael Scriven, an expert in program evaluation, suggests that any statistical test you can't do with a simple hand calculator may be too complex to yield practical results. We tend to agree, though there are occasions—say, when you have 250 surveys to compile and analyze—when a computer might be an expedient.

Generally, I feel I can do a rather good job of problem analysis using *simple descriptive statistics;* some appropriate *adding, subtracting, multiplying,* and *dividing;* some tips and tricks for looking at descriptive data; and a clear head. It has been my experience that being able to build good charts, graphs, and tables is a valuable skill. So is the simple skill of being able to calculate *mean, median, mode, range,* and, occasionally, standard deviation.

3. PILOT-TEST TO AVOID PITFALLS

We pilot-test new products, work systems, and training programs, so why not questionnaires? There's nothing more embarrassing than a phone call informing you, "There's no box to check for my department" or "I can't figure out how I'm supposed to answer question seven." And how does it feel to receive a return-mail survey with red-penciled grammar and syntax corrections? According to John Anderson, pilot-testing a survey often shows you ways to shorten and simplify the final instrument, just as pilot-testing a CBT course or workshop shows you where the fat and skinny areas are.

I recommend a three-step pilot test. First, photocopy your finished masterpiece and test it in a one-on-one situation with three specially selected people: (1) a member of the client staff (frequently a DP person), (2) a member of your own staff, and (3) a member of the population under study. Ask these guinea pigs to read the survey aloud and talk their way through the answers. That way, you can pick up any ambivalences or misinterpretations and can use the testees to help correct the problem on the spot. Second, after appropriate wailing and gnashing of teeth, the survey is cleaned up, and a small sample goes out to the target group. Third, when these come back, do a dry run on the scoring, compiling, and interpreting. This is where you find out that your instruction to "pick the one answer that best represents your . . ." was completely ignored, and most of the ungrateful wretches pick three items from the list. Though this debugging process is a pain, it saves you from the ignominy of having to throw out cases, invent silly scoring protocols to compensate for bad questions, and generally lose confidence in your own results.

Overall, I feel that statistical tests of significance are valuable, pure research tools, but most HRD situations rarely demand them. Instead, use the "Inter-Ocular Trauma Test": If the results hit you between the eyes, they probably have practical import. *Don't confuse significance with importance.* Results can be statistically significant but trivial nonetheless.

SOME FINAL DO'S AND DON'TS FOR BUILDING AND USING SURVEYS One of the finest assortments of tips and tricks for survey design and use came from the pen of Dr. Dean Spitzer, one of the true itinerant trainers in the world. He wrote this handful of handy reminders when he was teaching at the Western Australia Institute of Technology. When last heard from, he was preaching the gospel of good training technology at the Kuwait Institute for Scientific Research. This list of dos and don'ts was originally published in *Training* magazine.[2]

Survey Dos

▶ *Begin with a few nonthreatening, easy-to-answer items.* This ensures that respondents will continue to complete the questionnaire with a positive attitude. Threatening items at the beginning of a questionnaire can cause defensive—and frequently invalid—responses.

▶ *Make your items as brief as possible.* Filling out questionnaires can be a bore. Sometimes respondents will automatically turn off when they encounter tediously long items.

▶ *Emphasize the crucial words in each item.* If certain words

---

might change the entire meaning of the item when misinterpreted, italicize or underscore them.

▶ *Leave adequate space for respondents to make comments.* Although unstructured comments are often difficult to analyze, they can provide valuable information that might not otherwise be collected. Plenty of white space also makes the form appear less cluttered and more professional.

▶ *Group items into coherent categories.* This makes the respondent's job easier because he or she won't constantly shift mental gears, become fatigued, and make a mistake. Categories don't have to be labeled, but similar items should be grouped together.

▶ *Provide some variety in the type of items used.* This keeps respondents from becoming fatigued and bored and is particularly important for long questionnaires. Alternative types include: multiple-choice, true-false, short-answer, open-ended items, ranking items, and items that are contingent upon previous responses.

▶ *Include clear, concise instructions on how to complete the questionnaire.* Heed Murphy's Law here, too. Be sure that your instructions will inhibit any attempts (conscious or otherwise) to complete the questionnaire incorrectly.

▶ *Specify what to do with the completed questionnaire.* The return address should be clearly identified on the cover letter and on the form itself. Should the questionnaire be returned in a self-addressed envelope? What's the deadline for completing it? (By the way, deadlines increase questionnaire response rates.)

▶ *Provide incentives for a promptly completed questionnaire.* This doesn't mean you should "bribe" respondents, just that you should make every effort to motivate them to respond. Help respondents realize the importance of collecting this information, and explain how it will be used to benefit them. Sometimes the clout of a questionnaire signed by a highly credible person can promote responses. This device should be weighed against that of an anonymous questionnaire, one that will encourage more candor on controversial items.

▶ *Use professional production methods.* The more professional your questionnaire looks, the more likely you will get a high response rate. A printed questionnaire is easier to read and respond to.

▶ *Provide a well-written personal cover letter.* Questionnaires should always be sent with cover letters explaining their purpose and the reasons respondents were selected. Personal letters are best; if this isn't feasible, have the letter printed to match the type in the address and salutation. Never use a form letter.

▶ *Include other experts and relevant decision makers in your questionnaire design.* This helps assure that your questionnaire is comprehensive and technically correct. It will add credibility to the project and will give you a head start toward utilizing the completed data.

▶ *Plan how to analyze and use the data when designing the questionnaire.* Consider the analysis and use of data from the start. What might be a good question can result in meaningless data. Consider the nature of responses as carefully as you design the questions.

▶ *Be prepared to handle missing data.* Invariably, there will be incomplete responses and missing data on the returned questionnaires. Unless you have a plan for dealing with this missing data, you'll be stymied. Anyone who has used a five-point (or seven-point) rating scale knows that missing data cannot always be treated as though they were 3s or 5s (the midpoints of the scale).

▶ *Test your questionnaire on representatives of the target audience.* You may be surprised how many serious errors went undetected during the most careful and systematic design process. Perhaps the best way to test a questionnaire (without involving complex statistics) is to watch a few respondents complete it. If they're having difficulties, question them in detail to determine the source. Questionnaire designers frequently find that a single ambiguous word can invalidate even the best questionnaire item. A little time spent in pilot testing can eliminate lots of problems later on.

▶ *Number and include some identifying data on each page.* It's possible that the pages of the questionnaire may come apart, causing problems for the respondent. Avoid this by numbering and identifying each page.

Survey Don'ts

▶ *Don't use ambiguous, bureaucratic, technical, or colloquial language.* Don't give Murphy's Law an opportunity to sabotage your study. Pilot testing the questionnaire can help avoid this error.

▶ *Don't use negatively worded questions unless absolutely necessary.* Negatively worded items can easily be misinterpreted or clue respondents into a "desired" response. Most negative-sounding items can be reworded positively.

▶ *Don't use double-barreled items that ask respondents to re-*

spond to more than one statement or question. Such items can be confusing, especially when the respondent feels differently about each part. Instead, make each item a simple, discrete question or statement. When in doubt, make two items.

▶ *Don't bias respondents by hinting at a "desired" response.* For questionnaire results to be valid, respondents must not be biased by the way the items have been written. Again, pilot testing is the best way to avoid inadvertently biasing respondents.

▶ *Don't ask questions to which you already know the answers.* Don't waste respondents' time—and your own—by including items with only one realistic response. The inclusion of such items will bore respondents, needlessly increase the length of the questionnaire, and cause more work for those analyzing the data. The only exception to this rule is when you need documentation for the item in question.

▶ *Don't include extraneous or unnecessary items.* Make sure all the items on your questionnaire will yield useful data. Otherwise, you may overwhelm or unnecessarily fatigue the respondent. Check for this error by practicing tabulating and analyzing the data yourself.

▶ *Don't put important items at the end.* Items at the end of a questionnaire rarely get the same kind of attention that earlier items get. Save the least significant items for the end.

▶ *Don't allow respondents to fall into "response sets."* When a great many questionnaire items call for similar responses, respondents tend to continue responding in the same way. Item variety will counteract this tendency, as will a conscious decision to vary response formats and probable responses for consecutive items.

Even this extensive list of dos and don'ts doesn't cover the whole waterfront of designing, piloting, and administering a survey study. Rather than reiterate what I've gleaned from friends, colleagues, and our old college texts, I prefer to give you some references.

The single best source of tips and tricks on survey building is *Questionnaires: Design and Use* by Douglas R. Berdie and John F. Anderson (Metuchen, N.J.: Scarecrow Press, 1974). Another good resource for survey design is *Organizational Surveys: An Internal Assessment of Organizational Health* by Randall B. Dunham and Frank J. Smith (Glenview, Ill.: Scott, Foresman and Co., 1979). This is a fairly complete how-to for doing your own survey design, administration, and analysis. The emphasis is on job-satisfaction studies, which we designated earlier, but don't let that stop you.

There is good advice here. Finally, there is *Questionnaire Design and Attitude Measurement* by A. N. Oppenheim (New York: Basics Books, 1966). Don't let the date fool you—this is one of the standard survey texts and just as relevant today as when it was written. There's more emphasis here on Likert-type scales than I think is necessary, but there's also plenty common sense and good guidance.

SOME SPECIFICS ON CLNA SURVEYS

I have found the survey a useful way to gather information about a large population—a population too large for one-to-one interviews with all potential trainees—on a number of computer-literacy training issues. Key among these are the following.

▶ *Expectations* of individuals seeking out computer literacy training on their own and the type of applications would-be trainees are interested in being trained on. Indeed, it is important to determine whether such individuals have any expectations beyond the simple directive to "get thee hence and become computer-literate."

▶ *Trainee background,* specifically the amount of computer experience and exposure in the population. But in addition, it is useful also to determine the general background of the people who will be taking part in the training. An audience of ham radio hobbyists should be approached rather differently in training from an audience of linguists.

▶ *Feelings* of those who are going to have computer training for the first time in their lives. This topic is explored in more depth in chapter 5, Computerphobia: Measuring and Dealing with Reluctance.

▶ *Knowledge* of specific computer terminology and operations. Actually, this is only slightly useful. It has been my experience that members of subpopulations tend to rate their knowledge of a topic in relation only to their most immediate peer group. Thus, we sometimes are faced with such peculiarities as a senior data-processing officer rating his knowledge of computer operating systems as "below average," while a junior clerk in the shipping department who is a hobbyist feels fine about rating his knowledge of operating systems to be "above average." Nonetheless, the "estimate your knowledge of _____" query is a somewhat helpful first step—as long as it is followed somewhere in the process by some form of objective testing.

▶ *Learning preferences,* as in "What media/method of instruction are you most comfortable with?," is also an important factor. Chapter 6, Computer-Literacy Training and Learning Style, is devoted to the topic.

Beginning on the facing page is a sample computer literacy needs assessment survey. It is an early version of the one I am using now, and, as you will note, was obviously designed for a specific client. It covers all five of the major areas just specified, and obeys most of the dos and don'ts I've been preaching in this chapter. Notice, for instance, that not all possible computer terms are covered in the knowledge section. Content came from discussions with the client and interviews with the potential trainee population.

THE NEW COMPUTER USER SURVEY

INTRODUCTION This survey is designed for Big Bucks Bank employees who are exploring the possibility of using desktop or microcomputers on the job. It is composed of questions that will help the Information Center Staff develop a curriculum of microcomputer familiarization and training that will be most effective for you. To do that, we need to know what you *already* know about desktop computers and business applications of desktop computers and microcomputers, as well as your experience with and views of computers in general.

Your answers to the items on this survey will be kept confidential and used only for program-design purposes. In addition, be assured that the course of familiarization or training that is designed for you by the Center Staff must meet with your complete approval. It can be amended if it proves unsatisfactory to you.

About You

Name: _____

Title: _____

Years with the Bank: _____

Your specific reason for exploring desktop computing: _____

_____

_____

_____

_____

_____

_____

_____

_____

What you expect to be able to do as a result of taking part in a computer-familiarization program: _____

_____

_____

_____

_____

_____

_____

_____

Your Computer Background/Experience

Please read through the following list of statements that may or may not relate to your background and experience with computers. Place an X in the blank to the left of any and all statements that apply to you. Some items may seem a bit "odd" to you, but experience has shown them to be helpful in designing individualized familiarization and training.

Which of the following are true of you?

1. _____ I have never used a microcomputer in my life.
2. _____ I own and use a microcomputer in my home.
3. _____ I once took a course in computer programming and did well in it; passed.
4. _____ I can operate a word-processing terminal.
5. _____ I can type well enough to do personal correspondence.
6. _____ I enjoy tinkering with mechanical devices.
7. _____ I am a ham radio operator.
8. _____ I once took a course in information management and data processing.
9. _____ I have attended the bank's Data Processing for Non-DP Managers course.
10. _____ I haven't the vaguest idea how a computer does what it does.

What else about your background and experience with computers would be helpful for us to know?_____

_____

_____

_____

_____

_____

_____

Your Opinion

The following questions concern your feelings about the introduction of desktop or microcomputers to your specific work environment. Some people believe they will be very useful, while others haven't the slightest idea what they would want a computer around for. There are no right or wrong answers here, just your feelings and opinions about computers and the possible implications they have for your job.

1. I am not convinced that a computer would be of much use to me in my work.   SA A N D SD

2. Even if computers have some value to my kind of work, they are more trouble to master than they are worth.   SA A N D SD

3. Most managers would be reluctant to use a small computer because of the typing required.   SA A N D SD

4. I am not at all sure I can master this technology.   SA A N D SD

5. I am looking forward to learning more about computers.   SA A N D SD

6. I think a computer would overcomplicate my job.   SA A N D SD

7. I am concerned that a computer will take the "feel" away from my work.   SA A N D SD

8. I think we have to be careful about the way we introduce these things into the workplace.   SA A N D SD

9. I am concerned that a computer might someday replace me.   SA A N D SD

10. The advent of personal computers may be the best thing that could have happened to the banking industry.   SA A N D SD

Some Computer Specifics

To help us provide the most efficient training possible, we need some idea of what you already know about desktop computers, microcomputers, and computing. Below is a list of microcomputer terms. Some refer to concepts, some to specific kinds of equipment, and some to programming. Read through the list and indicate how much you feel you know about each item. Don't be forlorn if you know next to nothing about any or all of them. No single individual would ever have a need to know a lot about any of these items unless he or she were teaching data processing professionals. We need this information so that we know where your familiarization should start and what does and doesn't need to be covered.

TERM OR CONCEPT	*WHAT I KNOW ABOUT IT*					
1) Computer	1	2	3	4	5	6
2) Floppy diskette	1	2	3	4	5	6
3) Disk drive	1	2	3	4	5	6
4) Bit	1	2	3	4	5	6
5) Byte	1	2	3	4	5	6
6) Baud rate	1	2	3	4	5	6
7) Disk operating system (DOS)	1	2	3	4	5	6
8) Electronic spreadsheet	1	2	3	4	5	6
9) Database	1	2	3	4	5	6
10) Software	1	2	3	4	5	6
11) Interface	1	2	3	4	5	6
12) Modem	1	2	3	4	5	6
13) Random access memory (RAM)	1	2	3	4	5	6
14) Read only memory (ROM)	1	2	3	4	5	6
15) Lotus 1-2-3	1	2	3	4	5	6

1 = Know quite a bit about this; 6 = I never heard of this before

Your Learning Preferences

The following questions have to do with your preferences in learning. Not everyone likes to learn on his or her own and not everyone likes to or learns best, as part of a group. The following questions will help us meet your learning preferences.

1. I find I learn best when I work alone.   SA   A   N   D   SD

2. I find that working in a group helps because I see other people's views.   SA   A   N   D   SD

3. Learning by doing has always been a good way for me to learn.   SA   A   N   D   SD

4. To me, a picture is definitely worth a thousand words.   SA   A   N   D   SD

5. Lots of examples makes learning easier for me.   SA   A   N   D   SD

6. Being able to ask a lot of questions helps me grasp new and difficult ideas.   SA   A   N   D   SD

7. If I can tinker with a thing and read the manual, I can usually figure it out.   SA   A   N   D   SD

8. I prefer very specific instructions to general guidelines and concepts.   SA   A   N   D   SD

9. I like to know a lot about the principles behind a thing before I try putting it into practice.   SA   A   N   D   SD

10. I have no use for the theories and principles behind a thing. I just want to know how to use it to get what I want from it.   SA   A   N   D   SD

The foregoing survey, or some variant of it, plays a very specific role in our approach to conducting a computer-literacy needs assessment. The results of administering such a survey to a trainee population, when combined with all the other information gathering that has preceded it, will yield:

1. A general "feel for" the scope of knowledge, understanding, expectations of, and feelings about computers and computing within the work group you are considering training

2. Information that will tell you whether your *first-phase training* or *introductory session* should be pitched to a sophisticated or very unsophisticated audience—or if, indeed, you need to consider having sessions for *both* a technically sophisticated *and* technically unsophisticated audience

3. The kinds of computer uses or applications your introductory or first-phase session(s) should focus on

4. Whether or not you need to be addressing computer reluctance or the social consequence of computerization in the introductory session(s)

And that is really pretty much the extent to which the results of this survey should be put. You *could* press the results a bit further and use the *individual* responses to (a) establish content for the *second-phase* or *operational level* of training for specific individuals, and (b) determine the instructional methodology to prescribe for a given individual. You could, but I suggest that you don't. I suggest that you consider, instead, administering a specific content knowledge *test* to your trainers at the end of the introductory or first-phase training *and* a learning-style *instrument*. The results of these last two assessments are your guide for individualized prescriptions.

These two topics, tests and instruments, are the concern of the remainder of this chapter.

TESTS

By the book, a test is "a set of standardized questions administered to an individual for the purpose of measuring his aptitude or achievement in a given field."[3] But as with all things touched by the psychological community,

---

[3]The specific book I have in mind here is *The Dictionary of Psychology,* by J. P. Chaplin (New York: Dell Publishing, 1968).

the definition is simpler than the reality. The literature on testing refers to many types and categories of tests and testing. There are individual tests, group tests, verbal tests, performance tests, instructional tests, mastery tests, measurement tests, and psychological tests. Here we are talking about mastery tests; tests designed to tell you what the trainee does and does not already know and understand. Before any instruction is undertaken, a mastery test helps us define what the content of training should look like and what topics may be deleted or left out of the instruction. After the training has taken place, the mastery test tells us how well the instruction taught what it purported to teach. We will consider, in brief, the construction and use of two types of mastery tests; the performance and the verbal. But first, a little on the rationale for testing anyone at all.

WHY TEST?   It is important to consider testing to determine the entering knowledge and skill levels of your computer-literacy trainees, for two reasons. First, unlike so many other programs you might conduct in your organization, you can make absolutely no assumptions about the baseline or entry-level knowledge of your potential trainees. Few, if any, of your current co-workers were hired for their computer skills, the data-processing pros excepted, of course. On the main, your soon-to-be trainees were hired for their management or accounting or engineering or financial or training skills, but certainly not for their computer knowledge and skill. At the same time there is a nagging second factor: the advent of the hobbyist. The advent of computing as a hobby, something virtually nonexistent before 1979, has made it difficult to simply assume the computer knowledge and skill level in your organization to be zero. Besides, somebody out there is reading those millions of computer books and magazines that are rolling off the presses every month. It is a safe bet that more people are reading about computers than are buying and using them. This phenomenon alone means that you are going to have to do some "gating" or testing to ensure that your training is neither above nor below the level of your trainees, but pitched directly at their "comfort zone."

This set of concerns is less important if your organization is using specialized remote terminals or personal computers as remote or "dumb" terminals. If your major task is to train end users in such dedicated and specialized remote-computing circumstances, then the hobbyist problem is obviously blunted a bit. The procedures, processes, and protocols of a dedicated end user or remote-computing system are usually organization-specific and inaccessible to the hobbyist. This said, it is still important to identify the hobbyist or otherwise computer-savvy individuals. These may prove to be individuals for whom a remote-computing application will be very easy to learn and assimilate. What you won't want to bother with is testing their specific background knowledge level. You will still want to identify and isolate them. That task can probably be adequately addressed by the survey or questionnaire approach, which we looked at in the last section.

If your organization is supporting personal computing and desktop microcomputers such as Apple, IBM-PC, Digital, and Radio Shack, the problem of trainees' entry-level knowledge is going to sit right there in front of you and not go away. You are going to have to find ways to match your training to the varieties of experience with and knowledge of computers that probably exists within the trainee population. And that means some form of pre-training testing.

THE PERFORMANCE TEST

A performance test is the simplest, most direct, and, some say, the *best* way to determine what a person knows and can do. In performance tests, testees are required to manipulate objects and equipment, demonstrate operations, and generally "show their stuff." If you are working in a fairly small organization, one with about 100 or fewer employees, or perhaps even as many as 250 employees, performance testing is a feasible approach. But because performance testing requires that you sit down and interview and test each member of the population to be trained, you soon need to consider some form of paper-and-pencil (or computerized) knowledge testing as an alternative.

If you are considering some form of performance testing, there are a few prerequisites. For your performance testing to be effective, you need to know:

▶ The hardware operating systems and applications software that each trainee must master and that the organization is willing to support
▶ The specific uses to which the trainee will put all that hardware and software
▶ Lacking access to successful incumbents, the knowledge and skills, and knowledge and skill levels hypothesized or estimated by appropriate subject-matter experts as the minimum necessary for mastery of the specific applications (tasks) the trainee(s) must perform

In addition, you will need (a) to have available actual or simulated work tasks that accurately represent the range of tasks the trainee(s) must be able to perform on the job and, therefore, must master in training, and (b) a detailed checklist for evaluating and recording trainee responses and performances to the test stimuli.

While there is much intuitive appeal to performance testing, it is only really practical (a) when the potential trainee population is fairly small *and* there is time for such individualized testing; (b) when the tasks the trainees must master can be specified and defined prior to the assessment. Unfortunately, these conditions are seldom obtained. The more frequent case is that (a) the number of people to be trained is only vaguely identifiable, (b) the range of specific applications to be mastered is in the same state, and (c) more frequently than not the training is expected to define application potential for the trainee. In other words, for better or for worse, computer-literacy training, especially microcomputer-literacy training, is frequently expected not just to train employees in specific on-the-job applications of the computer, but to give them enough information and training so that they are encouraged to exert effort toward finding additional ways that computers and computing may affect (simplify) their jobs.

(I certainly don't encourage this something-for-nothing, "cross your fingers and hope" kind of training objective, but I understand it. If indeed you are being asked to make this sort of thing a goal for your training, please exert pressure to make it either an advanced or a secondary goal, not the primary goal of your introductory computer-literacy and beginning computer-skills training. Or are you comfortable having your next performance review tied to somebody's assessment of somebody else's "creative and innovative use of computers?" . . . I didn't think so.)

PAPER-AND-PENCIL TESTS The paper-and-pencil, or objective, test permits reliable measurement of an extensive sample of factual material. But at the same time a good paper-and-pencil test is difficult to construct, *especially* if the goal is to sample more than rote recognition and memorization. Complex understanding and problem solving are very difficult to sample reliably with a paper-and-pencil test; why else would the professional test-development folks be able to demand what they do for their services?

A good paper-and-pencil test does the following:

- ▶ Identifies present skills of people related to need performance
- ▶ Provides important guidance to trainer and trainee alike
- ▶ Provides a baseline to evaluate training and development

At the same time, there are limitations:

- ▶ Many individuals, up to one out of four, perform differently under the stress of testing than on the job.
- ▶ The reliability of tests for making decisions about individuals is sometimes questioned.
- ▶ Validation of a test is time-consuming and not inexpensive.

A SHORT PRIMER IN
TEST-ITEM DESIGN
If you are an old hand at test design, you can skip this section. If you need a primer or refresher in knowledge test design, you've come to the right place. The following well-chosen 1,500 words are adapted from a nifty little "everything you ever wanted to know about test construction" article by Marc J. Rosenberg and William Smitley. The original article appeared in the September 1983 issue of *Training* magazine.

Constructing Tests That Work[4]

Constructing effective tests requires subject-matter expertise, clear and concise writing, and considerable time and effort. Above all, it requires that each test item be designed so that every student interprets it in exactly the way the designer intends.

The four most common types of written tests—multiple choice, dichotomous, matching, and short answer/completion—are all variations of the same basic, two-part format: first a stem, which is a statement or question that provides the stimulus to the student; then two or more alternatives, often called distractors, from which the correct response to the stem is selected. The alternatives may be provided directly as in the case of multiple choice, dichotomous, or matching items, or, as in the case of short answer/completion questions, they may be implied. In the latter case, the "distractors" are all of the imaginable answer choices the student must filter out in order to provide the correct response. The format you choose should reflect your analysis of the specific content you wish to test and the learning objectives of the training course.

Multiple Choice

A multiple-choice test item consists of a stem, in the form of a statement or question, followed by more than two distractors. A key point in the design of multiple-choice questions is that all distractors should be plausible. Here are three examples:

Question format: What cartoon character was Walt Disney's first commercial success?
   a. Donald Duck
   b. Goofy
   c. Jiminy Cricket
   d. Mickey Mouse

Marc Rosenberg, Ph.D., is staff manager, instructional technology, AT&T Data Systems Education Center, New Brunswick, N.J. William Smitley, Ph.D., is staff manager–instructor with American Bell in Orlando, Fla.

Incomplete Statement Format 1: Walt Disney's first commercially suc-cessful cartoon character was:
a. Donald Duck
b. Goofy
c. Jiminy Cricket
d. Mickey Mouse

Incomplete Statement Format 2: The cartoon character
_____ was Walt Disney's first commercial success.
a. Donald Duck
b. Goofy
c. Jiminy Cricket
d. Mickey Mouse

Major advantages:

1. Test scoring is simplified because possible bias by the test administrator cannot influence a student's score. And because all distractors are provided in the item, an answer key can be developed to allow anyone to grade the tests—you don't need a subject-matter expert to do the grading.
2. When more than two distractors are provided for each item, the train-ee's chances of *guessing* the correct answer are reduced.
3. When enough plausible alternatives are available to be used as distractors, multiple-choice items are relatively easy to construct.

Major limitations:

1. Since the answer is provided among the distractors, it *can* be guessed; you can't be certain that the student really knew the answer to a given question.
2. The format relies on recognition, rather than "production" of the answer by the student. It is generally agreed that recognition reflects a lower level of learning than does production.
3. When enough plausible distractors cannot be identified, the development of quality multiple-choice items can become very difficult.
4. Since several distractors must be provided for each item, the format uses more space than some of the others.

Dichotomous or Two-Choice Items

The stem of a dichotomous, or alternative-response, test item is typically a declarative statement but can be in the form of a question. The stem is followed by only two mutually exclusive distractors (yes/no, true/false, right/wrong, cold/warm).

Major advantages:

1. The dichotomous format is useful for distinguishing fact from opinion, right from wrong, or in any other situation where there are two, and only two, mutually exclusive alternatives.
2. As with multiple-choice items, scoring is simplified and unbiased.

Major limitations:

1. Since only two choices are provided, the student has a 50% chance of guessing the correct answer. Therefore, the dichotomous format usually requires more test items than other formats to measure the student's knowledge accurately.

2. Few important statements are *absolutely* right or wrong, true or false. Therefore, dichotomous test items can be difficult to construct. It usually is a mistake to try to "qualify" the stem with words such as "always," "usually," "never," and so forth; such qualifiers provide clues to the correct answer, as in these examples:

    _____ T _____ F   An open style of supervision is always the better way to deal with subordinates.

    _____ T _____ F   It never rains in California between the months of June and September.

    If the test item doesn't fit the dichotomous format, don't force it; choose another format.

3. As with multiple-choice questions, the dichotomous format does not force the student to "produce" the correct answer.

Matching Items

In the matching format, a series of stems, usually called "premises," is listed in a single column, while the possible distractors are listed in a second column. All of the distractors in a matching series should be plausible answers for each stem or premise. In other words, all the premises and all the answer choices must be similar, or homogeneous.

In a matching exercise, stems should contain the majority of the information to be tested, while each distractor should be short, containing only a key word, number, or phrase. This reduces the burden on the student of repeated reading of a long list of distractors.

Example of a matching format:

Match the type of frame joint with the correct method of nailing that should be used.

Frame Joint	Nailing Method
Soleplate to joist	a. Blind
Rafter to valley	b. Edge
Rafter to rafter	c. End
Header to joist	d. Face
	e. Toe

Major advantages:

1. Since the matching format allows all the distractors to be used as possible answers for all of the stems, a lot of test items can be covered on a single page. Matching tests also can be completed more quickly than tests using other formats.

2.   The format measures factual knowledge and the student's ability to recognize relationships and make associations.
3.   As with multiple-choice and dichotomous items, scoring is simplified and unbiased.

Major limitations:

1.   As students complete the items they know to be correct, the possibility of making a correct guess increases through the process of elimination. This limitation can be reduced by providing more distractors than stems.
2.   Stems and distractors in a matching group must be homogeneous. That is, they must relate to the same concept and must be phrased in basically the same way. If the designer isn't careful, students will be able to reduce the number of plausible distractors.
3.   Again, the matching format relies on recognition rather than production of the answer by the student.

Short Answer/Completion

Short-answer test items, also referred to as "completion" or "fill-in-the-blank" questions, have stems constructed in the same manner as multiple-choice items. But, instead of choosing from distractors supplied by the designer, students must come up with a specific word, number, or symbol on their own.

Major advantages:

1.   Short-answer items are relatively easy to construct since distractors do not have to be created.
2.   They are very effective in measuring recall.
3.   Unlike other formats, the short-answer item requires the student to produce the correct response rather than simply to recognize it. Thus, the possibility of guessing the correct answer is drastically reduced.

Major limitations:

1.   The range of distractors depends upon the "mind-set" of the student at the time of testing. This mind-set may be different from the trainer's without being "wrong." Thus, the student might produce an unanticipated response which is arguably correct.
2.   Scoring is more difficult due to potential subjectivity in the interpretation of responses. A subject-matter expert may be required to determine whether the response is correct.
3.   A short-answer format should be used only when the correct response is, indeed, a significant word, number, symbol, or short phrase. Here are two inappropriate items:

1. A telescope is _____.
2. A tool used by astronomers to observe planets and _____ is a telescope.

Here is how the item might be improved:
A tool used by astronomers to observe planets and stars is a/an _____.

4.   Short-answer items that are poorly developed may measure the wrong things—by asking the student to recall an insignificant aspect of some important concept, for example.

Organization

Another important concern in the test-design process is that of layout. The organization of a written test centers around four major areas: the cover page, general test directions, specific directions, and item groupings.

The cover page: At least two matters should be addressed clearly and concisely on the cover page of any written test: the *purpose* of the test itself, and a reminder of the *objectives* of the lesson or course which the test covers.

General test directions: These give the student any information necessary to complete the test. General directions should include: total time allowed; any resources the student is permitted to use during the test; whether any group work will be allowed; how to complete a separate answer sheet, if necessary; suggestions to help the student complete the test efficiently; scoring procedures and values for each test item; and instructions about what the student is to do at the conclusion of the test.

Specific directions: Each set of test items, multiple-choice, matching, dichotomous, or completion, requires specific directions as to how the student is to respond. It also may be appropriate to provide practice items. If the procedures by which students indicate answers vary throughout the test (e.g., circle the letter, write in a number, or write in an answer), those procedures must be explained.

Whenever possible, however, construct tests in a manner that relies on as few differing procedures as possible. Don't forget to repeat your directions if the same types of questions appear in more than one place in the test or if a given format continues on following pages.

Item groupings: The placement and grouping of test items is an important consideration. Some general recommendations:

1.   If possible, group all items according to content.
2.   Within each content area, group all items according to type (i.e., keep all multiple-choice items together, etc.).
3.   Provide more space between items than within items.
4.   Try to disperse the easier test items uniformly throughout the test.

TYPES OF COMPUTER-LITERACY TEST ITEMS As you have observed, there are a variety of possible knowledge and skill items for probing computer-literacy levels. Here are some of the distinctions I have seen.

Fill-in-the-blank. James Farmer, a computer-literacy consultant with Sigma Systems, Toronto, favors fill-in-the-blank items for assessing both pre- and post-training knowledge levels. Here is a sampling of the kinds of items he uses for these purposes.

What is the fundamental language in which all computers work?

Name at least two programming languages and state their preferred usage.

_____

_____

Name at least three things an operating system can do.

_____

_____

_____

What is the typical speed of a high-speed line printer?

_____

Disk drives and printers are connected to the CPU by parallel interfaces. What does that mean?

_____

_____

_____

_____

Clearly, Farmer will brook no guessing on his quizzes! The advantage of this sort of test item is that you will know that the trainee or candidate *really* knows or understands something of computers if he or she is able to pass this test. The down side is that getting a correct answer is very dependent on (a) understanding the context—the stem—and correctly guessing the nature and content of a correct answer, and (b) having some idea of the test writer's assumptions about the content of the item. All in all, while such items are useful for pre- and post-training measures, they have limited needs-assessment value; they are "too hard," that is, they require a level of knowledge few proficient performers are likely to have. In the statistical sense, these sorts of items are very likely to create "false negatives," to classify learners as less knowledgeable than they actually are.

Definitionable items. The most basic of multiple-choice items is the definitional item. It asks the respondent simply to identify an example or nonexample of a term in the item stem. Here are a few definitional items:

Which of the following is an example of an applications software package?

a. Wordstar
b. UNIX
c. FORTRAN
d. MS-DOS

The purpose of a computer's Boot or Bootstrap routine is to:

a. Activate the printer
b. Load the operating system

c. Reset the computer clock
d. Load utilities into the CPU

Which of the following is a concept or an idea *not* generally associated with the word-processing function?

a. Word wrap
b. Edit
c. Decision table
d. File

Which of the following is a computer programming language?

a. CP/M
b. MS-DOS
c. BASIC
d. UNIX

Which of the following is an example of computer *hardware?*

a. Command structure
b. Baud rate
c. Floppy diskette
d. CPU board

Which of the following is an example of computer *software?*

a. Disk operating system (DOS)
b. Central processing unit (CPU)
c. Input/output (I/O) interfaces
d. RGB monitor

Such items certainly tell us whether or not the respondent can recognize the idea, topic, or thing under consideration. They do not tell us much about the *conceptual depth* of the respondent's knowledge.

Conceptual items. Douglas M. Bonham, director of Health/Zenith Educational Systems, prefers computer-literacy test items that require more thought, or that are more conceptual in nature.

The microprocessor can be thought of as:

a. A computer on a tiny chip of silicon
b. A universal logic element
c. A new way of designing digital electronics devices
d. All of the above

The characteristics of microprocessor-based device can be updated or changed quickly and easily by changing:

a. The CPU
b. The RAM
c. The firmware
d. The bus structure

The "power" of a microprocessor is determined by:

a. Its clock speed
b. Its instruction set and addressing modes
c. Its word size
d. All of the above

A plus for these items is that they tap "understanding" on the down side, they are hard to design—it is easy to make such items "giveaways"—and don't necessarily tell you much about specific knowledge or knowledge of specifics.

Our preference is, in fact, for the use of *both* of the last two types of items. A mix of vocabulary and concept items, we feel, will tell you whether a trainee is knowledgeable of the concepts but in need of specifics and vice versa.

VALID, RELIABLE, USABLE   A good test, one that tells you whether an individual fits into Group A or Group B, has three important characteristics: it is *valid* (it measures what it purports to measure); it is *reliable* (it gives the same scores for the same individuals on repeated administrations); it is *usable* (it can quickly and easily be administered to the people you want to measure). In other words, a good test is truthful, consistent, and practical.

Of these three qualities, validity is the one we are most interested in for developing a test that will tell us who is and is not already computer-literate. Validity comes in several colors. Content validity tells us how well a test covers specific material; construct validity speaks to the ability of a test to measure theoretical factors such as personality; and predictive validity tells how well a test forecasts future success and failure of groups of test takers. The specific type of validity we are interested in here is *concurrent validity*. What that means in this context is that your test must be developed so that people in your organization who score high on the test are the same people who know the most about computers. Without launching into a diatribe on statistical procedures, concurrent validity is established by administering your test to two groups—the certifiably computer-literate, those who are adjudged competent computer users in your organizations, and the certifiably illiterate, those who cannot use computers in an acceptable fashion. The procedure is pretty simple. Give your test, keep the items the computer-literate group can answer but the computer illiterate cannot, and toss the items both groups can answer correctly. (Realistically, you may want to leave some of the non-discriminating items in the test so that test takers aren't discouraged by the encounter. You simply don't score the nondiscriminating items.)

The difficult part is ensuring that your criterion—your computer-literate group—is really representative of minimum computer literacy in your organization. In other words, the computer-literate group *must* represent the scope of computer literates in the organization, and not just the heavyweights. If your trainee population is very large, you may be able to establish three populations: the computer illiterate, the computer aware, and the computer knowledgeable.

There are a number of statistical procedures you can utilize to establish the validity of your test. If you are comfortable with statistics, either of the following sources will give you valuable step-by-step help:

> *Essentials of Psychological Testing* by Lee J. Cronbach (New York: Harper & Row, 1960)
>
> *How to Measure Achievement* by Lynn Lyons Morris and Carol Taylor Fitz-Gibbon (Beverly Hills, Calif.: Sage Publications, 1978)
>
> *How to Calculate Statistics* by Carol Taylor Fitz-Gibbon and Lynn Lyons Morris (Beverly Hills, Calif.: Sage Publications, 1978)

In general, what you are looking for is a *correlation* between test scores and level of computer literacy as adjudged by some agreed-upon second standard. The first step in developing that correlation is to *table* scores and ratings like this:

	X	Y
Person	*Computer Literacy Rating*	*Test Score*
Merrill	High	42
Lynch	High	40
Pierce	High	39
etc.	°	°
etc.	°	°
Winken	Medium	25
Blinken	Medium	20
Nod	Medium	19
etc.	°	°
etc.	°	°
Moe	Low	3
Larry	Low	2
Curly	Low	1
etc.	°	°
etc.	°	°

The second step—if you are going to use a statistical or correlational approach—is to find a statistical test that fits the data in your table. In the specific case modeled in the table above, an appropriate statistic would probably be a Spearman's Rank Order Correlation Coefficient (Rs). But there are other situations and other statistics to consider, and they are beyond the scope of our discussion. My personal approach, by the way, is very straightforward: I call in the best statistical consultant I can find, and hand the ball off. It's called knowing your strengths and weaknesses, and managing your resources.

INSTRUMENTS

Sometime within the last two weeks—the last month at the outside—you have tested some aspect of your self-concept against some form of instrumental feedback. It may have taken the form of the most recent *Reader's Digest* Marriage Happiness Quotient quiz. It could have been in the guise of an advertisement challenging, "Do you have what it takes to start your own business? Take this simple test and find out." It could even have been some form of a "What's your management style?" inventory passed out in a seminar or workshop.

Regardless of where or how you encountered it, if you took the quiz, scored your answers, and compared your score to the printed norms, you have a feel for what an instrument is and how instruments can be useful in training. The capacity of these seemingly simple paper-and-pencil devices to rivet trainee attention to task has made them a favored tool of many trainers. Test publishers and vendors have seen the interest grow and have responded in kind. Today, whether you want to give feedback on management style, stress level, communication skill, or career advancement capacity, you can almost certainly find a commercially produced instrument that will query it for you.

Instruments can also be used in the needs-assessment process. If your concern is over the communication style or management style of your trainee population, then measuring a sample of the population against a good instrument is appropriate.

In the computer-literacy needs-assessment there are two instances where instrumentation would or could be appropriate. The first is in the area of computer fear or reluctance and the second is learning style. Both of these topics are treated in separate chapters later on. Very briefly, there are data to suggest that some people are reluctant to become involved with, or even afraid of, computers. If your face-to-face and focus-group interviews suggest that computer fear may be a factor in your organization, you should consider constructing an instrument to measure the extent of the problem in the organization. The items on page 72 are designed to measure computer reluctance. If you are concerned with this factor, you are going to have to develop your own instrument. As of this writing, no standardized computer reluctance measurement instrument exists.

Learning style is another matter. Several good learning-style instruments exist. (The items on page 74 are learning-style items.) The arguments for using a learning-style assessment in your computer-literacy needs assessment are in chapter 6.

EVALUATING INSTRUMENTS When looking at instrumentation, there are some specific checkpoints to bear in mind:

▶ *What is the theory behind the instrument?* Instruments test a theory of some sort—a set of constructs—against your trainee population. Find out *exactly* what that theory is.

▶ *What do high and low scores indicate?* The purpose of an instrument is to plot people against some theoretical continuum. What can you assume about people who "have a lot" of the theoretical construct, and what can you assume about those with a significantly lesser amount of the variable? How will these people differ on important job tasks?

▶ *Who was the instrument validated on?* Somebody's scores were used to make the instrument scoring key. Who were they? Are they like your trainees? Is the number large enough for you to feel comfortable with the reliability of the factor? If the instrument designers *can't* show you validation data—forget it! You can make up an instrument on your own, and for less money.

▶ *Is it usable in your context?* The best data won't make the best instrument if the instrument is hard to score, hard to administer, or "odd-looking" to your population. The best approach is to pilot-test the instrument with your population to find out how usable the instrument really is.

CHAPTER 5 COMPUTERPHOBIA: MEASURING AND DEALING WITH RELUCTANCE

THE "PROBLEM"

For the past few years we've been hearing an awful lot about something called "computerphobia." Not long ago, while attending a major computer-training conference, I watched a fairly well-known microcomputer consultant use the issue to grind her heel into her listeners' consciousness. "Computers are here to stay," she intoned menacingly, head bent forward, eyes glaring over her horn-rims. "You can run but you can't hide. There is a computer in your future, and you had better get with it before you get lost in the backwash."

Score one for the concept of microcomputers as the nerds' revenge.

And the articles! It sometimes seems that no self-respecting computer magazine or Sunday newspaper supplement is allowed to go more than a month without at least one story examining this modern plague. For a while there it looked as if computerphobia might even leap ahead of relationship-mending as the number-one topic in the Lifestyle section. Here is a random sample of some articles I stumbled across in 1983:

Do Women Resist Computing? (*Popular Computing*, Jan. 1983)

Computer Shock! (*Portable Computing*, Feb. 1983)

Striking Back at Technological Terror (*Personal Computing*, Feb. 1983)

Second-Class Citizen? (*Psychology Today*, Mar. 1983)

Computerphobia: Modern Malady Spawns New Industry Offering Cure (*Los Angeles Times*, Mar. 1983)

Fear of Trying (*Business Computer Systems*, July 1983)

Some People Should Be Afraid of Computers (*Personal Computing*, Aug. 1983)

Fear and Loathing in Computerland (*Executive Fitness Newsletter*, Aug. 1983)

Fear and Loathing at the CRT! (*Desktop Computing*, Nov. 1983)

The distilled wisdom of these articles and a few hundred others like them is that an enormous number of people are scared stiff of computers, and that if they can't overcome their irrational fear they will be left behind—just like the small-town kid in the television commercial whose parents see him off to college with such high hopes, only to have him flunk out in disgrace, slinking off the train fat, ugly, stupid, and forever unemployable because his parents failed to buy him a Commodore before he left.

Note that while they are presented as a single concept, two entirely separate assumptions actually are at work above. Assumption 1: Many or most of the people who aren't chomping at the bit for a chance to learn all about computers are *afraid* of computers. Assumption 2: Those who fail to master the computer had better learn to make clay pots or demonstrate medieval weaving techniques, because the doors to mainstream employment opportunities for computer illiterates are about to slam shut.

These two notions are blended together in much of the talk we hear about computerphobia—and each is open to question. This fact underlies quite a bit of what you're going to read here.

First of all, is computerphobia a real, important, and widespread phenomenon, or is it largely a figment of the collective imaginations of a group of headline-hungry pop psychologists looking for a hot topic to get them back on the TV talk-show circuit? A straw man propped up by the usual gaggle of sensation-mongering journalists? A paper tiger created by an unholy union of the Andy Warhol Principle and the Phil Donahue Effect, which results in the proposition that every issue will be famous for 15 minutes? Okay, that's overstating the case. While there are serious questions about whether computerphobia is as rampant a disease as many ask us to believe, any number of perfectly respectable people do insist that it is, indeed, a very real problem.

In January, on the television program *New Tech Times*, University of Pittsburgh psychologist Joseph Weinberg reported to host Lou Wattenberg that one-third of us are, to use his word, "*cyberphobic*": afraid of computing machines.

Another believer is Richard Byrne, a professor at the University of Southern California's Annenberg School of Communications. "For centuries," he says, "age, tenure, experience counted for a lot. The longer you were on the job, the more you knew how the company ran. Now, the younger you are, the more powerful you are because you adapt so quickly. There are executives out there looking forward to their retirement with the idea that maybe they can avoid learning to do this [run a computer] by retiring in time."

Thomas McDonald, a clinical psychologist based in La Jolla, California, claims that his entire practice is built around people experiencing computer-related problems he calls "techno-stress." McDonald reports seeing patients with fears ranging from vague discomfort with change to very specific anxieties about being left behind and outperformed by younger, more techno-savvy co-workers.

Byrne, who also runs a training company specializing in seminars promoted as "helping corporate executives overcome computerphobia," cites a Booz, Allen & Hamilton study which claims that one in three executives will resist computers and office automation, and one in ten will refuse to convert under any circumstances. Byrne attributes this to fear of magic: "Any sufficiently developed technology is indistinguishable from magic."

Perhaps it strikes you that a hauntingly familiar refrain is being replayed here. Every few years we hear a new arrangement of the tune "Be there or be square." Whether it's in the area of management theory or training and development, someone is always ready to tell you that if you aren't extremely careful, you are going to be caught wearing the organizational equivalent of a Nehru jacket when everyone else has switched to Italian suits and narrow ties. But then, this version of the song clearly has more validity and urgency than most: Computers are, indeed, opening doors to newer, faster, better ways of doing a lot of things, and they are changing the ways organizations operate. But as for computerphobia . . . well, maybe I'm jaded, but I humbly suggest that more people are going to make money "curing" computerphobia than will ever actually suffer from it.

Karl Albrecht is a San Diego–based psychologist and consultant who has both followed and contributed to a number of emerging ideas and movements in the HRD business over the years and who, as publisher of a newsletter called *Computers in Training*, is about as enmeshed in the computer revolution as one can get. He puts the whole issue in a nutshell by pointing out that there is a world of difference between a simple reluctance to drop everything and learn computing, and true computerphobia. "I believe we are doing a great disservice to people," Albrecht says, "if we don't recognize that some of them are very reluctant to be involved with computers. But to accuse these people of having a phobia is too strong. No normal person is phobically afraid of computers. A phobia is a debilitating psychological condition that requires professional treatment. I have taught dozens of executive-awareness seminars and have yet to meet anyone I would even suspect of being that debilitated."

Wait a minute, you say. This is making too much of a catch phrase that was never meant to imply a pathological disease. People who talk about computerphobia don't suggest that its victims are being committed to mental hospitals in droves. They just mean "fear of computers." Fair enough. But the word does suggest an unnatural degree of fear—a fear that seriously cripples one's ability to deal rationally with the idea of computers or to learn how to use one.

James M. Jenks, chairman and CEO of the Alexander Hamilton Institute in New York City, is fed up with the computerphobia scare, finding it both derisive of executives and condescending to the human ability to adapt and change. In an invited commentary in *Today's Office* (November 1983) entitled "Fear of Micros Is Microfear," Jenks mounted an indignant rebuttal: "To say that fear of computers is stalking executive suites is nonsense. The fact is, never before has any office tool been so warmly received by so many managers." From there he gets feisty:

Consider:

> ▶ One of American Management Association's most popular seminars is "Fundamentals of Data Processing for Non Data Processing Executives." It's not fear that's making managers storm AMA's walls, it's the desire to learn what computers can do for them.
>
> ▶ According to Dataquest, a market-research firm in Cupertino, California, the number of personal computers shipped has jumped from 1.4 million in 1981 to 2.8 million in 1982; shipments for 1983 are estimated at four million. One-third of these computers landed—and will continue to land—on executives' and managers' desks.
>
> ▶ The number of installed business microcomputers will reach fifty million by 1990, predicts International Resource Development, a market-research group in Norwalk, Connecticut.

In fact, my experience is that many managers are buying personal computers (and even learning to create programs for them) because it takes so long for the corporate DP department to meet their information needs.

Managers also complain that, because they can't communicate exactly what they want to their DP departments, they'd rather do it themselves. That's not fear, that's initiative.

It's true, though, that not all managers are pounding their desks, demanding that a computer be installed immediately. Why? Most managers lack firsthand experience with computers; many are indifferent, others unknowing. This should not automatically be interpreted as fear.

The three main charges that have been leveled against managers are: They are afraid that they won't be able to get the computer to do what it's supposed to do, thus looking incompetent or inept to their subordinates; they are afraid that they'll have to relearn math because computers deal mostly with numbers; and they are afraid that they'll be replaced by a computer.

This is ridiculous, I say. First of all, people who plan, organize, control and direct others have long passed the stage where they fear looking silly in front of others. I suggest that those people who haven't overcome feelings of shyness are not truly managers.

Distaste for math should not be confused with fear of it. Most of today's managers, in fact, feel undressed without a pocket or wristwatch calculator. Besides, it's roundly accepted that computers relieve managers of the math burden rather than demand more math knowledge of them.

Finally, the charge of fear of replacement comes from the tales of reduction in a work force due to automation. It's not the managers who have been replaced, of course, but clerical workers and staff members.

When looked at this way, it seems clear that if today's managers have anything to fear, it's being force-fed remedies for a nonexistent disease.[1]

SO WHERE ARE WE?

Let's take this to the functional level. The question before the bar is whether enough people are actually afraid of computers so that computerphobia represents a significant training problem—a looming menace for which one should be on the lookout when conducting a CLNA for the purpose of developing an end-user training program. Is it possible that the few available facts and a little common sense can solve the dilemma?

Fact 1: A lot of consultants and other people who make a living from this sort of thing consider computerphobia a lucrative new area.

Fact 2: Research by some pretty respectable firms and organizations suggests there is enough measurable resistance to office automation for the matter of resistance to be taken seriously.

The aforementioned Booz, Allen & Hamilton study is one example. Another source of information is academic research. Though very few systematic studies exist, those we have tend to support several conclusions:

1. People without computer experience are more anxious than people with computer experience (in general) when confronted by a computer-based training task.

2. Regardless of previous experience with computers, people faced with a new and unfamiliar computer task are measurably anxious.

3. Hands-on experience with the specific computer tasks creating anxiety tends to reduce that anxiety.

4. People with a tendency to have anxious responses to other situations, such as taking tests and facing changes in their personal

---

[1]Reprinted with permission from *Today's Office*, 1983, Hearst Business Communications.

lives, also tend to become anxious about computers and tasks that involve computers.

Notice, however, that these findings are virtually the same you would expect to get if you erased computers from the picture and replaced them with any number of new or unfamiliar or challenging tasks—driving a car, learning to conduct a performance review, learning to play tennis. Nothing on that list even hints at any widespread, crippling phobia.

The most recent research I have seen suggests that the problem is more important in the eyes of trainers and DP specialists than in the eyes of end users. A study conducted in December 1983 by Exxon Office Systems Company, Stamford, Connecticut, and the New York City consulting company The Omni Group Ltd. found that "corporate representatives responsible for office automation training significantly underestimated the actual level of computer literacy among office workers, and overestimated the degree of fear or other negative attitudes of company personnel." Specifically, the Exxon-Omni study found that trainers and MIS people believe that 30 percent of would-be users are fearful of computers, but that only 3% of people falling in that class expressed agreement to survey items of the "I am afraid of computers" type.

Conclusion 1: Some genuine reluctance, uneasiness and, yes, fear, is present out there. It is possible some people in the ranks of your organization are fearful of, and hostile toward, computers. But no convincing evidence supports spending vast amounts of time and money looking for phobias under every desk.

Fact 3: Apprehension over one's ability to master and use computers productively is not the same thing as being afraid of computers. This distinction shows up clearly in a Computer Awareness and Literacy Study conducted by the Minnesota Educational Computing Consortium (MECC) between 1978 and 1980. MECC surveyed and tested several thousand grade school and high school students. They concluded that *anxiety*—a particular kind of stress associated with using or dealing with computers—is a different matter from, and largely independent of *efficacy*—a student's sense of confidence about his or her ability to use computers.

Fact 4: Until very recently, computer manufacturers have done little or nothing to dispel doubts about efficacy. Just the opposite. Traditionally it has been considered gauche to aim even one's advertising—let alone one's manuals and instructions—at civilians. Witness the fact that an estimated $3 billion of books, manuals, audio tapes, video tapes, disk tutorials, and how-to classes were sold in 1983 to make computers sensible to non-data-processing managers and computer hobbyists.

Fact 5: Manufacturers of computers and software still haven't awakened completely to the fact that there is a problem. In the May 1983 issue of the *Training and Development Journal*, Malcolm Knowles, one of the deans of adult-learning theory, recounted his experience attempting to suggest to someone at Apple that the company's documentation left much to be desired from a learning standpoint. The reply he received was a curt "Others seem to have no trouble mastering . . ." et cetera, et cetera.

Manufacturers, Apple among them, are starting to come to terms with the fact that it's usually a mistake to let techies write manuals for novices, but most documentation is still inadequate. Sheila Tucker, a New York textbook editor, evaluated a number of software manuals for *PC* magazine and concluded that many "appear not to have been designed for human consumption."

Conclusion 2: Viewed from the perspective of the non-technically-trained nonhobbyist, there is legitimate reason to be concerned with one's ability to master the personal computer—be it at home or on the desk at work. Exasperation that your bicycle-assembly instructions are written in Japanese is not the same as being afraid of bicycles.

Fact 6: Some very real questions of *value* can and should make potential computer users hesitate when considering the machines' application to their work. A lot of people, it should be remembered, have no more intrinsic interest in computers than they do in ham radios, hang gliding, spelunking, or plumbing. Even to most people who already *use* them in work settings, computers are simply tools: possible problem-solvers, better typewriters, and so on. These relatively uninterested pragmatists realize that in many applications, computers have yet to evolve into more than gimmicks: it really *doesn't* make sense in cost-benefit terms to buy a $2,000 computer system to organize your meatloaf recipes. Do not confuse the "appliance users" and "tinkerers" with "reluctants" and "non-reluctants."

But it is *easy* for the specialist, hobbyist or zealot, who characteristically *sees* everything as fertile ground for some computer application, to mistake a perfectly rational disinterest in computers for a sign of reluctance or fear.

Conclusion 3: In some cases, resistance to computers is really just good consumer sense in action. Not everyone wants or needs to be computer-literate—especially not in the bit, byte, Pascal-versus-BASIC sense. A considerable chunk of the so-called reluctance out there is nothing more than logical concern over factors of cost, benefits, and effort. If your scatter-gun computer-literacy program is trying to force electronic spreadsheeting down the throats of people who have perfectly good reasons for not giving a damn and wishing you'd let them get back to work, ask not after phobias: trainer, heal thyself.

Fact 7: In the words of Charles Ruhbin, an editor of *Personal Computing* magazine, "one of the biggest mistakes prospective computer users make is thinking they are going to 'get a computer' in the same way they would get a stereo system. They don't realize that what's involved is learning to use a computer, and that means a lot more than simply plugging in the device. Learning to use a computer is more like taking up a musical instrument than learning to operate an electrical device."

In other words, unlike an electric coffeemaker or a food processor, a computer does not instantly make life easier; it instantly makes it harder. Regardless of the simplicity of your application (and programs are getting easier to use everyday), some sort of learning curve is involved. Anyone not expressing some concern once he or she understands the need for this level of commitment may be suspect.

Fact 8: Common perceptions aside, we are not a broadly technical people. Math and science education has been on the wane for many years in this country; witness last year's report by the Presidential Commission on Excellence in Education. Most of us slipped through high school, college, and even graduate school without much more than a semester or two of chemistry, physics, and math. It is a basic axiom that adults learn best when the new material overlaps or is similar to information they already have or past experience. The problem with computers for most of us is that we have so few past experiences or previous knowledge to help us deal with the new information.

Fact 9: Resistance to change—any change—is normal. There is a large and respectable literature pointing out that resistance to change is a fact of human existence. In his book *Overcoming Computer Fear*, Jeff Berner attributes much of the reluctance he has encountered to the fear of looking like a jerk to others when one can't immediately make the computer do handstands.[2]

Fact 10: With all the publicity about grade school kids learning BASIC and Logo and becoming software millionaires, a widespread impression is that one must learn to program to use a computer. Most business people have been around enough to know that a lot of programmers and systems people are, if you'll excuse the Merrill-Lynchism, a breed apart. And even if it weren't so, media images of nerds, rich nerds, and power-crazed nerds could give any normal mortal second thoughts.

Conclusion 4: Resistance is a normal part of the change process. You see it in training every day. There is no reason to blow it out of perspective

---

[2] I know the feeling well. The primary reason I won't play computer mystery and adventure games has to do with "jerkophobia." My first encounters with Castlequest and Adventure ended with the computer telling me I was a hopeless boob. "You shot the butler you idiot! Now the werewolves will eat you! Good riddance!" Shades of Woody Allen! Who needs abuse from appliances? The programmers may have thought they were being cute; I didn't. And now I don't play their games anymore.

or howl that it is abnormal or suicidal just because the subject is computing. Learning to use a computer to do one's work is not all that easy, and apprehension is fed by the common misrepresentation that one will be—must be—instantly more productive with a computer on one's desk.

Summation: If it please the court, I think we have come to four reasonable conclusions that give us a decent perspective on computerphobia for our needs-assessment work.

1. Some amount of genuine, irrational computer fear exists. How many people we're talking about is anybody's guess. Want mine? There are too few honest-to-goodness phobias to worry about if you're designing training for typical groups. For people fearful enough to require some kind of special—but not extraordinary—attention, *maybe* as many as one in ten.

2. Concern over one's ability to master computer use is different from computer fear and should not be confused with it.

3. Some people don't want or need computers. Others can't cost-justify them. These people aren't ill, they're either uninterested or prudent.

4. Resistance to change, and to learning something new and foreign, is natural and normal. Ever try to get a group of managers to participate in a role-playing session?

In general, recognize that resistance, reluctance, and a few pockets of fear may exist in your organization. But don't blow it out of proportion in your findings or in your program planning.

MEASURING RESISTANCE

There are two ways to measure the level of computer reluctance or resistance in your organization. The first is through focus-group and one-on-one interviews. In these discussions, confront the issue directly. Ask questions such as:

How do you feel about the idea of having a computer in your department/on your desk?

Do you think the *idea* of having computers in the office makes people uneasy?

How reluctant are people in your department to working with computers?

How confident are *you* that you can learn to use the XYZ Tech in your work?

Are you concerned that computers are going to make your work *harder* instead of easier?

Remember, you are trying to tap *three* specific issues to see whether or not they must be addressed in your training:

1. *General concern and anxiousness.* Are the people you will be training concerned with the computer in a general sense? Do they see computers as a personal or societal threat of some sort?

2. *Personal or departmental efficacy.* Are people concerned with their own ability to learn to use computers? Are they concerned about other people they work with?

3. *Propriety of the business decision.* Are people concerned that the decision to computerize or make computers available to their unit is a sound one? Are they concerned that productivity and control over their work will be negatively affected?

These same issues can be dealt with in survey and questionnaire form if appropriate. The previously cited Dr. Albrecht prefers to query people's attitude toward technology in general. He prefers, then, items like these:[3]

Do you actively read about scientific subjects, research, or investigations?
1 = a great deal
2 = fairly often
3 = not much
4 = not at all

Can you disassemble and repair various simple mechanical things like toasters, lamps and children's toys?
1 = very skillfully
2 = fairly well
3 = moderately well
4 = not very well
5 = I would never try it

The MECC inventory took another approach to the problem of measuring reluctance. Their items look like this:[4]

I feel uneasy when I am with people who are talking about computers.
1 = strongly agree

---

[3]From "Technophobia Quiz," copyright © 1982, Karl Albrecht and Associates, San Diego, California. Reprinted with permission.

[4]Reprinted with permission of Minnesota Educational Computing Consortium from "Minnesota Computer Literacy and Awareness Assessment," copyright © 1979, MECC, St. Paul, Minnesota.

2 = agree

3 = undecided

4 = disagree

5 = strongly disagree

It is my guess that I am *not* the kind of person who works well with computers.

1 = strongly agree

2 = agree

3 = undecided

4 = disagree

5 = strongly disagree

Just to be difficult, I've taken a slightly different approach.

Which of the following are true of you:[5]

_____I have never used a microcomputer in my life

_____I am a "ham" radio operator

_____I enjoy tinkering with mechanical devices

_____I can operate a word processing terminal

There is something to recommend each approach. The important thing is to be able to identify (1) whether or not you have a pervasive computer reluctance problem, and (2) whether there are specific individuals who should be sorted out and given special training and help.

DEALING WITH COMPUTER RELUCTANCE

In his book *Overcoming Computer Fear*, Jeff Berner takes the view that knowledge overcomes fear. "You aren't the one who is 'computer illiterate.' When it comes to getting their message across, it's the computer industry, its advertisers, and its technical writers who are *people* illiterate." Berner then launches into his own discourse on what is and is not important to know and his folksy explanation of all those confusing terms those nasty computer people use.

There are two or three pretty good analogies in Berner's book, and the tone is nice. Pick up a copy of it to use as a model of how you might want to present material to a computer reluctant audience. At $3.95, it's worth the price. At ninety-two paperback pages, it's easy reading.

Richard Byrne, who is the most unbridled and insistent promoter of the computerphobia concept, also turns out to be one of the people with the most positive advice on overcoming reluctance. He offers these ten hints for

---

[5]Reprinted from "The New Computer User Survey," copyright © 1983, Performance Research Associates, Minneapolis, Minnesota.

overcoming one's *personal* reluctance, that can easily be modified for use in a training program.

1. *Be willing to start ignorant.* It's okay to not know anything about computers. Let yourself know that and let your trainees know that as well.

2. *Define your purpose.* Why do you and your trainees want to learn *anything* about computers? The best development objectives—at first—have to do with improving something you are already good at through the use of a computer.

3. *Ask kids.* Byrne suggests you ask your kids, nephews and nieces, the neighbor's young—whatever small non-rent-paying organism you can find who is into computers—to give you a lesson. Of course, it won't do to drag a gaggle of twelve-year olds into your classroom to act as computer-age role models (or would it?) but you *can* encourage your students to make the effort on their own.

4. *Let go.* Don't expect yourself to know everything, and don't insist on hanging on to old ways. If you *like* writing on a legal pad and scattering pages around the table when you are working on a report, fine. Give yourself permission to be skeptical of new procedures the computer imposes. But at the same time, decide to keep an open mind about the possibility that a computer *might* have a positive impact.

5. *Find a partner.* Jeff Berner also suggests having a learning partner as well as someone a bit better to call on when you are stuck. For your trainees, *you* may have to be the good and kindly Sherpa. But if that is impractical, you might want to create such a person for the people in the departments or units you are training. And lashing students up two to a terminal not only saves training expense, but also gives each person a peer to work with after the training.

6. *Share wins.* Find a way for the learning partners to stay in contact. Encourage them to call each other not only with problems but with successes as well. *You* might get into the act by polling graduates and publishing the progress for each class, and even passing out kudos in a newsletter for six months after the program.

7. *Celebrate little victories.* You must know how well this principle works in the classroom already. Just double it up for the class of

computer reluctants. For instance, warn them that you are a cheerleader and that you believe every step along the computer mastery route deserves a rousing cheer. *Then* come through. Applaud, whistle, and cheer when they all have successfully booted up, loaded a program, got something to print out. And mean it! Sure, it seems hokey; better to have them think *you* are a little nuts than think *they* are stupid.

8. *Follow the news.* You know how important it is to keep up with a new subject and how, when you do, it really pays off. Reward graduates with a one-year subscription to *Business Computing* or *PC* magazine, or *Personal Computing*, and keep that in-house newsletter idea in mind as well.

9. *Teach somebody.* You know this in your bones. It wasn't until you started teaching Basic Supervision that you really *understood* basic supervision. Maybe you *can't* have your trainees teach someone else, but don't dismiss it out of hand as an idea. Why not rotate teaching between yourself and the trainees in some fashion? Perhaps you could even assign topics for them to teach one another. Helping others learn something well enough to teach it to someone else is hard, intense work. But look for disk tutorials, books, and manuals you can use to coach your new trainees before you dismiss the idea.

10. *Laugh a lot, it always helps.* Does it ever! Think through using one of the training films that pokes fun at computers for use in your program. There is one starring Monty Python alumnus John Cleese that is a hoot. But most of all, keep the atmosphere as accepting of fun as possible. The humor will rise up from the group once they know that this *isn't* life-or-death training.

Byrne has one other suggestion that bears some consideration. The trainee, he urges, should "actively enter the learning process." By way of example he cites the case of a friend who encouraged employees to take a portable computer home and "headbang in private" with it. That's a bit unstructured for some, but the idea of letting someone feel out the keyboard in private is a good one. Consider purchasing a portable or at least establishing a private carrel and making available a good overview-type disk tutorial for prework. Something like Knoware or Blue Chip or one of the other "Welcome to the Computer" disks in Appendix C, would work well for this brief introduction because of the ease of operation and gamelike aspects of these packages. In any case, look at disk tutorials and audio tutorials as precourse work. You *should* find something useful for that "try it alone" strategy.

POSTSCRIPT

Notice one thing about all of these prescriptions for overcoming computer reluctance. Each piece of advice is based on the assumption that *doing* and *knowing* will overcome fear. What research there is tends to support these assumptions.

But notice something else. All of these tips and tricks could serve as guides for virtually any training-design effort. Perhaps the best advice one can follow when trying to create computer training with the computer-reluctant person in mind is just to build the best *training* you can. After all, every trainee—fearful or not—deserves the best you have to offer.

CHAPTER **6** COMPUTER-LITERACY TRAINING AND LEARNING STYLE

If ever a hackneyed old phrase deserved resurrection, it is that 1960s shibboleth "Different strokes for different folks and different ways on different days." Data-processing trainers are finding that they must modify techniques and approaches that have stood them in good stead over the years when they embark on "end-user" training for non-data-processing professionals. To their surprise, they find that they sometimes must modify their approach for each new group of end users. The style of instruction appropriate for one group of learners isn't necessarily appropriate for another. Within that discovery, trainers claim, lurks a learning-style stumbling block.

A PERSONAL PERSPECTIVE

Frankly, I have long been skeptical that learning style or any of its sundry correlates are highly influential learning variables. I have never doubted the *existence* of learning style, cognitive style, and individual media-method preference factors. I simply have had trouble considering learning-style factors of primary importance in the training design and development process—until now.

Reports from others in the training world certainly influenced my thinking, but it was my own experience learning to use a microcomputer that first suggested the impact that learning style might have on the computer-literacy learning puzzle.

Normally, I can get a handle on almost anything new I want to learn through reading and through interviewing experts. That's what reporters and researchers are good at and get paid for—lapping up information and turning it back out in a new form. But my first microcomputer proved intractable to that approach. I was especially surprised because over the years I have worked on my share of computer operator, data entry, and reconcilement clerk-type training projects, have authored a little CAI (before it became

CBT), and even participated in developing training for one of the first magnetically programmable desktop calculators, the Olivetti Program 101.

After some trial and error, I found that a combination of one-to-one tutoring, disk tutorials, and audio-tape tutorials worked best for me. For me, it was most effective to walk through several examples of a procedure or practice a series of commands with the audio or live tutor, and then pop a disk tutorial into the computer to learn the conceptual information. Now I can make sense of most of the books, articles, lectures, and napkin notes people commend to me, but it took time.

On reflection, of course, I realized that there is a great similarity in the way I learn anything new and different. As a training program designer and developer, I had always had equipment available to play with and a subject-matter expert to badger to death. Once I had the basic ideas down, I could get all the enrichment information I wanted through almost any communications channel: lectures, books, films, puzzles, you name it.

"VELCRO LEARNING"   I have come to think of this learning-something-new phenomenon, to characterize or conceptualize it to myself, as Velcro learning. You know Velcro fabric don't you? It's that wonderful material that holds coats closed and mittens on, that isn't a button or a snap or a zipper, but a couple of fuzzy strips of stuff that cling to each other when they touch. (If this modest plastic metaphor eludes you, think of wool skirt or suit and a Persian cat. Cat rubs against wool, purrs, saunters away, and leaves suit/skirt in need of dehairing.) Most of what we adults have to learn—when we have to learn something new—is like that Velcro snap, that cat-hair-on-wool experience. The "something new" rubs up against the "something old" we already know a lot about, and sticks. Most of the new we are expected to learn in life is intrinsically related to the same general conceptual mass of what we already know. Bankers learn more banking, managers learn MOR managing, and so on. The "new" we are exposed to in most training is not brand-new, but a new tweak or twist on information that is essentially logically and conceptually consistent and related to other things we already know. Learning something new under these circumstances is interesting, stimulating, and often fun and easy.

Pay attention . . . here comes the point of this rambling! For many people, the computer has no correlate in their personal knowledge base. It is woefully unlike anything they have ever had to learn to handle before! There are no hook-and-eye, Velcro-like associations, no commonly understood cat-hair-and-wool ideas and structures to tie understanding of the computer to for non-DP-trained trainees. Under these circumstances, learning style, cognitive style, and all that literature about individualized prescriptions and approaches become major design considerations, a major variable to be accounted for in the computer-literacy learning formula.

Another trainer who has spoken out on the importance of the learning-style variable on computer-literacy learning is Ronnie Colfin, president of Edutrends, Inc., a New York City–based company specializing in personal computer training, including seminars, videotapes and coursebooks. In a recent issue of *Data Training* Colfin made the following observations:[1]

> Because the data processing professionals in your company are a relatively homogeneous group, you [DP trainer] probably need only a limited number of methods for training them. When you find yourself responsible for training people to use personal computers, however, you face a different situation. Some of your old techniques and approaches might work, but some won't. The needs and learning style of, say, a company president are quite different from the needs and learning style of a programmer. At the same time, they are probably quite different from those of any other end-users in your organization.
>
> End-users are not only different from data processing professionals, they are different from each other, too. In dealing with them, you have to put aside your tried-and-true techniques and draw on the entire spectrum of training methods. Public seminars, in-house seminars, one-on-one instruction, videotape, computer-based training, interactive video—each has a place in personal computer training.

After discussing the pros and cons of various media and method and the fit with different audiences, she concludes:

> Use a holistic approach in your user training, remember you're dealing with people who learn best in their own way, and provide a variety of training tools in a non-threatening environment. Match the training to the user and you are already more than half-way to success.

TRAINING BY JOB TYPE

Colfin's approach to solving the "different strokes" problem is a *job-centered* one. This strategy suggests that by treating managers and sales reps and clericals and others as independent groups, you can strike a strategy that will be appropriate for the people in that group. Some of her specific suggestions are:

> *The public seminar* can be very useful for high level executives because it can put them among their peers, a situation that you can't always

---

[1]Reprinted with permission from the December 1983 issue of *Data Training*. © 1983 by Warren/Weingarten, Inc.

create within your organization. The public course is often a forum where people from many different companies can exchange ideas freely. If a person feels intimidated by the computer, the seminar provides a safe environment in which to explore. This kind of course can also target specific groups, with offerings such as "A Cost Accountant's Use of VisiCalc."

An in-house seminar might be appropriate when you have the resources to develop it for some specific group in the company. You might well find yourself giving three or four different courses on the same software package. "An Introduction to Lotus 1-2-3" might acquaint the student with basic commands for that program, but you could have an advanced seminar geared to marketing people as well. For a word processing program, you might have one class for secretaries and another for managers who want to learn how to create reports using data from their databases. You might want to consider bringing in an outside instructor for your in-house seminars.

One-to-one instruction is effective for obvious reasons. The key to success with this training method is a sensitive instructor. This person must be patient and understanding and must know the software "inside and out." A business person often has the most credibility with users, and it is especially important that the instructor understands how the specific software relates to the user's job. The one-on-one instructor should be a problem solver. Computer jargon is not acceptable in this type of training. The instructor should explain technical concepts in an easy-to-understand way using everyday language. And this person must create an atmosphere in which the user feels free to ask questions and is not made to feel stupid or inadequate for asking questions as basic as "where's the enter key?"

Videotape is the next best thing to a live instructor. In studies done at Purdue University, video was shown to be more effective for learning and retaining material than any other training medium. The combination of moving pictures and sound make the deepest and most long-lasting impression. As children of the television age, we are extremely receptive to this kind of input, and more and more information is being disseminated this way.

Videotape is especially appropriate when you have a large number of prospective trainees and you are particularly concerned about cost. Dividing the purchase or rental price of a tape by many students can keep the cost per student quite low. In addition, people can often learn with video at their own pace; you can even send a tape home with a student who has a player. When you can arrange private viewing of the tape by trainees, they are free to stop and rewind for any difficult spots, without the embarrassment of "classmates" knowing about it.

This by-job-category approach is a reasonable approach in the small-to-medium organization where the trainer can be available to help those who need more attention and tutoring than a course can provide, or than the individual is willing to ask for during a formal program. In large organizations you can't afford to have people leaving training untrained. In that situation, you should at least consider a more formal media method matching, one based on cognitive or learning-style constructs.

THE COGNITIVE OR LEARNING-STYLE APPROACH

Let's start with a quick overview of cognitive-style theory. The root concept couldn't be much simpler. "Cognition" refers to a common activity, one we all do *every* day: thinking. To be more precise, it refers to the activities of thinking, knowing, and processing information. "Style" refers to the possibility that you, me, and the guy down the hall do all that a bit differently, if not idiosyncratically.

So far, so good. Nice idea. Beyond this point, however, things become a bit more murky.

Kenneth M. Goldstein and Sheldon Blackman, co-authors of *Cognitive Style* (New York: John Wiley & Sons, 1978), define the concept as one that refers to "the structure rather than the content of thought, the ways in which individuals conceptually organize their environments."

In *Learning How to Learn* (New York: Cambridge: The Adult Learning Company, 1982), Robert M. Smith defines learning style, a blood relative of cognitive style, as "the individual's characteristic ways of processing information, feeling, and behaving in learning situations."

What does that mean, exactly? "It has long been apparent to teachers, educators, and observers," Smith says, "that people differ as to how they go about certain activities associated with learning. They differ as to how they approach problem-solving. They differ as to how they go about 'information processing,' or putting information through their minds. Some people like to 'get the big picture' of a subject first and then build toward a full understanding of that picture by details and work through to some kind of meaningful construct, or way of looking at an area of knowledge, out of these details. Some like theory before going into practice. Others don't."

It seems almost self-evident that the notion of cognitive style has a lot of implications regarding the design and delivery of training programs.

As compelling and interesting as the general idea of cognitive style may be, there is little agreement among researchers on the particulars—how it works or how important it is compared with other variables. Technically, cognitive style is an intervening variable, something not directly observable but assumed to exist as a result of indirect evidence. So it should be no surprise that one researcher has catalogued nineteen separate approaches to the study of cognitive style. There is plenty of room for model building and theorizing about the nature of the beast.

Goldstein and Blackman suggest that there are five major approaches to the study of cognitive style. Three of these provide some flavor of the concept's history and content.

Authoritarianism. The first concerted studies of cognitive style were really studies of leadership style. Appalled by the atrocities and inhumanity exhibited in Nazi Germany, several groups of first-rate social scientists and psychiatrists—among them Kurt Lewin, Erich Fromm, Wilhelm Reich, and Erik Erikson—began to look at factors involved in prejudice and anti-Semitism, and structural differences between authoritarian and democratic leaders. These studies eventually led to the conclusion that authoritarianism, prejudice, and so on are not isolated beliefs and behavior patterns, but consistent, personality-based ways of thinking, feeling, and behaving. During the course of these studies, two important correlates of authoritarian behavior and attitudes were discovered: rigidity and intolerance of ambiguity. These two factors eventually were placed on the extreme end (the authoritarian end) of a continuum of mental strategies for understanding and dealing with the information and events of day-to-day life. At the other end of this particular scale is the laissez-faire individual.

Field-Dependence/Independence. Another of the early serious cognitive-style researchers, Herman Witkin, believed cognitive style to be based in personality in general and directly related to the way we are "wired" to perceive or "see" our surroundings. Witkin's theory placed people on a continuum. Those with a tendency to view their surroundings in an analytical or bit-by-bit fashion he dubbed "field-independent," while those who take a global or all-at-once view of their surroundings he called "field-dependent."

The field-independent individual approaches situations in an analytical way, separating elements from their background. Tending to see the whole rather than the parts, the field-dependent person approaches things in a global way. In learning situations, field-dependent people are more sensitive to social aspects, while field-independent people are more likely to ignore what the group is thinking or feeling and remain focused on the content.

Conceptualizing/Categorizing. A third major approach is represented by Jerome Kagan, who studied the tendency of people to be consistent in the way they form and use concepts in interpreting information and in problem-solving. Kagan also proposed a scale or continuum of styles. On one end he placed those who practiced relational-contextual categorizing, or the tendency to use patterns of functional or thematic similarity to combine bits of information into a consistent whole. On the other end is analytical-descriptive conceptualizing, or the tendency to find similarity in things based on external, objective attributes. Here, key observable characteristics are used to group things as opposed to making a single idea of them. Robert M. Smith illustrates the two styles this way: "Confronted with three items—meat, cheese and bread—the relational-contextual person (also called global) might describe them as a sandwich, while the analytical-descriptive person might simply call them edibles."

Other interesting models of cognitive and learning style have been developed by David Kolb and Robert Fry, who talk about four cognitive styles in terms of a model of learning and a learning-cycle concept; R. A. Cohen, who categorizes people as "lumpers" or "splitters"; and Joseph Hill, who says that people function according to three modalities of perception: "kinesthetic," which leads to physical or "motoric" thinking; "visual," which leads to spatial thinking; and "auditory," which leads to verbal thinking.

RELATIONSHIP TO LEARNING

Huey B. Long, author of *Adult Learning* (New York: Cambridge: The Adult Education Company, 1983), has looked carefully at the research on style and adult learning and found four general relationships.

1. *Age.* Younger learners (under twenty-four) prefer to learn in peer groups, to work with inanimate devices, to listen, to use iconics (pictures, charts, graphs, etc.), and to learn through direct experience. Older learners (over twenty-four) prefer traditional class organization, detailed explanations, interpersonal competition, qualitative emphasis, and listening and reading activities.

2. *Aptitudes.* The field-dependent/independent factor is related to career selection and academic majors among college students. Also, teachers and learners matched in cognitive style tend to evaluate each other positively, whereas teachers and students who are mismatched tend to evaluate each other negatively.

3. *Achievement.* Field-dependent people do less well on mathematical tasks. Achievement on standardized paper-and-pencil tests is related to cognitive style.

4. *Instructional Techniques.* Research on the relationship between specific instructional techniques, learning, and cognitive style has yielded interesting but inconclusive results. Kolb's contention of such a relationship is currently a subject of hot debate and intensive research.

The chart at the end of this chapter, from Smith's *Learning How to Learn,* shows some of the more popular cognitive/learning-style instruments being used in current research on style and learning achievement.

BEYOND THE PSYCHOLOGY OF STYLE

Although the concept clearly has been with us for some time, there are those who believe that it has only begun to be understood and exploited. Among them is Dudley M. Lynch of Brain Technologies Corporation in Lawton, Oklahoma. "The concept of cognitive style is greatly colored by the traditional paradigms of psychology," Lynch says. "Traditional researchers are just beginning to understand the core of cognitive style."

He points to the work of Harvard University researcher Howard Gardner on differential intelligence. "Cognitive style," says Lynch, "is really an indicator of different types of intelligence." As Lynch reads Gardner's research, there are at least six types or "styles" of intelligence, each related to specific brain tissues and each complete with its own capacity for the perception, processing, and storing of information. The six types of intelligence are *language facility,* the encoding and decoding of auditory stimuli; *logical reason,* the ability to order abstracts; *musical capacity,* melodic reasoning and memory; *spatial relation skills,* three-dimensional reasoning; *sensory/motor skills,* "movement intelligence"; and *feeling skills,* ability to access and assess the emotions of oneself and others.

Does it matter whether Gardner considers these *intelligences* rather than *cognitive styles?* Yes, it does. If they are styles, they are variables to be considered in the areas of learning, problem solving, and relating to other people. If they are intelligences—fixed attributes that differentiate inextricably among individuals—they *are* the game.

Obviously, the issue of cognitive style is far from settled. There is much to be learned and many researchers to be heard from. But research results aside, the renewed interest in cognitive style is one of the most interesting outcomes of the current rebirth of thinking as a subject to think about.

USING COGNITIVE AND LEARNING STYLE TO PRESCRIBE TRAINING

Humorist Robert Benchley once suggested that "There are two kinds of people in the world. Those who put everything in groups of two and those who don't." Think twos, for here come some. There are *two* ways to use the cognitive and learning style concepts to shape your training. One is to add a cognitive or learning-style instrument to your overall surveying effort. This should prepare you with information about the distribution of learning styles in the organization and give you some help planning the kinds of training options you need to have available for the populations to be made computer-literate.

The second way to use "style" in training is to prescribe in-depth training for specific individuals based on their specific styles. We recently used learning style assessment in this way with a small direct-sales company. The organization wanted to have all the sales reps supporting their selling with a small IBM-compatible computer. After having shelled out the two thousand and change for the units, somebody thought it would be nice to train the reps. The problem was that the fifty-five salespeople worked out of their homes and only got together as a group twice a year. Our solution was to find someone to run a one-day seminar on the computer, give all fifty-five reps a standardized learning-style test, and prescribe in-depth individualized training based on the results. Actually, we simply "suggested" some things each individual might try, based on the inventory results. The reps are independent contractors, so suggest was all we could do. Our very informal evaluation indicated that the individual sales reps found the suggestions useful. These same reps, by the way, use a social-style selling concept in their daily work, so the "different strokes" idea wasn't new to them, only a new and obvious wrinkle.

The second couplet to consider is the "build" or "buy" option. You could simply sit down and make up a style questionnaire of your own. Some common sense, a microcomputer, and a Likert scale is about all it takes to pull your own style inventory together. Don't believe it? Here are nine items you can use for starters. They were put together for use in an organization where standardized instruments have a bad reputation. You could do the same.

Your Learning Preferences
The following questions have to do with your preferences in learning. Not everyone likes to learn on their own and not everyone likes to learn or learns best as part of a group. The following questions will help us meet your learning preferences.

1. I find I learn best when I work alone.	SA	A	N	D	SD
2. I find that working in a group helps because I see other people's views.	SA	A	N	D	SD
3. Learning by doing has always been a good way for me to learn.	SA	A	N	D	SD
4. To me, a picture is definitely worth a thousand words.	SA	A	N	D	SD
5. Lots of examples makes learning easier for me.	SA	A	N	D	SD
6. Being able to ask a lot of questions helps me grasp new and difficult ideas.	SA	A	N	D	SD
7. If I can tinker with a thing and read the manual, I can usually figure it out.	SA	A	N	D	SD
8. I prefer very specific instructions to general guidelines and concepts.	SA	A	N	D	SD
9. I like to know a lot about the principles behind a thing before I try putting it into practice.	SA	A	N	D	SD

The interpretation is also commonsensical. Items 2, 4, 6, and 9 suggest a small-group classroom experience, while items 1, 3, 5, 7, and 8 tend to suggest a tutorial or self-study approach. By the way, don't take that interpretation as gospel, because we've yet to gather enough data on these items to say they are valid predictors. The point is simply that you can make up a preferred-method-of-learning instrument of your own if you like and go with an intuitive interpretation of results.

The other approach is to use one of the standardized style instruments. There are at least two that merit your attention (and this will be the third and final twosome).

LEARNING STYLE INVENTORY (LSI) Developed by Psychologist David A. Kolb to help individuals understand the way they learn, and teachers and trainers to understand their students better, the LSI is probably one of the best-researched instruments around. The LSI can be completed, scored, and profiled in about thirty minutes. Tacked onto the end of an overview or orientation seminar, it could be a nice bonus to trainees, and an opportunity for them to take some control over further learning.

The LSI assesses for four learning styles;

Participation—use of ongoing events

Observation—reflection, examination of experiences

Theory—use of readings, lectures, models

Experimentation—practice of new skills

The self-scoring version comes with an explanation of learning style and its importance for training education and career development. The trainer's manual gives aid in using the LSI in a prescriptive fashion.

For more information on this specific inventory, contact:

McBer and Company
137 Newbury Street
Boston, MA 02116
(617) 437-7080

MINDEX THINKING STYLE PROFILE Mindex is an instrument designed and developed by Dr. Karl Albrecht. It is also highly useful in a self-assessment discussion mode. The one hundred items on the instrument tell you whether you are:

Blue Sky—Left-brained—abstract

Blue Earth—Left-brained—concrete

Red Sky—Right-brained—abstract

Red Earth—Right-brained—concrete

Albrecht's instrument goes on to also give feedback on Sensory Mode Preference, Structure Preference, Mental Flexibility, and Thinking Fluency. (I bring up the Mindex instrument because I am in the preliminary stages of trying it out as a screening instrument for prescribing specific computer-literacy training techniques for individuals. It looks very promising, but it is too early to be more definitive about the matter.) For a closer look at the Mindex, contact:

Karl Albrecht & Associates
P.O. Box 99097
San Diego, CA 92109
(619) 272-3776

MUST YOU DO STYLE?

Must you do style analysis as part of your computer-literacy needs assessment? Nope. In fact, there are some who are as "down" on learning style as I am "up" on it. But if you are concerned about the fact that so many of the people who are going to need computer-literacy training in the next three to five years have no current context for understanding computers and computing, then you should think seriously about adding the learning/thinking style dimension to your assessment procedure. Whether you choose to build a commonsense learning-preferences instrument or pick up one of the standardized instruments, the consideration of learning style can't hurt your efforts and might help with some of those tough-to-teach cases that have eluded you in the past.

For more on cognitive and learning styles, pick up a copy of *Cognitive Style, Learning Style, and Transfer Skill Acquisition* (1979) by Patricia Kirby. It is available through:

The National Center for Research in Vocational Education
National Center Publications
The Ohio State University
1960 Kenny Road
Columbus, OH 43210

The last purchase price I saw was $10, a decent price for 113 pages of everything you could care to read about learning style—and in intelligible English, no less.

A SAMPLE SELECTION OF LEARNING-STYLE INVENTORIES

Cognitive Aspects of Learning Style

Name of Inventory	What It Assesses	Format	Sources of Further Information
Embedded Figures Test	Field-dependence/independence (perceiving and getting meaning)	A booklet with 25 designs hidden in the marble	Consulting Psychologists Press, 577 College Ave., Palo Alto, CA 94306
Kolb's Learning Styles Inventory	How an individual adapts or learns from experiences	Rank ordering the words in nine 4-word sets	McBer and Company, 137 Newbury St., Boston, MA 02116
Conceptual Styles Test	Analytical versus relational (thinking and grouping things)	Select two pictures from sets of three	Goldstein and Blackman 1978
Matching Familiar Figures Test	Reflectivity versus impulsivity	Pictures of sets of objects only one of which is identical to the standard	Krumboltz 1965, pp. 133–61; NASSP 1979
Transaction Ability Inventory	"Your Natural Means of Transacting with Your Environments"	Rank ordering the words in ten 4-word sets describing oneself (e.g., intake information "randomly" or "sequentially")	Gregorc 1979

Broad-Gauged Inventories

Name of Inventory	What it Assesses	Format	Sources of Further Information
Canfield Learning Styles Inventory (CLS)	Preferences for structure, environment, climate, sensory modalities, expectations	Forced ranking of four choices in 30 questions	Humanics Media, Liberty Drawer 7970, Ann Arbor, MI 48107
Productivity Environmental Preference Survey (PEPS) (children's version available)	How adults prefer to function, learn, concentrate, and perform in occupational or educational tasks.	Reaction to 100 items on a Likert-type scale	Price Systems, Box 3271, Lawrence, KS 66044
Grasha-Riechmann Student Learning Styles Questionnaire	Preferred styles: competitive, collaborative, avoidant, participant, dependent, independent	Reaction to 90 items on a Likert-type scale	Faculty Resource Center, University of Cincinnati, Cincinnati, OH 45221

Miscellaneous Inventories

Name of Inventory	What It Assesses	Format	Sources of Further Information
Self-Directed Learning Readiness Scale	Extent of capability for exercising autonomy when learning	Self-report questionnaire with 58 Likert-type items	Guglielmino and Associates 734 Marble Way, Boca Raton, FL 33432
Myers-Briggs Type Indicator	Preferences for thinking, feeling, perceiving, intuiting, sensing, judging together with extroversion versus introversion	Forced-choice questionnaire with 166 items	Consulting Psychologists Press, 577 College Ave., Palo Alto, CA 94306
Learning Preference Inventory (Adult Basic Education)	Student preferences when learning tasks, skills, and knowledge	Pictures of learning situations and a set of related questions	Manzo 1975
FIRO-B	Three characteristics of interpersonal relations—behavior expressed toward, and wanted from, others—inclusion, control, affection	Forced-choice questionnaire with 54 items	Consulting Psychologists Press, 577 College Ave., Palo Alto, CA 94306

Miscellaneous Inventories			
Name of Inventory	**What It Assesses**	**Format**	**Sources of Further Information**
Learning Activities Opinionnaire (Vocational Education)	Preferences for concrete versus symbolic and structured versus unstructured instruction	Self-assessment on 22 Likert-type items	Oen 1973
Life Styles Inventory	Twelve basic styles of behavior toward the world	Self-assessment through forced choice	Human Synergistics, 39819 Plymouth Road, Plymouth, MI 48170
Adaptive Style Inventory	The way one characteristically adapts to different situations—toward concrete experience or reflective observation, abstract conceptualization or active experimentation	Self-description test with eight items; six sets of paired statements requiring a choice to go with each item	McBer and Company, 137 Newbury St., Boston, MA 02116

CHAPTER **7** PRESENTING RECOMMENDATIONS TO MANAGEMENT

Perhaps the most important part of a needs-assessment study is delivering the results to management. You may have performed the best study in the history of the organization. The results and findings may be overwhelming in implication. But if your presentation of those results is poorly positioned and lacks persuasive power, nothing, but nothing, will change in your organization.

There is an old adage about the infinite number of slips possible twixt the cup and the lip. The slip we've observed trainers make most frequently—and most unnecessarily—is that of presenting the results of a professionally done, first-rate study in a lackluster, amateurish fashion.

But don't results speak for themselves? No way! As a consultant, I am hypersensitive to the image I project to clients. I am always striving for credibility in the clients' eyes. In a sense, I'm always selling. What I don't understand is why organizational staff people, who are also consultants, internal consultants, totally neglect their client image. As an in-house person, you have to compete for organizational resources with not only outsiders but other staffers as well. You must be able to sell your ideas to gain the resources you need to solve the problems you find.

Like it or not, the results of a mediocre study or a mediocre plan, persuasively presented, are more likely to generate management action than are results of excellent work poorly presented. My guiding principle is: The quality of a results presentation is more important than the quality of study that produced the results. To be blunt, I am convinced, as are others I know who make a living doing training and development work, that it is the quality of our presentations, not the quality and thoroughness of our work, that gains us kudos and repeat business from our clients. Experience has taught us that we must put as much thought and cleverness into the communication of results as we put into the design and conduct of the project.

Toward that end, we have developed eight guidelines to bear in mind when attempting to communicate and sell results and proposals to management.

1. DEFINE THE PURPOSE

You may be getting tired of this line, but it's as true for presentations as it is for anything else: If you don't know where you're going, you'll probably end up somewhere else. You wouldn't start a needs study, or any other important project, without defining your goals. The same applies to a results presentation and a project plan. John F. (Jack) Anderson, of Anderson & Berdie Research, puts it this way:

> When you're commissioned by an organization to do an evaluation or any kind of program or personnel research, it's because someone wants an answer to a question. But beyond that, they are usually anticipating the need for some course of action. So we have an obligation to present the results of our work in a way that allows the decision makers in the audience to determine that course of action. If, six months after you've presented your findings, nothing has changed, you haven't really done the job you were commissioned to do.

Though some we've talked to have said it differently, the essence is usually the same. To be precise, the purpose of any presentation of field research findings—be they findings from an evaluation study, a needs analysis, or a climate study—is to communicate so that others can formulate and instigate a course of action. When we report findings to a sponsor or client, our pervasive goal should be to cause someone to do something. If we are also *recommending* a course of action such as a training plan, the presentation is just that much more important.

Until you can answer the question "Who do you want to have do what, and how do you get them to do it?," you can't start planning a presentation. At least not a presentation that will communicate something specific and dynamic to the intended audience.

Anderson and Berdie suggest that you try to state, in twenty-five words or less, the action you want the participants to take as a result of your presentation. If you can't, I question whether you began your work by asking, "What is the problem I'm looking at, and why is it important enough to warrant this study?" And I question as well whether you took time to sit back when the work was finished and answer the question "What did I learn about the need for computer-literacy training in this organization?"

2. KNOW THY AUDIENCE

When you develop a training program, you do your best to make it audience-sensitive. Educational level, vocabulary, background, and experience, among other factors, should be seriously considered when designing training.

The same treatment applies to designing a results presentation. Among the important audience questions to ask are these:

▶ Will the audience for the presentation be decision makers, technical people, or a mix of both?
▶ What kinds of results presentations have they favored in the past?
▶ Do they prefer written results to oral presentations?
▶ How do they respond to charts and graphs?
▶ Have they ever totally panned a presentation of results?

I used to believe that you could psyche out an audience at arm's length. I accepted, for instance, the assumption that decision makers are more receptive to big-picture results presentations than to reams of charts, correlations, and printouts. However, a mortifying misreading of one of those rare data-cruncher decision makers—the type who likes to impress the room with his or her mastery of Statistics 201—cured that bad habit. Don't try to outguess your audience. No one expects the fry cook to guess how you want your eggs, so don't try to guess how the powers that be want their presentations cooked and served.

Generally, the best source of this sort of intelligence is the study sponsor. After all, he or she authorized your work and is on the line with you. So ask. And ask your liaison as well. The person who has been helping you connect with the right people and generally expediting your work is likely to know the sensitivities and preferences of the decision makers.

3. COMMUNICATE AS YOU GO

Communicating results is not a one-shot affair. Douglas R. Berdie, of Anderson & Berdie, believes that part of the communication job is to keep the client posted on everything that's happening. Send the sponsor and key decision makers copies of surveys, work schedules, and your routine field communiques about the project. Pen some sort of FYI on their copies. As results accumulate, share bits and pieces with your key person(s).

Why this emphasis on communicating as you go? Five reasons:

1. The sponsor is paying for your time and effort, and needs to see energy being expended. Call it a need for positive feedback. But it is also true that communication and observable effort build credibility and trust. Your sponsor is your best friend, if you keep him or her abreast of what you are doing and learning.

2. The results of your work will be more easily accepted by those who have ownership feelings toward the study. Asking the sponsor for advice and making brief, informal interim reports help build that sense of ownership.

3. The sponsor and some of the key decision makers can give you valuable feedback when you have questions about findings. An unexpected, unusual, or especially damning revelation needs validation. A sympathetic sponsor can tell you if your findings make sense in light of his or her experience and intuition. And sponsors often have access to other information that they can use to judge your unusual findings. *Note:* I am not suggesting you give the sponsor veto power over your findings. I simply believe the sponsor is a great sounding board.

4. The sponsor knows who should see your results, who will need to concur with them before action can take place, and how you should package that information for those key decision makers. He or she can tell you, for instance, who needs a private preview beforehand and who must be catered to during a public presentation.

5. Sponsors don't take kindly to public surprises, especially disagreeable surprises. By giving sponsors and key decision makers a sneak preview of any bad news, you give them time to accept it, think about implications and ramifications, hypothesize causes and remedies, and generally plan a response strategy they can unleash when you *publicly* present the bad news. Sponsors and key decision makers want to be on your side. After all, they are asking you to give them a reading about how things are going and what needs to be done. A tactical information leak gives them the lead time they need.

4. TAILOR YOUR REPORT FOR THE AUDIENCE

When you read presentation of results or presentation of proposals, what do you think of? A written report? A group of people sitting around a walnut conference table? A presenter with flip charts, overheads, and grand graphics?

I've noticed that most presentations follow the rule of tradition. If the client organization traditionally writes 200-page results reports, I write 200-page results reports. If most results presentations are delivered orally to small groups, I follow this organizational formula as well. If the folks like those long reports or cozy meetings, great. But remember, a two-day presentation and a 200-page report may be too little for some groups and studies, while a two-hour presentation and a 20-page report may be too much for others.

The trick is to tailor your efforts to the need. If you plan to present your findings report to six people, find out as much as you can about the communication styles and organizational and personal needs of those individuals. What issues are they sensitive to? What vested interests do they have that relate to your study? What outcomes do they expect and what results will be rejected out of hand? What are the "we tried that" or "oh, no, we don't" issues? What are the local taboo words, ideas, concepts?

Regardless of the particular needs, expectations, and communication comfort zones of your clients, there are some generally accepted givens for effective client communication.

▶ If you find you must prepare a written report, do so in unadorned English. The object is to communicate, not to overpower.

▶ In both written and oral communications to mixed audiences of decision makers and technical people, use the *Wall Street Journal* or pyramidal format. Organize the report in this order:

a.   A brief statement of the problem under investigation

b.   Findings

c.   If appropriate, conclusions and recommendations

▶ In written form, this "executive overview," as it is sometimes dubbed, will be two to five pages long. In oral presentation, it should take less than an hour to establish rapport, set a workable climate, and get to the punchline. The subsequent parts of the report simply elucidate the executive overview and, if necessary, explain methods, data reduction procedures, and the like.

▶ Most audiences prefer a descriptive results report as opposed to correlational or complex tabular presentations. If you are an in-house or trusted investigator, you are probably accepted as a competent expert. So spare your audience the details of your design and analysis steps, and keep your computer runs to yourself.

▶ Clearly separate findings, interpretations, conclusions, and recommendations. Dr. Darwin Hendle, of the University of Minnesota Measurement Services Center, suggests that while clients want to hear your solutions, they need to know what is supportable fact or finding and what is your own informed conjecture. Separate the two so that you don't dilute the impact of the facts and findings.

▶ Accuracy is another key to credibility. Spelling and organizational title errors, tables that don't total 100 percent, wrong dates and misattributions, all these undercut your credibility with the audience. When in doubt, use phrases such as "it is our understanding" or "it is our perception of the situation," rather than "the problem is . . ." or "since the goal of your division is to . . . ." Acknowledging that you might be wrong is always preferable to being overly self-assured.

▶ Think your way through the media and choreography of the presentation. Use the same media-method savvy you use when designing a training package, a sales presentation, or any sort of media show. "Why," Jack Anderson asks provocatively, "do we assume that a report is a written mini-thesis or that an oral presentation requires an armful of unreadable tables on mylar sheets? How about presenting results in skit form or as poetry or in a cartoon or slide show format? People somehow have the idea that reports should be dull to be legitimate."

5. PILOT-TEST THE PRESENTATION

We pilot-test training, don't we? Isn't a needs-assessment report or a training proposal just as important to your success? Get your department's two biggest nitpickers and the coordinator from client department together for a dress rehearsal. Only during a dry run will you realize that your findings aren't as crystal-clear as you thought or that "end user," "workstation," and "remote computing" are taboo expressions in the client organization, but that "desktop" and "personal computer" are acceptable. You'll also get a reaction to the "sell power" of your presentation from the client rep, as well as some thoughts about who will react negatively to the presentation and how to mitigate that response.

6. LEAVE NOTHING TO CHANCE

Nitpick both your presentation and written material relentlessly. You may have conducted the best study in the world and developed strong, compelling results and findings, but a third-rate presentation can make a mockery of all your hard work.

Use sharp, word-processed copies of written materials instead of poor photocopies of memos. Package written materials in attractive binders. Use professionally prepared visuals. These little things gain you important credibility points. Making certain that presentation rooms are clear and comfortable, that appropriate audio-visual equipment is on hand and functioning, and that chairs and tables are suitable for the group, are examples of thoughtfulness that can gain still more credibility points. Reports peppered with misspellings or smudges, malfunctioning overhead projectors, and a pile of party hats and empty champagne bottles in a corner of the presentation room are unfortunate little touches that do not gain you credibility points.

Your professionalism is being tested during a face-to-face results presentation. You'll be questioned about your findings and occasionally challenged. How you react will affect the reception of your report. You have only one opportunity to make a positive, credible impression, so don't leave that impression to chance.

7. KEEP THE BALL IN THEIR COURT

Your job as presenter of results and proposer of solutions can't be overruled by your natural inclination to nurture. Sure, you should counsel and be empathetic if the client starts bemoaning your findings or ideas, but focus your counseling on the meaning and implication of results. Direct challenges to your methodology should be answered in a calm, rational way. Any show of impatience with the client's questioning can only make matters worse. It might even be wise to assume a fairly unemotional, detached manner during the entire results presentation period. If you appear too "high" on your results, you might be misinterpreted as a lightweight.

Definitely avoid prolonged discussions about why things turned out as they did. Everybody has a story to tell and a rationalization to make. You erode your findings by sympathizing with those "If you worked here, you'd understand" stories.

If you've done your work carefully and well and presented your report competently and confidently, you're on solid ground. You have nothing to be defensive about, explain away, or react emotionally to.

8. EVALUATE

One way to evaluate a needs study is simply to stand back and watch. If you see activity taking place around the neighborhood of the problems you elucidated, that's a nice indicator. Or, after some time has passed, you might want to come right out and ask what happened as a result of the study, report, and presentation. If the answer is, in so many words, "Not much," you have just inherited a new study. That's the one you are going to have to do to find out why the results of your original study didn't produce the results you planned, or any results at all. After all, if your study was on target and your presentation followed these guidelines, it should have had an effect.

When analyzing an old study that went sour, there are two important questions to ask and answer for yourself:

Did I study the wrong problem, come to the wrong conclusion, or recommend the wrong course of action? If your answer to all or any of this is yes, then your best bet is to simply shake it off, learn from your error, and try again. If the answer is no, then ask this second question:

Is it possible that, regardless of what I find or recommend, nothing will ever happen around here? If your answer to this testy little query is affirmative, you would be well advised to keep your résumé up to date—and your head down.

CHAPTER **8** DESIGNING YOUR COMPUTER-LITERACY TRAINING PROGRAM

This book is *not* about designing training. When pressed, I easily admit my forte is assessment, not design. I marvel at the training skills of the Goeff Bellmans, Forest Belchers, Dana Gaines Robinsons, Dugan Lairds, and Martin Broadwells of the world. *They* know how to make a classroom hum! Just the same, I feel it's appropriate to pass along what I've learned looking over the shoulders of some very able computer-literacy training types.

A TWO-STAGE PROCESS

One of the most frequently used and apparently successful computer-literacy training designs I have seen calls for a two-stage strategy. Stage One is an awareness or overview session, or series of sessions, while Stage Two is focused on specific skills, operations, and applications. Obviously, this strategy is both consistent with and reinforced by our approach to computer-literacy needs assessment.

Characteristically, the Stage One training is small-group-oriented and short—no more than one day, and in most instances two to four hours. Obviously, it is not exceptionally cost-effective to take even this much time on a fairly mundane overview and "welcome to the computer" training. But there are considerations I think override bucks and make this a "smart money" approach just the same. Because of all the critical human factors or "person" variables we have been discussing—almost to distraction—in this book, I think it is wise to make sure that your first stage of training works well at a variety of levels. Consider this list of just a few of the more obvious issues that need attending to before your training can effectively address skills:

▶ Trainees must be brought to a uniform, minimum computer technology background level. That bugaboo of so many people coming from so many varied specialty backgrounds necessitates that you attend carefully to basic concepts and jargon early on in the training.

▶ There is as much misinformation about computers as there is information floating about these days. It is important that learners have an opportunity to address their conceptual misunderstandings and have help in reforming their thinking prior to skill training.

▶ Though I've gone to great lengths to dispel the computerphobia myth, I still acknowledge that there is a certain level of anxiety and antagonism toward computers and computing that must be dealt with—especially among the ranks of those with very little previous exposure to computers. This, of course, militates strongly against expecting to accomplish much skill training until such issues are put to rest.

▶ Organizational policy and procedures need to be explained and discussed with managers and professionals who are learning about personal computing for the first time. This subgroup of computer-literacy trainees must deal with both the technical and the organizational aspects of personal computing. Mixing heavy hands-on work with the organizational issues slights both.

In short, because there are so many nonskill issues to be dealt with, the first stage, or at least the early part of your computer-literacy training, should be anything *but* a heavy hands-on, learn-the-commands sort of program. It should be, instead, the sort of program that deals with and works through *every* issue that can *interfere* with effective learning of skills.

I have seen considerable variety in the structuring of Stage Two training. So much so that I tend to see Stage Two as the product of what is learned about the learners from the needs assessment *and* from the Stage One process itself. In fact, I am suggesting that, when convenient, you might consider the awareness stage to be a *part* of the needs assessment—the individual prescription part.

USING STAGE ONE TRAINING TO PRESCRIBE
Four of the needs-assessment issues we have been discussing in this book can be dealt with very handily in the computer-awareness (Stage One) training phase:

- ▶ Trainee knowledge level
- ▶ Trainee reluctance level
- ▶ Previous experience and current interest level
- ▶ Trainee learning style

Following this approach, you would end your Stage One training with hands-on experimentation. During this "play-with-the-computer" period, the Stage One instructor can be about the business of prescribing Stage Two training for the trainees on an individualized basis. If you have administered knowledge quizzes and reluctance and style inventories prior to the Stage One training, the instructor can use these results, along with a one-to-one discussion, to prescribe the learning strategy best suited to individuals on an individual basis. If you have had to rush into your Stage One training without doing learning style, knowledge level, and reluctance level testing on an individual basis, you can do so at this point.

Even if the idea of so much individualized assessment seems unrealistic, or unnecessary, for your situation, or if you just don't go for the approach for some purely personal reason, *do* think carefully about separating completely the *awareness* and *hands-on* phases of your computer-literacy training. What you lose in administrative and trainee travel time, you gain in clarity and quality of learning.

MISCELLANEOUS TIPS AND TRICKS
There is a lot to be learned from trainers already involved in computer-literacy and computer-use skills training. Here for your edification and guidance, and in no particular order, are a handful of helpful hints for computer-literacy training I have accumulated from discussions with those hardy souls "out there" on the front edge of the surfboard:

▶ Senior executives prefer their computer training one-to-one. They do *not*, it seems, play well with others. Marian L. Saunders, assistant manager for educational development, U.S. Senate Computer Center, Washington, D.C., assures us that this principle applies in government as well as in corporate life. The bigger the wheel, the more important behind-closed-doors, one-to-one training becomes.

▶ For more normal humans, two trainees to one computer seems a pretty comfortable arrangement for introductory hands-on training. That, at least, is the opinion of David O. Olson, president of Computer Workshops and Seminars, Philadelphia. For an overall head count, he prefers an even dozen trainees, but definitely no more than twenty. Olson adds these rules of thumb:

1. "Don't get carried away with hands-on training—especially with managers and professionals. Being able to play a computer like a piano doesn't make someone computer-literate. What's important (for these groups) is being exposed to what computers can do."

2. "Ninety to ninety-five percent of business applications are covered by spreadsheet and filing systems. Interest in charting and graphing comes mostly from middle and senior managers. Word

processing on a personal computer is mostly for small businesses."

▶ Joyce and Robert Killian, professors at Southern Illinois University and John A. Logan College, respectively, have been involved in microcomputer skills training for engineers, and from that base of experience, they send along the following tips:

1. To force an adult into participation is to risk resentment. If at all possible, let participation be voluntary.

2. Don't assume that any given group is "naturally" more computer-literate than the average. The Killians find that only 35 percent of engineers have ever keyboarded data and only 24 percent have ever written a program.

3. Allow trainees to be actively involved and as self-directed as possible. The Killians' experience suggests that learner-centered sessions result in better-focused training and more satisfied trainees. In addition, they observe that trainees with some previous computer exposure tend to be more specific in their statement of personal learning needs.

4. Training should take place in the job setting and provide opportunities for practice on job-related tasks. Frequent review/evaluation of progress adds to student motivation.

▶ Gary D. Brown of CRWTH Computer Coursewares, Santa Monica, California, cautions that the focus of a computer literacy program should be "head skills" in preference to "hand skills." Brown's approach emphasizes general as opposed to specific computer operations. "Many people teach the computer as a solution—it isn't. The computer is an organizer that gives you ideas. It should be seen as a catalyst for the end user. I direct my teaching at the commonalities, the things every computer can do. People are flexible. With that sort of information they can cope with any tool."

▶ Edward B. Yarrish, Executive Technology Associates, Allentown, Pennsylvania, warns against a "data entry, machine operator" approach to computer-literacy training. In his words, "You can choose to teach the specifics of machines A and B and C, or you can choose to teach computing generally and let people experiment from there with your help. I prefer the latter. . . . We have to remember that managers are still inventing uses for this technology, and accept the confusion and uncertainty this causes. People have to find their own level of computing literacy. To use the automobile analogy, basic driver's training is good for most people. But some want to go on to the race car or moving van or motorcycle. We aren't confused by that. Eventually, computer literacy will seem as clear and unconfusing and commonsensical as that to us.''

▶ Diane McInerny and Robert Pike of Communication Consultants, Manhattan Beach, California, conduct a seminar in developing computer-literacy training. Among their many guidelines, are these:

1. Start with a needs assessment.

2. Classify the type of training indicated by the needs as:

   a. *Briefing*—an overview of the kind of computers and software used by the organization. The briefing is for top management and other people not directly involved to gain support and provide general knowledge.

   b. *Literacy*—a more in-depth overview of the kind of computers and software used by the organization. This level of training is for managers and supervisors of the people who will be using the computers.

   c. *Competency*—in-depth training on the specific computers and software for the people who will actually be using the computers.

   d. *Fluency*—a total training on the specific computers and software that includes all beginning and advanced features for people who must be experts.

3. If you decide to use data processing personnel instead of acting the expert, be prepared to police the individual. Toward that end McInerny and Pike offer these nine suggestions:

   a. *Maintain control.* Make it clear that you are in charge and material must be clear to you before being presented to trainees.

   b. *Define roles/commitments.* Establish roles, work to be done, and deadlines.

   c. *Prepare the outline.* You must prepare the outline. The DP person doesn't have your skills, so don't expect to get what you want if you don't ask for it.

   d. *Monitor progress.* Set checkpoints for your on-loan DP people. Monitor their progress by meeting with them to see how they are doing.

e. *Coach 'em in instructional techniques.* Give them tips on working with beginners. Perhaps even a dry run is in order.

f. *Guard against terminology.* One of the problems of working with a data-processing professional is their familiarity with the material. Make sure your expert defines all terminology to your satisfaction.

g. *Be in classroom to assist.* You must be present to help the DP person out if he or she gets into trouble, goes astray, or panics.

h. *Reward help.* Make sure trainees and management know the role played by the DP person. Making the person look good in his or her home department is more important than money.

i. *Have DP coach you.* If all else fails and you find the DP department has no one who can do what you want done, contract with the DP people to coach you on content.

As you can tell, computer-literacy training is an area in flux. No one is 100 percent sure of what should be in the training or how it should be approached. We are *all* feeling our way into the future. There is certainly no reason for you to feel that you don't know or can't learn enough to handle your organization's training needs. If you are already personally computer-literate, you are a step ahead. After you have taught a program or two, you'll see that it's not nearly as complex or hard to do as you expected. With a little effort, and some practice, not only will you be competent in yet another technology—one of the continuing benefits of being a training professional—but you will be out there on the front edge of the computer expertise surfboard, helping your organization make the transition to the twenty-first century: a genuine, bonefide Shockwave Rider.

A GUIDE TO COMPUTER LITERACY LEARNING RESOURCES

OVERVIEW

One of the narrow bridges facing the headlong gallop of the personal computing revolution is user training: learning to make the computer do the things it's supposed to do.

Pioneers of the microcomputing age like to point out that back in the "old days" (usually defined as sometime between 1978 and 1981), the proud new PC owner mastered his or her machine through perseverance, trial and error, stubbornness, and help from fellow computer fanciers.

Today, by comparison, there is almost an embarrassment of riches. Your local bookstore has at least one rack of "how to" books on personal computing. Seminars, workshops, and micro "schools" abound. And what major city doesn't have a plethora of computer-user groups, rivaled only by the number of local McDonald's outlets? And that, too, can be a problem since once you have determined your organization's computer-literacy learning needs, you must tackle the task of specifying appropriate learning resources for meeting those needs. Appendices A through E are a modest catalogue of programs and other resources you may find of help in starting your search. Here is what you'll find on the next pages:

Appendix A:	Courses, Classes, and Schools
Appendix B:	Films, Videos, and Other A/V Learning Aids
Appendix C:	CAI and Disk Tutorials
Appendix D:	Audio Tutorial Options
Appendix E:	Books, Magazines, and Manuals

Each Appendix is self-explanatory. I have taken a little space at the beginning of each to tell you where I found the materials and what is and is not included and why. I *am* a bit squeamish about the schools and courses section since, as you well know, schools can be here today, gone tomorrow. They seem to make a slicker, quicker exit than used-car lots. I have more faith, though, in *every* other resource. The personal computer book won't be out of print tomorrow.

Do not expect these appendices to be exhaustive. They aren't. So do me a favor! When you find your favorite book or most useful film missing, don't just squawk about it! Educate me! Send a note to me at:

> Computer Literacy Learning Resources
> c/o Performance Research Associates
> P.O. Box 10068
> Minneapolis, MN 55440

Tell me about this wonderful piece of stuff you have been keeping to yourself. In return, I'll be glad to send you a summary of the results of everything I learn from what is sent me *if* you (a) ask for it and (b) include a self-addressed, stamped envelope. If you are feeling really magnanimous, send along a buck to defray photocopying and handling. If you think that idea is an affront coming from a guy who is getting rich from publishing books, (a) *you* have a lot to learn about who makes the money in book publishing, and (b) don't get overheated and *don't* send the money, but send the request anyway. Since this book is slated for publication in early 1985, don't expect a reply *before* June 1985.

A FINAL THOUGHT

It is very, very tempting to wax poetic—and smarmy— about the pitfalls of this task. Cutsie analogies and metaphors come quickly to mind; journeys through uncharted jungles, visits to Mad Hatter tea parties, and dalliances at traveling patent medicine shows are but a few of the tempting ways one might go about lampooning the never-never land (see what I mean?) of computer-literacy learning. Let it suffice to say that the field is full of well-meaning, hard-working, young (and some not so young) entrepreneurs who believe they have discovered/invented/developed the one true way to salvation: the very best and only consequential computer-literacy training program/videotape/disk tutorial/audiotape/manual/book your organization will ever need. As you already know, I don't believe in one-stop shopping, or that there is a one-and-only something that you need to get the computer-literacy training job done. I have this ingrained bias that you need more than a single resource to meet your organization's needs. Of course, you are going to meet a lot of vendors who can't afford to hold that viewpoint. Okay. So humor them. They are well-meaning people trying to make a living. Don't begrudge that. Be glad they believe enough in what they are selling to stand up for it and tell you all about it. As long as ''it'' is technically accurate, meets your style and level of learning specifications, and has been tested, give it your consideration and ignore the hype. Better yet, relax and enjoy watching a true believer waxing enthusiastic and poetic about his or her cherished product. It's an endearing, enjoyable quality. It grows on you.

APPENDIX A COURSES, CLASSES, AND SCHOOLS

The most prevalent form of microcomputer tutor is the human. And the variety is mind-boggling! There are one-day classes, semester courses, and seven-day "seminars at sea." There are even services that sell you one-on-one tutoring in your home or office by the hour.

As is the case with all human instructors and trainer-based courses, the age-old consumerist warning "*Caveat emptor*" pertains—in spades. There are more horror stories told about fly-by-night computer schools and back-of-the-computer-store seminars than in an Alfred Hitchcock retrospective. In the early days of the microcomputer era the instructors, when there were instructors at all, were either computer heavyweights, mainframe programmers, and technicians who moonlighted teaching hobbyists, or enthralled hobbyists teaching other hobbyists. So what if they didn't know John from Thomas Dewey? It was their technical acumen that made them valuable. Today, however, the average in-need-of-instruction individual is more than likely not to know a byte from a boll weevil, and the hi-tech and super hobbyist turned instructor is simply an overpowering overmatch for the trainee of this ilk. So check out the instructor(s) you will be working with carefully.

My bias in fixed-location schools is to go with those that are (a) licensed by the state they reside in, and (b) have courses of less than two days geared specifically toward business applications of specific hardware and software.

An exception is one or two of the national computer sales franchise outfits that require training to keep the franchise and then *police* their policy.

As far as computer courses brought into an organization are concerned, I have a weakness for courses offered by old-time training companies bringing new content to old clients. But even here, careful quality control and investigation of references—even some pilot testing—is in order.

MOVEABLE FEASTS: SEMINARS ON THE MOVE

The following are organizations that run either open seminars or closed in-house workshops. Though most have head offices, their forte is the road-show seminar, not running a fixed-location school.

Computer Workshops and Seminars
1701 Arch Street, 6th floor
Philadelphia, PA 19103
(215) 496-0323

In 1982 David O. Olson was a working trainer. Today, he heads a healthy little company that has put several thousand executives and business people through microcomputer orientation training. CWS, formerly the Computer Workshop, publishes a short public workshop offering schedules every quarter, but tends to specialize in at-your-shop programs.

▶ *Understanding and Using Small Computers.* A one-day seminar designed primarily to introduce trainees to small computers for the first time. Can be conducted with Apple and/or IBM equipment. Uses VisiCalc and PFS:FILE.

▶ *Business Applications for Small Computers.* A two-day workshop using Lotus 1-2-3 software and IBM/IBM compatible hardware. Workshop limited to eight people. Concentrates on using spreadsheet, database, and graphics programs to organize and operate an office or small organizational unit.

Software Education Corporation
Grace Building, 37th Floor
1114 Avenue of the Americas
New York, NY 10036
(212) 921–4744

A company with a lot of experience in the data-processing training business. Software recently began conducting micrcomputer seminars and workshops as well as DP and end-user training. Their programs are conducted on client premises only.

▶ *De-Mystifying the Computer Mystique.* A two-day "hello, computer" course. Focuses on mainframe computers and applications, though minis and micros are considered.

▶ *Understanding and Selecting a Microcomputer.* A one-day course designed for managers, supervisors, and executives who are considering microcomputers for their companies or departments. Also provides some basic microcomputer terminology and jargon.

▶ *Installation and Implementation (of Microcomputers).* A two-day course designed to provide the tools for effective installation and implementation of a microcomputer application. For managers and supervisors who have purchased a microcomputer and need to increase their own literacy skills. Also covers selection criteria for software.

▶ *Using Lotus 1-2-3.* Four to six days, depending upon the number of modules selected. Course aimed at the setup and use of 1-2-3. Twenty percent lecture, 80 percent hands-on training. Last two days are devoted to trainee applications.

▶ *dBase II.* Four to six days, depending upon the number of units scheduled. Similar in structure to the Lotus 1-2-3 course described above.

▶ *Using Your VisiCalc Software.* A two- to three-day course designed for the user of VisiCalc in a business environment. Thirty percent lecture.

Summit Micro Computer Learning Center
436 Springfield Avenue
Summit, NJ 07901
(201) 277-3837

Offers in-house seminars with a business orientation. Offerings cover Lotus 1-2-3, dBase II, WordStar, VisiCalc, Basic, and Introduction to the IBM-PC.

McGraw-Hill Training Systems
1221 Avenue of the Americas
New York, NY 10020
(800) 255-6324

▶ *Computer Literacy Seminar.* A two-day seminar for up to 20 people. Based on the program McGraw-Hill developed to train their own people on microcomputer technology. Covers basic micro hardware, word processing, telecommunications, and data analysis. Price varies with local and tailoring needed. Train-the-Trainer program also available.

Software Banc Seminars
661 Massachusetts Avenue
Arlington, MA 02174
(617) 641-1241

Offers four-day seminars on either dBase II or Lotus 1-2-3. Seminar conducted by Adam B. Green, author of best-selling book on dBase II. Instruction on videotape and hands-on.

Executive Technology Associates, Inc.
2357 Lehigh Street
Allentown, PA 18103
(215) 791-5555

▶ *Computer Literacy Training Series.* Offers two related two-day programs: Level I and Level II. Computer literacy—Level I focuses on the very basics. Level II moves into applications and problem solving.

ETA, founded in 1981, has been very aggressive and successful in offering in-house workshops for a variety of prestigious organizations, both corporations and associations. Instruction emphasizes hands-on work with computer.

CLASS Associates
P.O. Box 492
Wilton, CT 06897
(203) 762-2595

▶ *Making Small Computers Work for You.* A one-day introduction to microcomputers and applications. Conducted around New England at a variety of locations. Also provides custom seminars on an in-house basis.

CES Compulearning
680 KinderKarnack Road
River Edge, NJ 07661
(201) 599-9510

Company offers a wide variety of programs and teaches a variety of hardware configurations. Founder Ralph Ganger was in the management and supervisory training business before starting compulearning. Offers about 21 courses, majority under one day.

Title	Length (Hours)
Introduction to IBM PC	3
Desktop Computers	4
Basic Programming I	8
Basic Programming II	8
Writing Files in Basic	4
VisiCalc	6
Lotus 1-2-3	6

Multiplan	6
Spreadsheet Design	6
Introduction to dBase II	8
Atari Graphics	2
Intro to Microcomputers in the Office	10
The WordStar Program	6
Word Pro (advanced word processing)	44
Computerized Bookkeeping	8
How to Buy a Home Computer	2
Telecommunications	2
Using a Micro to Manage Investments	2
Microcomputers for Retailers	2
Computer Literacy for Trainers	8

National Training Systems, Inc.
1111 Broadway
Santa Monica, CA 90401
(213) 394-7685

NTS, one of the long-time, big-time training companies has gone into the computer training business. NTS clients kept coming up with a need for basic computer training, and, not one to look a good idea in the mouth NTS founder, Jay M. Sedlik, developed a customizable in-your-shop computer-literacy training program aimed at senior-level managers. (Two to three days, maximum 20 participants, hands-on, lecture, film/video.)

NTS also offers audio, interactive video, and videotape programs.

Forum/Nevison Executive Computing
84 State Street
Boston, MA 02109
(617) 523-7300

Forum Corporation has moved aggressively into personal computer training for executives business through acquisition of John M. Nevison Associates of Concord, Mass. At the same time, Forum/Nevison has gone into business with VisiCorp to offer the VisiTraining Program. The program is advertised as being specifically created to meet the microcomputer training needs of Fortune 1000 companies. Should be a very classy traveling show.

OTHER TRAINING GROUPS

AGS Computers, Inc.
111 Broadway
New York, NY 10006

Crozier-Smith, Inc.
512 West Hickory
Suite 113
Denton, TX 76201

Software Review Corp.
33 East Philadelphia Street
York, PA 17401

Portable Computer Training Associates
P.O. Box 85
Hamel, MN 55430

The Boston Systems Group
5609 Stearns Hill Road
Waltham, MA 02154

Hasiba/Harris Associates
152 Eighth Avenue
New York, NY 10011

University Seminars
9024 St. Charles Rock Road
St. Louis, MO 63114

FIXED-LOCATION SCHOOLS

A friend in the continuing-education division of a California university quips that anytime he finds a hole in his slate of offerings, or a program having to be canceled, he schedules another "Welcome to the Microcomputer" or "Using Microcomputers in Small Business" course. "There seems to be an unlimited appetite for the ninety-five-dollar Saturday morning microcomputer seminar," he says. It seems that every community college, junior college, vocational technical institute, and city university in the country has learned those truisms and has a robust slate of courses. It is close to impossible to catalogue and report university and other public school programs. By and large, they are an irrelevant force for meeting the computer-literacy training needs of business and industry.

What we *have* tried to get a handle on are proprietary schools and institutes that focus their training efforts on the small computer user in business and industry. This listing is far from definitive and is certainly *not* an endorsement. We do, however, have a bias toward schools with some sort of a certified or licensed staff, an association with a well-funded parent company, if possible, and a management that knows the difference between a computer hobbyist, a hacker, and a business user.

Accelerated Computer Training [ACT]
6071 Bristol Parkway, #4
Culver City, CA
(213) 215-3571

An ambitious one-store computer school trying to go national. Founded by a former airline pilot and flight instructor, the emphasis is on (a) business users and (b) making learning enjoyable. Founders claim all courses are developed by professional instructional designers used to designing training for professionals and executives.

Offers nine courses ranging from eight to sixteen hours in length. Three "tiers" of programs—introductory or computer basics, applications of popular software packages, and programming.

American Management Association
135 West 50th Street
New York, NY 10020
(518) 891-0065 (special registration number)

Offers a wide variety of "DP for the non-DP manager" courses as well as hands-on microcomputer training programs. The Grant Parent of management update training organizations. Ask for their catalogue.

ARES Schools
7640 West 78th Street
Minneapolis, MN 55435
(612) 332-6345

This school, itching to become a national chain, has an interesting gimmick—lab time with interactive video tutorials. A division of American Business Service Corporation and, yes, licensed to the teeth. Specializes in IBM-PC and business applications–oriented training.

COMMAND Small Computer Learning Center, Inc.
7400 France Avenue South
Edina, Minnesota 55435
(612) 835-7819

Another one of those small start-up schools working like heck to be a *big* computer-literacy school. Also another of those groups that has gone to the trouble of getting state licensing. Offers nine courses in the 3- to 12-hour range. Typical course titles: Introduction to Business Microcomputers, DOS Management, Introduction to WordStar, Advanced WordStar, Apple Writer, and Lotus 1-2-3. Instructors prefer small groups (6–10) and one computer to one student.

Control Data Business Center, Inc.
Minneapolis, MN
Boston, MA
Atlanta, GA
Milwaukee, WI
Chicago, IL
Dallas, TX
Denver, CO

There are CDC Business Centers in over seventy locales in the U.S. (listed in both White and Yellow Pages), and they have been moving more and more into the training business, especially computer-user training. As of this writing, they are offering a series of half-day, hands-on programs for learning to use specific microcomputer software programs. Lotus 1-2-3, WordStar, Condor, and MultiPlan programs have been widely advertised.

Logical Operations
240 East Avenue
Rochester, NY 14604
(716) 262-2226

Another young start-up company. Offers several interesting programs; Apple Literacy, IBM Literacy, MultiMate, MultiPlan, WordStar, Lotus 1-2-3, Advanced 1-2-3, dBase II, Introduction to DOS.

The Personal Computer Learning Center
1120 Avenue of the Americas
Seventh Floor
New York, NY 10036
(212) 840-6868

Located in midtown Manhattan, PCLC should be a convenient stop for busy management types who don't want others in the organization to see them learning to compute, for some reason or other. PCLC also brings their act into your organization if you really want them to. Courses offered are Visi-Calc 1, VisiCalc Applied, SuperCalc, Desktop/Plan II, Graphics (VisiPlot), Graphic Forecasting (VisiTrend/VisiPlot), VisiDex, VisiFile, Intercomputer Communication, WordStar, Dow Jones News/Retrieval, The Source. Obviously, the orientation is business first. The organization calls itself "the school for the busy executive" and advertises, "Your schedule is our schedule."

Personal Computer Library & Learning Studio, Inc.
1340 Hamburg Turnpike
Wayne, NJ 07470
(201) 696-7200

Another very business-oriented school. Uses only IBM-PCs. Nineteen courses available, from a "Computer Literacy" course to a very nifty "Systems Analysis/Design for Personal Computer Users" of three half-days' length.

Schaak's Computer Academy
2422 Transport Drive
St. Paul, MN 55120
(612) 452-0900

and

2138 Burnsville Center
Burnsville, MN 55337
(612) 435-5445

A pair of microcomputer schools catering to business-user needs. Offers small and large classes, two-to-one tutorials, and a variety of self-study practice options. Owned and operated by management of a midwestern regional microcomputer and consumer electronics store chain. Uses state-certified instructors and is licensed as a school under state law. Offers courses from 2 to 10 hours in length. Highly targeted curriculum from Introduction to Microcomputers (3 hours for $35) to DB Master Report Generation (3 hours for $50); over 40 programs in all. A couple of Fortune 500–size companies have contracted large blocks of instruction at the schools.

OTHER FIXED-LOCATION SCHOOLS

Accelerated Computer Training
18201 West McDurmott
Irvine, CA 92714
(714) 660-0455

Center for Computer Applications
334 Newbury Street
Boston, MA 02115
(617) 247-0538

ComputerPrep
10057 North Metro Parkway East
Phoenix, AZ 95021
(602) 944-8258

Computer Tutor
554 Washington Street
Wellesley, MA 02181
(617) 237-6061

Datel Systems
1211 Avenue of the Americas
New York, NY 10036
(212) 921-0110

Information Science Associates
676 North St. Clair
Chicago, IL 60611
(312) 787-2723

Instamation
131 Gould Street
Rochester, NY 14610
(716) 461-1800

Microcomputer Learning Center
120 West Madison
Chicago, IL 60603
(312) 332-0419

Personal Computer Training Center
2120 L. Street
NW Washington, DC 20001
(202) 466-7604

Prodigy Computer Learning Center
Colonial Square Mall
229 Route 22 East
Green Brook, NJ 08812

Susan Harmon Transitions, Inc.
185 Carey Road
Brookline, MA 02146
(617) 566-0596

COMPUTER STORE TRAINING

By and large, I am leery of computer store training. It can be perfunctory and uneven in quality. There are three general exceptions: ComputerLand

Computer Stores, Radio Shack Computer Academies, and Sears Business Centers. The Radio Shack Academies are a no-nonsense lot, but they tend to provide very good training. The ComputerLand in-store training, and especially the ComputerLand Training Academies, are quite good. The ComputerLand head office seems to police franchises closely and helps out with their training design and materials.

RESORTS, SPAS AND OTHER ODD PLACES TO LEARN ABOUT COMPUTING

Think I was kidding about computer cruises and the like? Nope. Here's the proof—hey, don't look down your nose at the possibility of a computer camp for big kids! You've considered sending your small fry, haven't you? What's good for the gosslings may be good for the geese as well! If you've a hankering for a vacation of mixed bits, bytes, and beluga, try one of these.

Class Associates, Inc.
P.O. Box 492
Wilton, CT 06897
(203) 762-2595

Runs a series of week-long Mississippi River cruises aboard paddlewheeler *Mississippi Queen*. Tax-deductible under odd-learning-on-a-riverboat exemption law.

Club Med
Punta Cana
Dominican Republic

Arranged through "normal" Club Med channels.

Computers Simplified
6515 Saroni Drive
Oakland, CA 94611
(415) 339-3392

Books camp and spa spots all over the U.S., but mainly uses the 1,200-acre Silverado Resort in the Napa Valley.

Executive Computer Camp
VROOM, Inc.
2516 Maple Avenue
Dallas, TX 75201
(214) 698-9182

Actually in the posh "old town" area of Dallas.

Jackson Hole Personal Computer Resort
Star Route
Box 362A
Jackson, WY 83001
(800) 443-8616

Midwest Computer Camp
9293 Lafayette Road
Indianapolis, IN 46278
(317) 297-2700

Dubbed "nature and microcomputers perfectly blended," actual site is at Old Acres, a 51-acre wooded estate.

Princess Cruise Lines
2029 Century Park East
Los Angeles, CA 90067
(213) 553-1770

Yes, that's right, software and softwinds aboard the Love Boat. Now *that's* computer dating.

CANNED COURSES YOU COULD CONDUCT YOURSELF

Off-shelf "you drive" computer-literacy training programs are beginning to surface. Not much data exist on the success of this approach, but if the work has been done well, buying into one of those could save reinventing the wheel. The following companies offer such programs; write for details.

Boeing Computer Services Company
P.O. Box 24346
Mail Stop 9A90
Seattle, WA 98124
(206) 575-7700

1975–1983, 23 video cassettes, color, 30 minutes each, instructor's print materials, learner's print materials. Purchase: $8,600 ($495 each). Rental: $1,500 ($80 each). Preview: $200 ($30 each).

"Making It Count" presents broad overview of data-processing concepts and problems. Covers fundamentals of hardware and software, programming languages, and logic. Introduces and defines data-processing terms in context. Shows role of computers in management decision making and how to acquire computing capability. Intended to help employees assume a more active role in defining their own computing requirements and evaluating systems. Boeing claims 60,000 people have made their way through this program.

McGraw-Hill
International Training Systems
1221 Avenue of the Americas
New York, NY 10020
(212) 977-6741

Seven video cassettes, color, $5\frac{1}{2}$ hours (total running time of series). Purchase: $4,200; 3-month rental: $1,600; 1 month rental $630.

"Introduction to Data Processing" is a top-end, heavy-duty, supertech program. The stars are John J. Donovan and Stuart E. Madnick of the MIT Sloan School of Management. Advertised as a "brief self-study course designed to take a person from a position of little knowledge of data processing to one of solid understanding of basic concepts.

John Wiley & Sons
New York, NY 10158

Package course called "Introduction to Business Data Processing" can be used to hold DP for non-DP managers program.

Public Media, Inc.
Films, Inc., Division
1144 Wilmette Avenue
Wilmette, IL 60091
(312) 256-3205

Has a program called "The Computer Seminar." Heavily film/video-based. A spinoff of BBC series *The Computer Programmer.*

United Education & Software
3600 South Minnesota Avenue
Sioux Falls, SD 57105
(800) 843-9970

Actually provides a turnkey computer-literacy learning center operation. Focuses on ten student projects and two-to-one hands-on work.

APPENDIX B FILMS, VIDEOS, AND OTHER COMPUTER-LITERACY A/V AIDS

There have been "welcome to the computer" audio-visual materials almost as long as there has been something definable as a computer. The "why" is dead-simple. The first big-time digital computers—the first *any* kind of computer, for that matter—moved from the drawing board and concept paper to reality at the behest of the War Department, the Pentagon's predecessor, during World War II. That may *seem* odd to someone under thirty, but World War II was a consuming holocaust, and just about *every* man, woman, and child on the planet was in some way involved. So *anyone* with an idea that might give the "good guys" an edge could get research and development funding. Radar, rockets, jet aircraft, nuclear power, television, infrared, fiber optics, and the modern computer all advanced during that period. The digital computer, as a machine of war, was sold as a *device* that promised to generate more accurate gunnery tables for long-range artillery. So it goes.

The first real working digital or "electronic" computer, ENIAC, didn't really come of age until after the war was over, and then was really just a giant calculator. (Don't worry, I'll get to the point—and there *is* a point—in a minute.) Anyway, it and the other computers of that first era were behemoths. ENIAC filled rooms and needed a crew of fast-moving technicians on roller skates to keep it running for more than a few minutes at a stretch. Needless to say, those first computers were a little big to drag around for show and tell. Enter the training film.

During the war, the Army Signal Corps had discovered the training film. John Huston, among others, got his start making training films. With peace breaking out all over, the market for "Know Your Enemy" and "Social Diseases and You" movies diminished considerably. What to do with all those studios, crews, and budgets? Aha! Let's document all the new technology that was invented to win the war. Enter the first computer film. Between 1950 and 1960, by one estimate, the Army Signal Corps *alone* produced 500 films on computers, computer technology, and, when it was finally invented, computer programming.

Whether today's computer-literacy flick makers learned anything from the Army Signal Corps types is moot. The whole training film industry is really an offshoot of that origin. So when the current computer age shifted into high gear, so did the training film industry. And we're the better for it.

Back to the point. You don't have to look at too many "welcome to the computer" movies and videos to discover that, as with books, courses, and disk tutorials, there are a multitude of meanings lurking under the unpretentious descriptor "Computer Literacy Film."

There seem to be three types of computer-literacy films available today:

1.   All About Big Computers

2.   All About Little Computers

3.   Using Little Computers

TYPE 1: ALL ABOUT BIG COMPUTERS

By and large, these are the classic "what's a computer?" and "welcome to computing" films. They tend to be "gee whiz," "modern miracle," and "will wonders never cease" in tone. They generally feature a baritone narrator and lots of voice-over, long-shots of giant computer rooms with a teletype background sound. Frequently there is a lot of animation; always these films are in color and feature classy graphics. But for some reason, every time I see one of those animated sequences showing the bits and bytes doing their thing, a *must* in these films, I flash on those old Bufferin versus Aspirin commercials with little A's and B's fighting to get through the trapdoor into the bloodstream.

And for some reason, a lot of these Big Computer movies and videos end by drifting off into social relevancy and ask nagging questions about the implications of computers to man's sense of humanity. The last line is almost invariably "The Future is in your hands!" *Yawn.*

This sort of film is more—or less—relevant, depending on your approach to structuring a computer-literacy training program. If you are working with mainframes and remote, fourth-generation-language, end-user access systems, these sorts of films will probably be of considerable value. If you are strictly into microcomputer training as computer-literacy training, then these will probably not be as useful to you. And since I couldn't think of any place else to put them, you will also find listings for not only films and videotapes but for filmstrips and slide/tape presentations here as well. (The check mark next to some entries means I have viewed them myself and they seem okay to me; pilot testing advised, of course!)

▶ *How Does a Computer Work?* Seeks to solve a major computer problem—underuse—by helping managers understand computer basics and see how computers fit into business. Uses animation and humor to present the computer as a positive influence to help managers improve their own effectiveness. Intended for nonspecialists.

> Xicom-Video Arts
> Sterling Forest
> Tuxedo, NY 10987
> (212) 989-2676

1981, 16mm film or video cassette, color, 16 minutes.
Purchase: $390. Rental: $100. Preview: $35.

▶ *Basic Computer Terms.* Introduces beginners to the parts, processes, and terminology of today's computers. Large and small computers are being used in many professions for routine tasks. Humor is used to remove the mystique surrounding computers.

> Pyramid Films
> Box 1048
> Santa Monica, CA 90406
> (213) 828-7577

1976, 16mm film or video cassette, color, 16 minutes.
Purchase: film, $250; video, $235. Rental: $30.

▶ *Computer Basics for Management.* Emphasizes use of computer as a management tool. Video supplements expand material in AMA course of the same title which is included in printed materials that accompany the video. Shows hardware, charts, slides, and other visuals to make concepts clear.

> American Management Associations
> 135 West 50th Street
> New York, NY 10020
> (212) 586-8100

1982, 6 video cassettes, color, instructor's print materials, learner's print materials.
Purchase: $1,585 (for 5 people). Preview: $50. Other cost factors: AMA members, $1,385 (preview: $40).

▶ *Computers in Your Life.* Intended for those with little or no technical knowledge about computers. Illustrates how computers are productive tools within the society. Offers an introductory examination for general audiences. Includes humorous touches.

Association for Computer Machinery
111 West 42nd Street
New York, NY 10036
(212) 586-8100

1982, 16mm film, color, 13 minutes.
Rental: free.

▶ *Information Processing and the Computer: A Survey.* Provides a basic introduction to computers—their history and applications today, including science, the arts, and business. Addresses information processing, computer concepts, and societal implications.

Charles E. Merrill Publishing Co.
1300 Alum Creek Drive
Columbus, OH 43216
(614) 258-8441

1979, 15 video cassettes, color, 15–30 minutes each, learner's print materials.
Purchase: $2,495. Preview: free.

▶ *What Is a Computer?* Designed for training staff who are coming into contact with the computer for the first time or who work alongside it without really understanding just what it does or is capable of doing. Humorous cartoon explains the relationship between the central processing unit and the computer's peripherals—the video console, the printer, card reader, magnetic tape unit, and disk unit. Deals with software, hardware, and data preparation.

Xicom-Video Arts
Sterling Forest
Tuxedo, NY 10987
(212) 989-2676

1979, 16mm film or video cassette, color, 18 minutes, instructor's print materials.
Purchase: $390. Rental: 3-day, $100. Preview: $35.

▶ *Matter of Survival.* Portrays a situation in a company where the computer methods that are about to be introduced to take over much of the paperwork will result in a surplus number of responsible, long-time employees. Poses the problem from the points of view of management and of the employees concerned.

National Film Board of Canada
1251 Avenue of the Americas
New York, NY 10020
(212) 586-5131

16 mm film, color, 26 minutes.
Purchase: $350. Rental: $30. Preview: free.

▶ *Silicon Factor: So What's It All About?* Looks at how evolution has become revolution as the silicon chip continues to become less expensive and more sophisticated every year. Provides a detailed look at the silicon chip—its development, design, production, and mushrooming applications. Examines the potential gains in levels of productivity and competitiveness with microelectronics as well as what long-term effects this revolution could have on employment, life-styles, and the economy. Asks how far computer-controlled machines can go on imitating human functions.

Films, Inc.
733 Green Bay Road
Wilmette, IL 60091
(312) 256-3200

1981, 16mm film or video cassette, color, 40 minutes.
Purchase: film, $690; video, $345. Rental: $75. Preview: free.

▶ *Now the Chips Are Down.* Shows how microprocessors are made and the different kinds of applications already in use or being researched. Surfaces issues and problems that arise from sophisticated machines such as the choice whether to advance applications of the computer or to stop the advance.

Films, Inc.
733 Green Bay Road
Wilmette, IL 60091
(312) 256-3200

1981, 16mm film or video cassette, color, 50 minutes.
Purchase: film, $860; video, $430. Rental: $100. Preview: free.

▶ *Computers at Work.* Capsule glimpse of some of the many ways computers are being used in a variety of fields. Companion film to *You and the Computer.*

Creative Venture Films
P.O. Box 599
Springhouse, PA 19477

16mm film, color, 12 minutes.
Purchase: $175. Preview: free.

▶ *Silicon Factor: And What of the Future?* Raises issues about the effects of microelectronics on employment, life-styles, and the economy over the next few years. Gives examples of computers at work in a variety of settings.

Films, Inc.
733 Green Bay Road
Wilmette, IL 60091
(312) 256-3200

1981, 16mm film or video cassette, color, 40 minutes.
Purchase: film, $690; video, $345. Rental: $75. Preview: free.

▶ *Computers at Work: A Complete Video Course.* There is a lot to pick and choose from in this 15-cassette series. Though there is a $25 sampler tape available, you would be better served to preview before buying—some units are better than others, some more relevant to business settings than others.

Lansford Publishing Co.
P.O. Box 8711
1088 Lincoln Avenue
San Jose, CA 95155
(408) 287-3105

15 cassettes, color, approximately 30 minutes each, student guides, instructor's manuals, self-quizzes available.
Purchase: $295 per unit, $4,300 per set.

Titles and brief descriptions:

Evolution: Computers, Yesterday and Today (from Babbage, through Fourth Generation applications)

The Computer System: Machines and People (computers on campus and basic data processing)

Hardware and Software (from interface to operating systems)

Sequential Processing Applications

Direct Access Applications (users and experts tell why it's important)

Systems Development: A Case Study (a for-real case of a company trying on computing)

Computers in Business (tiptoe through the applications, once over lightly, please)

Computers in Society (nonbusiness but interesting applications in medicine, law, engineering, etc.)

Teleprocessing Systems (case study of an unusual business application)

Database Processing Systems (database versus file processing systems; a bank application)

Distributed Processing Systems (all about remote processing)

The Automated Office (Hello, word processing.)

Computer Crime and Security (Let's not give people ideas, now.)

Computer Careers and Your Future (Lots of folks testify that there ain't nothing like a mainframe.)

▶ *Input and Output Units.* Discusses the structure of digital computers and the role of peripheral devices. Describes the appearance and use of typical input and output units. Enables a computer user to make a knowledgeable, rational choice of an input/output unit. Audio Visual Library of Computer Education Series, No. 7.

Prismatron Productions, Inc.
155 Buena Vista Avenue
Mill Valley, CA 94941
(415) 383-0449

Video cassette or 60 slides and audio cassette or 2 filmstrips, 20 minutes, instructor's print materials.
Purchase: video, $99.50; filmstrips, $65; slides, $75. Preview: free.

▶ *Human Side of Computer Graphic Design.* Developed to assist managers and users of computer graphics in how to deal with the new pressures this system creates. A help to identify problem areas before they boil over and to reduce skepticism about the system, allowing it to operate as it was designed.

Society of Manufacturing Engineers
P.O. Box 930
Dearborn, MI 48128
(313) 271-1500

1981, video cassette, color, 16 minutes.
Purchase: $150. Rental: $40. Other cost factors: SME members, $120
(rental: $35).

▶ *Understanding Computers.* Uses a mix of cartoons and photographs. Describes in clear nontechnical terms exactly what computers can and can't do. Examples show why computers are more suitable for some applications than others. Emphasizes the programmer's responsibility for efficient utilization of the computer. Audio Visual Library of Computer Education Series, No. 2.

Prismatron Productions, Inc.
155 Buena Vista Avenue
Mill Valley, CA 94941
(415) 383-0449

1981, video cassette or 60 slides and audio cassette or 2 filmstrips, 20 minutes, instructor's print materials.
Purchase: video, $99.50; filmstrips, $65; slide, $75. Preview: free.

▶ *Computer.* Provides a highly visual introduction to the world of computers. Diagrams demonstrate the fundamental structure of digital computer systems. Describes how computers can be used to process information. Shows computers at work in laboratories, factories, and offices. Audio Visual Library of Computer Education Series, No. 1.

Prismatron Productions, Inc.
155 Buena Vista Avenue
Mill Valley, CA 94941
(415) 383-0449

1981, video cassette or 60 slides and audio cassette or 2 filmstrips, 20 minutes, instructor's print materials.
Purchase: video, $99.50; filmstrips, $65; slides, $75. Preview: free.

▶ *Computer Terminals.* Utilizes both diagrams and photographs to explore characteristics of online computing. Describes the use of terminals and the nature of communication channels. Illustrates terminal applications by examples that include real time, information retrieval, program development, and CAD. Audio Visual Library of Computer Education Series, No. 8.

Prismatron Productions, Inc.
155 Buena Vista Avenue
Mill Valley, CA 94941
(415) 383-0449

Video cassette or 60 slides and audio cassette or 2 filmstrips, 20 minutes,
instructor's print materials.
Purchase: video, $99.50; filmstrips, $65; slides, $75. Preview: free.

▶ \ *GIGO*. Takes the viewer into the world of the computer to
see what it is, how it works, and, most important, how it will affect our lives
and our jobs. Designed to allay fears and doubts about what's going on. Intended for all employees and community groups.

Dartnell
4660 Ravenswood Avenue
Chicago, IL 60640
(312) 561-4000

16mm film or video cassette, color, 30 minutes.
Purchase: $525. Rental: $120.

▶ *Understanding the Computer*. Introduces the computer and
demonstrates its wide range of applications. Includes programming basics
and computer languages. Surveys computer's present and future impact on
society.

Ibis Media
Box 308
Pleasantville, NY 10570
(914) 747-0177

157 slides and 2 audio cassettes, instructor's print materials.
Purchase: $165.

▶ *Central Processor*. Describes the structure of digital computers
and the role of the central processor. Discusses computer binary devices.
Considers program execution and the function of registers. Explains read/
write operations and reviews semiconductor memories. Audio Visual Library
of Computer Education Series, No. 10.

Prismatron Productions, Inc.
155 Buena Vista Avenue
Mill Valley, CA 94941
(415) 383-0449

Video cassette or 60 slides and audio cassette or 2 filmstrips, 20 minutes, instructor's print materials.
Purchase: video, $99.50; slides, $75; filmstrips, $65. Preview: free.

▶ *Fundamental Computer Concepts I.* Basic ideas behind programmable digital processors. Large computers versus small computers. Makes an analogy between computer block diagram and post office box.

> Lifetime Learning Publications
> 10 Davis Drive
> Belmont, CA 94002
> (415) 595-2350

Video cassette, color, 37 minutes.
Purchase: $471. Rental: $76.

▶ *Computer Hardware and Software Jargon.* Basic computer vocabulary, including hardware and software terminology. Discusses input/output, mini and micro systems, memory and data channels.

> Lifetime Learning Publications
> 10 Davis Drive
> Belmont, CA 94002
> (415) 595-2350

Video cassette, color, 40 minutes.
Purchase: $300. Rental: $75.

TYPE 2: ALL ABOUT LITTLE COMPUTERS

In this category of films and videos, you find two extremes, the overly cute and the "techie-to-the-max," with very little in between. Among the overly cute are the "cute people" and "cute sets and scripts" subvarietals. Cute people are guys with funny hats, and ex–Monty Python stars who are basically saying to the viewer, "If I (dummy that I am/cool guy that I am/laid back and nonthreatening as I am) can master these little buggers, so can you." Cute sets and cute scripts are the type that go, "Well, boys and girls, you all know what this is—it is a bright, shiny, red, ripe apple. Well, guess what this [point to the machine] is, an apple too. But it is a very special kind of apple. You don't eat it, for one thing. Do you know what else? Yes! It's a computer. Can you say *computer*?" I guess the theory is that saccharin overload is a cure for computerphobia.

Supertechie flicks are characterized by guys in shirtsleeves and paisley ties giving overhead projector-aided lectures (yes, and recorded live on video!) on such scintillating topics as "Telenet vs. Tymnet: The Debate Rages On" and "The Intel 8080 and You." Most have some general audience soft-shoe up front that makes you *think* the whole film is going to be in English—and a few minutes later you start to think your ears have gone bad.

Luckily, these two extremes in flicks are easy to spot from their promotional literature. And for the right audience, as in "take this audience—please!," both varieties *are* very useful.

▶ \ *Adventures of the Mind: A Computer Literacy Film Series.* Actually a series of six films, *Data Processing, Control, Design; Speaking the Language; The Personal Touch; Hardware and Software; For Better or for Worse; Extending Your Reach.*

Developed by Johns Hopkins University's Applied Physics Laboratory, this series is an almost perfect introduction to personal computing for the absolutely illiterate. The films are designed to put the most computerphobic audience at ease.

The key tool for this task is the narrator/hero. Our bumbling leader is about as no-tech a human as you're likely to come across. From word one you just know that if this guy, with his L. L. Bean Wardrobe, one foot in the sixties and the other in the cab of a Kenworth truck, can handle a personal computer, so can you.

These films are good, but it's pretty obvious that "low thread" was an uppermost concern to the writers and producers. The production values are first rate, though some of the writing is aimed at adolescents: "Why, you could even put a directory of your whole rock-music collection on a personal computer!" Those bits and pieces that *are* specific to the high school and collegiate sets are few, brief, and tastefully done for the most part.

In *Data Processing, Control, Design* we see list storage by a club of some sort, customer-account storage and parts inventory in a sports-car repair shop, a hospital room with computerized controls for paraplegic patients, an automated weather station at an airport, and a group of students designing experiments and models in a class. In other words, in 15 minutes a lot of introductory—and even slightly more advanced—conceptual stuff gets covered. This unit shows both the strengths and weaknesses of the series. On the plus side are clarity and simplicity of examples and explanations. On the minus side are the total lack of hard-core business application and the college-course tone to the storyline and cases. Definitely worth previewing or even testing on a small group. But don't jump into a commitment to using these films until you have previewed them carefully.

Indiana University
A/V Center Video
Bloomington, IN 47405
(812) 335-8087

16mm, color, 15 minutes per unit (6 units).
Purchase: $150 per video unit; $240 per film unit. Rental: $15 per unit.

▶ \ *The Computer Programme.* This ten-film series presents the basic concepts of the microcomputer in pretty straightforward British English. Talks down just a tad when explaining why we should be going to computers. Application examples are clear and concise, as is most of the exposition. This series and another ten-film series called *Making the Most of the Micro* are actually a repackaging of a highly lauded BBC series on the microcomputer. Made for adults, but not necessarily managers or technical people.

Films, Inc.
733 Green Bay Road
Wilmette, IL 60091
(312) 256-3200

1982, 10 16mm films or video cassette, color, 25 minutes each.
Purchase: films, $4,995 ($500 each); video, $2,990 ($400 each).

▶ *Promedia 1: The Video Computer Primer.* A spinoff from the Texas Personal Computer Show—A PBS television program, slick, good graphics, not cheap, but popular despite that. Divided into eight easy-to-understand segments, a demonstration of the capabilities of a personal computer. The segments are (1) a display of a computer system, including keyboard, display screen, disk drive, floppy diskettes, and printer; (2) the functions of word processing; (3) various uses for numerical manipulations; (4) how to use DataBase information systems; (5) the benefits of intercomputer communications; (6) educational programs for learning about computers; (7) an introduction to programming and computer languages; (8) color demonstrations of games and entertainment.

Promedia, Inc.
Dallas, TX
(800) 531-5074

Video cassette, color, 60 minutes.
Purchase: $99.

▶ *Introduction to Industrial Microcomputers.* Discusses the basics of microcomputers and their use in manufacturing. Offers an understanding of the abilities and limitations of microcomputers as well as information to correctly identify successful applications. Includes the technology review of microcomputers, fundamentals of microprocessor operation, simple programming structures, estimating software costs, input and output elements, and future trends in industry. Goes step by step through the development of a simple program for a PET microcomputer. Designed for the practicing engineer.

> Society of Manufacturing Engineers
> P.O. Box 930
> Dearborn, MI 48128
> (313) 271-1500

20 video cassettes, color, 60 minutes each.
Purchase: $1,250.

▶ *Industrial Microcomputer Systems.* Examines the programming techniques for using microcomputers to control machine tools and monitor processing and inspection devices. Describes memory technology, programmable controllers, and writing programs. Emphasizes basics and application in manufacturing situations. Microcomputer training unit can be used to program, debug, and run actual automation exercises.

> Society of Manufacturing Engineers
> P.O. Box 930
> Dearborn, MI 48128
> (313) 271-1500

36 video cassettes, color, 40–50 minutes each, learner's print materials.
Purchase: $1,500. Rental: $50.

▶ \ *Microcomputers: An Introduction.* Introduces basic terminology and initial questions asked about microcomputers on the job. Shows the possibilities computers offer for word processing, accounting, and financial applications. Combines animation and live footage. Intended to create acceptance for computers in the workplace.

> CRM/McGraw-Hill Films
> P.O. Box 641
> 674 Via Dela Valle
> Del Mar, CA 92014
> (619) 453-5000

16mm film or video cassette, color, 26 minutes, instructor's print materials.
Purchase: $495. Rental: $75. Preview: free.

▶ *Microcomputers.* Explains the structure of microcomputers in clear, simple terms and includes pictures of the very latest equipment. Diagrams demonstrate how the different components of a microcomputer contribute to its operation. Shows examples of microcomputers employed in a range of situations.

> Prismatron Productions, Inc.
> 155 Buena Vista Avenue
> Mill Valley, CA 94941
> (415) 383-0449

Video cassette or 60 slides and audio cassette or 2 filmstrips, 20 minutes, instructor's print materials.
Purchase: video, $99.50; filmstrips, $65; slides, $75. Preview: free.

▶ *Powersharing: The Microcomputer.* A starting point for understanding the microcomputer—what it is and what it does. Demonstrates its power and versatility in action, using an Apple II as a representative system. Shows word processing, graphics, database management, spreadsheet, and new wire services.

> Martha Stuart Communications, Inc.
> P.O. Box 246
> 2 Anthony Street
> Hillsdale, NY 12529
> (518) 325-3900

Video cassette, color, 50 minutes.
Purchase: $225. Rental: $55.

▶ *What Is a Word Processor?* Dramatizes the difference in performance that a word processor can make from the office worker's point of view. Uses humorous, realistic office situations relating to keeping files, updating correspondence, and making corrections. Features John Cleese of Monty Python fame.

> Xicom-Video Arts
> Sterling Forest
> Tuxedo, NY 10987
> (212) 989-2676

1982, 16mm film or video cassette, color, 28 minutes, learner's print materials.
Purchase: $625. Rental: $120. Preview: $40.

▶ *Micro Revolution.* Discusses how microelectronic technology has revolutionized our lives. Describes the appearance and function of different types of integrated circuits. Explains why silicon chips have become so important and how they are used.

Prismatron Productions, Inc.
155 Buena Vista Avenue
Mill Valley, CA 94941
(415) 383-0449

Video cassette or 60 slides and audio cassette or 2 filmstrips, 20 minutes, instructor's print materials.
Purchase: video, $99.50; filmstrips, $65; slides, $75. Preview: free.

▶ *Introduction to Personal Computers.* Covers terminology, operations, applications, home and office use. Programming and complex vocabulary covered in the manual only.

Microlab, Inc.
2699 Skokie Valley Road
Highland Park, IL 60035
(312) 433-7558

Video cassette, color, 40 minutes, reference manual.
Purchase: $99.95 (1/2″); $129.95 (3/4″).

▶ *Office Information Processing.* An introduction to word-processing operations.

Bergwell Productions, Inc.
P.O. Box 238
Garden City, NY 11530
(516) 222-1111

3 color filmstrips, with 3 audio cassettes, (11–14 minutes each), with study guides.
Purchase: $149 for the set.

▶ *Guide to Microcomputing.* History of computer, hardware and software introduction. Applications and operations. Computers dealt with are Apple II and TRS-80 Model 11.

Bergwall Productions, Inc.
P.O. Box 238
Garden City, NY 11530
(516) 222-1111

4 color filmstrips, with 4 audio cassettes (12–16 minutes each).
Purchase: $219.

TYPE 3: USING LITTLE COMPUTERS

The emphasis is on the word "using". The films and videos we've been talking about up to now are basically conceptual or knowledge-centered. This last major grouping of films, videos and sundry A/V stuff, is skills-centered. Though many of these films and videos *do* talk about how computers work and why computers do "this" and need "that" to function properly, they are basically *keystroke* courses on film. "Push the keys labeled Control, ALT, and Delete simultaneously like this to reboot your system." The goals of these films and tapes, at the least, are very behavioral. "At the end of this program, you will be able to use VisiCalc to balance your checkbook and project the most likely date of your personal bankruptcy," and so on.

There tends to be a very big shortcoming in the structure of keystroke films and videos I have seen. While most do a perfectly fine job of introducing the viewer to this bit of software or that specific hardware system, I have yet to see one that is focused very well on introducing the learner to *applications* of the hardware and software being shown. And the two are very different.

No, I'm not splitting hairs. The difference between feature- and application-focused training is *real* and *important*. For instance, I was able to sit down and type and file a letter on my IBM-PC using my WordStar software long before I was anything approaching facile with it. In fact, it took several more months for me to learn to *apply* the WordStar software to the job of writing and editing a story or doing a report for a client. I had to figure out how to apply the features to my tasks, pretty much—though not totally—on my own.

If your goal is, say, to train real estate agents to use a microcomputer to write letters to prospective clients, to keep prospect lists on file, and to calculate closing and financing costs, then your training must revolve around *those specific applications* to be effective. If, however, your charge is to give a mixed group of learners—rich man, poor man, beggerman, thief, doctor, lawyer, Indian chief—an introduction to microcomputer-based word processing or data-based management, then you need feature-focused, *not* application-focused, training.

There are films, videos, and other A/V materials that can help you meet one, but not both of these different goals. You are going to have to settle for *feature-focused* films and videos for now, but I have been told that honest to goodness *applications-focused* films and videos are in production by a number of publishers (the number is two, to be exact). As of this writing you are going to have to be content with feature-focused flicks even though you may have an applications situation. So you need to remember that you will have to do quite a bit of supplementing to make your instruction as complete as it needs to be. You will probably have to add some of the newer disk tutorials and some one-to-one tutoring or small-group casework.

Another word of caution: Some trainers have told us that using keystroke-specific films and videos in a classroom setting—with more than four or five people—is a tough act. To be useful, they claim, the video playback unit must be much closer physically to the individual being trained than with interpersonal skills training or your run-of-the-mill "talking head" flick. On the other hand, those folks who have been able to spring the dollars for workstations, learning carrels, size playback units (like the little nine-inch color EIKI unit), report that their visually-oriented trainees find the learning experience very satisfying.

Not everyone agrees, by the way, with this contention. Gilbert Mann, president of LEARN-PC Video Systems, believes the small-group setting is an ideal format for using keystroke video tapes. "Reluctant learners can team up and support each other," he says. "And during pilot tests, I've even seen pairing total novices with more knowledgeable students work well."

Okay, *you* decide. Better yet, run your own pilot to decide which way works best in your organization with your trainees.

Following is a listing of the keystroke videos I have run across. Remember that they are all feature-focused and not applications-focused. Again, next to those I have looked at myself *and* think merit your consideration, I have placed a check mark. Those not checked aren't necessarily bad. The most likely case is that I have read about them or been told about them, but simply haven't been able to review them. And anyway, how many "To boot up your computer you turn this switch . . ." flicks do I have to sit through in one lifetime?

FEATURE-FOCUSED VIDEOS, FILMS, AND SUNDRY A/V MATERIALS

▶ \ *How to Use Your IBM-PC™ in Ten Easy Video Lessons.* This is an almost perfect product for those of us who know in our hearts that the only thing we'll get from the new, revised IBM-PC user-friendly documentation manual is a paper cut.

Kennen's ten-lesson cassette assumes only that you can get your new "Baby Blue" home from the computer store and out of the box. Beyond that, nothing is taken for granted. Not until Lesson 3 do you plug the thing into an electrical outlet, and the cassette even tells you how to do that: "Find one of these and plug it in here like this; no, turn it around, that's upside-down."

Lesson 2, the "All-about-Computers" section, comes closer to being one of those "more than you ever wanted to know about silicon" affairs, but it does stay this side of uselessness. If Lesson 2 is a bit patronizing, it is not as bad as many of the ''In the beginning, there was the abacus'' sorts of presentations one finds masquerading under the guise of computer literacy these days. And it is mercifully short.

Lessons on using the keyboard follow, along with some basic but important words of advice on using the computer's operating system (PC/DOS), the use of off-shelf software, and a smattering of basic programming. Music up, out, fade to black.

Kennen also publishes ''How to Learn in Ten Easy Lessons'' video cassettes for IBM-XT, Apple II+, Apple IIe, Apple III, Commodore 64, Sony SMC-70 and CP/M Computers.

> Kennen Publishing
> 150 Shoreline Highway
> Building E
> Mill Valley, CA 94941
> (415) 332-5828

Purchase Only: $69.50.

▶ \ *VisiCalc*™ *for the IBM-PC*™. VisiCalc for the IBM-PC in a sense picks up where ''How to Use Your IBM-PC'' leaves off. Using a very similar step-by-step approach, we waltz through the wonders of that most popular of electronic spreadsheets, the VisiCalc software program from VisiCorp. Just as in the previous tape, lessons are applications-oriented and keystroke-specific. VisiCalc for the IBM-PC comes with a workbook that takes some of the burden of memorization off the learner's back. Comprehension of spreadsheets is tough enough without adding memory drills to the task.

VisiCalc for the IBM-PC is *very* fast-paced. It certainly isn't a watch-once or watch-all-the-way-through-and-you've-got-it flick. I had to go back and back again to get all the nuances and understand all the examples. That doesn't mean this is a bad program. It is simply a very intense 35 minutes of running time. That 35 minutes doesn't represent the time to mastery needed or the amount of time a trainee will need to spend with this tape.

Video Initiatives also publishes *Guide to the IBM-PC*™, *Guide to Lotus 1-2-3*™, *Guide to dBase II*™.

> Video Initiatives, Inc.
> 345 Swett Road
> Woodside, CA 94062
> (415) 851-8437

Video cassette, 35 minutes.
Purchase Only: $300.

▶ *VisiCalc™: The Electronic Spreadsheet.* This tape was reviewed by Michael Hick, a sales promotion manager for Sperry Corporation, in the November 1983 issue of *Desktop Computing*. He ended the review this way:

> To summarize all the concepts presented, the instructor explains a job-costing template created with VisiCalc that gives you a real appreciation of the power of the VisiCalc program and the variety of problems it can help solve.
>
> My initial reaction to the Compuvid VisiCalc tape was that it was an unpolished presentation put together on a low budget, despite the cost to the consumer. But as I reviewed the amount of valuable information provided, it became obvious that much thought went into the design of the examples and the overall organization. You will come away with a better understanding of how VisiCalc works and the number of ways that it can be put to use.

Compuvid
815 North Royal Street
Alexandria, VA 22314
(703) 683-3234

Video cassette, 50 minutes.
Purchase: $175 (VHS or Beta); $225 (3/4″ U-Matic). Preview: $20.

▶ *Introduction to Lotus 1-2-3™.* This eight-lesson program focuses primarily on the use of Lotus 1-2-3 on the IBM-PC. The video program is accompanied by a demonstration computer disk to enhance hands-on learning. Disk contains unfinished worksheets, examples, and an answer guide showing the examples completed.

Learn-PC Video Systems
3601 Wooddale Avenue South
Minneapolis, MN 55416
(612) 532-7672

Video cassette, 60 minutes.
Purchase: $495.

▶ *Learning Concept: The VisiCalc Program.* This program shows the step-by-step of VisiCalc used on the IBM-PC in a "Stop the tape and do this on your computer now" fashion. Focuses on commands and features, very light on applications. Comes with a *Quick Reference Guide.* Micro Learning also publishes video learning tapes covering Lotus 1-2-3, MultiPlan, and WordStar.

Micro Learning Concepts
380 Lexington Avenue
Suite 1208
New York, NY 10017
(212) 687-0066

Video cassette, 58 minutes.
Purchase: $129.95 (add $30 for 3/4″ U-Matic).

▶ *How to Use the MultiPlan Software Package.* This "Big Eight" consulting firm has blitzed the possibilities by providing video-based programs on a broad matrix of hardware and software combinations.

MultiPlan training is available for Apple IIe, IBM-PC, Texas Instruments Pro, Hyperion.

VisiCalc training is available for Apple II+, Apple IIe, Apple III, IBM-PC, Texas Instruments.

Lotus 1-2-3 training is being made available for IBM-PC and a few others but will be more expensive than those now on the shelf (approximately $225).

> Arthur Young/Clarkson Gordon
> The Arthur Young Building
> 1950 Roland Clark Place
> Reston, VA 22091-1490

Color, video cassette, plus practice diskette.
Purchase: video cassette, $195 (adds $55 for U-Matic Tape); additional diskettes, $9.95; additional manuals, $19.95.

▶ *WordStar*™. Lansford publishes a raft of video-based programs. The tapes were actually produced by Anderson Soft-Teach, a computer consulting and training company. Five student workbooks accompany each tape. The whole Lansford list includes:

> *dBase II*
>
> *Lotus 1-2-3*
>
> *MultiPlan*
>
> *VisiCalc*
>
> *Introduction to the IBM-PC with DOS Commands*
>
> *SuperCalc 2*
>
> *PFS: An Introduction to Personal Filing System*
>
> *BASIC: An Introduction to BASIC for Business Applications*

> Lansford Publishing Co., Inc.
> 1088 Lincoln Avenue
> P.O. Box 8711
> San Jose, CA 95155
> (408) 287-3105

Video cassette, 45 minutes.
Purchase: $199.95.

▶ *dBase II: An Introduction to the Command Language.* Touted by one *PC Magazine* writer as the best video tutorial on dBase available. Quality of graphics low, close-ups of computer screen a bit muddy. Also from Soft-Teach:

> *IBM-PC: A Beginner's Guide*
>
> *DOS: Disk Operating System Commands for PC-DOS and MS-DOS*
>
> *1-2-3: An Introduction to Integrated Spreadsheet*
>
> *MultiMate: An Introduction to the Word Processor*

Anderson Soft-Teach
2161 Blossom Valley Drive
San Jose, CA 95124
(408) 356-3552

Video cassette, 42 minutes.
Purchase: $195.

APPENDIX **C** CAI AND DISK TUTORIALS: USING THE COMPUTER TO LEARN COMPUTING

One of the fastest-growing "delivery systems" for computer-literacy training, and perhaps the most logical and appropriate one, is the personal computer itself. Thanks to the "disk tutorial," a self-instructional program that runs on the computer you're learning about, the computer has become a viable candidate for the role of computer-literacy trainer.

The market already offers a wide variety of disk tutorials, and more reach the market every month. There are full-color, animated programs that teach you more than you ever wanted to know about computers in general and about broad applications such as data processing. There are extremely specific disks that teach you things like how to make your new Polar Bear 77 microcomputer load and run Sunshine Software's new Vegetable Management Program—the one that helps you work out optimum schedules for cultivating your cabbages and picking your persimmons. Whether you are interested in programming an Apple IIe in Pascal, learning to do cash-flow projections with a specific spreadsheet, deciphering the printed instructions that came with your word-processing system, or getting tips on how to combat eyestrain, there probably is a tutorial available to teach it.

The majority of disk-tutorial publishers are small software publishers, training companies, and aggressively managed book publishers. (Of course, a number of these small companies are going to cease being small at the rate disk tutorial sales are growing.) Hardware manufacturers and major software publishers also are coming to see that the "documentation" (manuals) they have been providing to their customers isn't instructionally adequate. They have learned the hard way that we the users—at least the noncomputerholics and hobbyists among us—need more and better information to take full advantage of our purchases.

That axiom has been hammered home to original equipment manufacturers (OEMs) and software publishers by the fact that an estimated $3 billion a year training business has sprung up around their products. Many are now joining the scramble to produce instructional material, frequently computer-based training material, to accompany their primary products.

VisiCorp, Inc., the San Jose, California, company that almost single-handedly invented the applications-software business by coming up with the electronic spreadsheet VisiCalc, has introduced a series of computer-aided, self-study programs called the VisiTutor series, which will coach the use of VisiCalc and other packages the company has since developed.

Ashton-Tate, based in Culver City, California, publisher of dBase II, the best-selling database management software program, is aggressively advertising the dBase II On-Disk Tutorial, a CAI program designed to teach the use of the dBase II software. When you buy the software itself, the advertisements promise, "at the same time you'll be getting the most advanced teaching tool for free." That line *should* worry CAI houses such as American Training International (ATI) of Manhattan Beach, California, and Cdex Corp. of Los Altos, California, the industry leaders, but it doesn't. In fact, the dedicated CAI houses are contracting with many of the big software houses to develop disk tutorials to include with their software packages.

ATI, for example, has developed disk tutorials for the PeachText 5000 by Management Science America. MSA used the inclusion of an ATI tutorial as a marketing plus and featured the combo in ad. It is also the case that many people are willing to invest $40 to $100, the price of a disk tutorial, to get a look at the capability of a software package without having to buy the software pig-in-a-poke fashion, as it were.

The hardware manufacturers are beginning to include disk tutorials with their machines. Buy an Apple computer these days and you get a disk called *Apple Presents Apple* to help start you off on the right foot. Since about October 1983, the same has been true of the IBM-PC. All new Baby Blue's come with a disk tutorial called *Exploring the IBM Personal Computer,* produced by Digital Learning Systems.

The purchase of disk-tutorial packages, like the purchase of any other training product, calls for some care and thought. Just as all seminars, books, and video tapes are not created equal, neither are all disk tutorials; some are well designed, some aren't. And even a well-designed package can't help you much if it is designed to do one thing and you expect it to do something else.

Joel Rakow, executive vice-president and cofounder of American Training International, cautions shoppers to do some homework before buying. "You have to ask some key questions and know something about the packages you are investigating to make an intelligent purchase," he says. "In some instances I would advise against a tutorial even though we publish seventy-some of them."

The key questions Rakow suggests revolve around the level of expertise the intended end users already have, the level of expertise you want them to develop, and the urgency of the training need. "You have to be clear," he says, "whether you are interested in software literacy, general computer literacy, or skills development. You need different training for each. If you are trying to help a manager develop skills with a specific piece of software on a specific piece of hardware, you wouldn't pick a tutorial package that features color graphics and animation and that starts with the history of computing. You'd want something that pretty closely simulates the computer in action the way the end user would see it performing every day.

"On the other hand," Rakow continues, "if you wanted to teach computer awareness and computing concepts, you might even opt for a seminar instead of a tutorial." As a rule of thumb, he says, a disk tutorial is most useful when "you have to teach the skills in a hurry and you can do it on the computer the person will be using every day. Of course," he adds, "I'm a little prejudiced since those are the kinds of programs we specialize in."

Bodie Marx, vice-president of the computer software division of Milliken Publishing Co. of St. Louis, claims that educational software—a common industry term for disk-tutorial packages—should be just as exciting, ingenious, and provocative as the games your kids play with their home video equipment. "These products [should] offer a fascinating blend of educational design and computer-generated entertainment," he said in a recent issue of *Leisure Time Electronics.*

David H. Ahl, an editor with *Creative Computing* magazine, suggests that the following criteria should be applied to an evaluation of educational software.

1. *Educational soundness.* Is the package tested? Are data available? Is there a glaring absence of clear objectives, rote and drill, practice and testing—the things you would expect in an instructional package?

2. *Appropriateness.* Is the package designed for your learners and their specific current needs?

3. *Challenge and progress.* Does the instruction proceed at a pace appropriate to your learners? Does it treat them as adults?

4. *Motivation and reward.* Does the program build competence? Does it reward competence? Is some appropriate fun built in?

5. *Correctness.* Are terms correctly defined? Do practice procedures actually work? Do examples look like the real screen displays, printouts, etc., that the trainees will be working with later?

6. *Compatibility with your system.* What are the exact requirements for hardware, memory, and peripherals? Does the program run all the way through on your gear?

7. *Instructions and hand-holding.* Does the package explain everything your trainees will need to know to load the program and run it successfully? Are appropriate workbooks, tip sheets, and job aids included? Can the learner use the package without already having mastered the material to be learned? (A disk tutorial on computer literacy for beginners should *not* open with instructions such as "Boot the system in the A Drive and this tutorial in B, then call up the Lesson Menu.")

As with all training tools, the value of a disk-tutorial package is determined by the rigor with which it was designed, developed, and debugged. Wise purchasing decisions require that you evaluate these packages with a critical eye. The package you buy should both teach effectively and show the computer off to its best advantage. Demand as much of the computer as a "trainer" as you demand of it as a management-support tool or of yourself in the classroom.

Since the publishers of disk tutorials generally publish multiple programs, I have constructed this listing by publisher rather than program. In the instance of those programs I have played with myself, I have included a short critique. Because there is a cookie-cutter kind of sameness to a CAI company's programs, what is true of one tends to be true of all.

Apple Computer, Inc.
20525 Marinani Avenue
Cupertino, CA 95014
(800) 539-9696

The following disk tutorial programs are available (some for disk-copying costs) through authorized Apple Computer dealers:

Apple Presents Apple: A highly regarded CAI introduction to Apple computing and keyboard functions.

Apple IIe: Business Applications (an introductory/interactive demo) provides the introduction to using AppleWriter, VisiCalc, and other business-oriented, software-driven functions.

Product Training Packages: Apple Computer supplies the following software-support disk tutorial packages through authorized dealers: AppleWriter II, AppleWriter IIe, Quickfile II, and the Apple III specific Businessgraphics, System Utilities, AppleWriter III, Mail List Manager, Senior Analyst III, and VisiCalc III).

CBS Educational and Professional Publishing
383 Madison Avenue
New York, NY 10017
(800) 227-1617, ext. 336

Publishes the following book/disk tutorials:

> *Using the IBM Personal Computer: WordStar*
> *Using the IBM Personal Computer: VisiCalc*
> *Your IBM Personal Computer: Use, Applications and BASIC*

Also publishes programming tutorials for the IBM-PC on Fortran 77, Pascal, COBOL, BASIC, UCSD Pascals, and Organization and Assembly Language

---

Cdex Corporation
5050 El Camino Real
Los Altos, CA 94022
(415) 964-7600

Publishes 23 disk interactive tutorials with workbooks for the following software packages: VisiCalc, WordStar, SuperCalc, SuperCalc 2, Lotus 1-2-3, MultiPlan, EasyWriter II, dBase II, DB Master—Version 4, IBM-PC DOS 2.0. Versions of these packages are available for IBM-PC, IBM-PC XT, Compaq, Apple II, plus Apple IIe. Cdex also publishes general orientation tutorials for the IBM-PC, Texas Instruments Professional, and Apple IIe.

Cdex is one of the first publishers to try building software-applications CAI. *Managing Your Business with SuperCalc or SuperCalc 2; Managing Your Business with Lotus 1-2-3 Program; Making Business Decisions Using Lotus 1-2-3 Program; Making Business Decisions Using the MultiPlan Program;* and *Making Business Decisions Using the VisiCalc Advanced Version Program* are made more than software tutorials. All go beyond the software to teaching an approach to applying the software.

The Cdex tutorials are generally some place between page turners and truly interactive simulations. Much of the information giving reminds me of Robert Horn's "Information Mapping" approach to individualized instruction.

CMA MicroComputer
5722 Santa Fe Trail
Yucca Valley, CA 92284
(619) 365-9718

Publishes *The Teacher PC*, a disk tutorial program, covering IBM-PC, DOS, DOS utilities, and three levels of programming. Leads learner through the OEM manual and all keyboard commands. Also covers basic data processing.

Comprehensive Software Support
2316 Artesia Blvd., Suite B
Redondo Beach, CA 90278
(213) 318-2561

Publishes the following disk-tutorial-centered learning packages:

> *PC Pal:* An introduction to using the personal computer. Uses games and animation to teach basic keyboard operations, introduction to hardware operation, role of software, introduction to word processing and spreadsheets. Available for both IBM-PC and TI Professional. Graphics, sound, and animation.

> *PC Tutor:* Teaches intermediate and higher-order computer concepts. Lessons on use of PC-DOS included. Will run on any MS-DOS-friendly system.

It is obvious that the designers and developers at Comprehensive like doing CAI and showing how good they are. In some ways the programs are a touch too flip for business settings, but what the heck, they are fun. *PC Pal* tends to be a little "parent" in tone. *PC Tutor* uses awfully full screens sometimes and small character size.

Computer Systems Research, Inc.
40 Darling Drive
Avon, CT 06001
(203) 678-1212

Publishes CAI programs that run on mainframe or IBM-PC. Relevant computer literacy titles are:

> *The IBM-PC Primer:* 6-module program covering IBM-PC capabilities. Focuses on features, functions and operation of the system.

> *VisiCalc Training on the IBM-PC:* 12 modules for learning the VisiCalc spreadsheet. Audio tapes, written pre- and post-tests, and disk exercises.

> *Data Processing Concepts:* Provides training for non-data-processing personnel in computer basics, computer capabilities, systems concepts, and benefit of on-line systems. Geared for people with little or no computer background.

Courseware, Inc.
10075 Carroll Canyon Road
San Diego, CA 92131
(619) 578-1700

Publishes the *PC-Master,* a 2-disk and workbook tutorial program that takes learners through basic personal computing functions on IBM-PC. Explains word processing, communications, data-base management, and electronic spreadsheets.

PC-Master has an awful lot of space-bar pressing (page turning); in the section discussing word processing, I counted 23 page turns/space-bar presses. The designers and developers have some very nice effects programmed into the lessons, but I was itching to interact a bit more. The section on choosing software is pretty good. A very menu-driven program that helps you move in and out of topics easily.

DELTAK Microsystems
1751 West Diehl Road
Naperville, IL 60566
(800) 282-5586

Publishes the following disk-tutorial exercise-centered packages, which feature color graphics and interactive practice:

Teach Yourself VisiCalc

Teach Yourself the IBM-PC

Teach Yourself VisiCalc-Extended Features

Teach Yourself VisiAnswer

Teach Yourself TutorMate

Teach Yourself MultiMate

Educational Courseware
3 Nappa Lane
Westport, CT 06880
(203) 227-1438

Publishes the *Basic Tutor Series,* 9 disks plus workbook covering systems commands, programming, creating graphics, music, sounds, shapes, pictures, files, and programming aids. Runs on Apple and Franklin hardware.

Individual Software, Inc.
24 Spinnaker Place
Redwood City, CA 94065
(415) 591-4166

Publishes the following disk tutorial programs:

The Instructor: Teaches first-time users to interact with the IBM-PC. Features graphics, color, and sound.

Professor DOS: For IBM-PC users who want to delve into higher-level PC concepts, including DOS commands. Graphics, color, sound, and animation.

Here is another company with designers and developers who like to have fun and show off a little. Both programs use light humor and very good graphics. After a right answer in one spot, the program replies, "Perhaps this is too easy?," and a couple of responses later offers, "Perhaps a good instructor?" The characters used for that are bold and clean, the screens seldom cluttered. *Professor DOS* assumes you really do want to know all about DOS, and in that sense it really comes at you.

Innovative Program Associates, Inc.
1 Airport Place
Princeton, NJ 08540
(609) 924-7272

Publishes the *Introduction to Computer Literacy,* a 4-disk/9-module tutorial plus workbook program that covers basics from "What's a Computer?" to personal computing principles and simple BASIC programming. Runs on Apple II or Apple IIe.

Knoware, Inc.
301 Vassar Street
Cambridge, MA 02139
(617) 576-3825

Knoware's only published CAI program at this writing is called *KNOWARE* as in "First there was hardware, then there was software, now there is *KNO-WARE.*" Get it? Knoware is a 3-diskette program that introduces the learner to the IBM-PC. (The program runs on any IBM clone and most MS-DOS operating system equipment, though.)

    InfoWorld called this "the world's best computer literacy learning program." That's a bit stiff. In actuality, it *is* a darn good intro to using the personal computer in business. The feature that makes people so wild about it is that it is pure fun. All the learning takes place in the context of a game. The goal of the game is to get from the mailroom to the chairman's seat, get rich, and retire. In some ways, the program gets close to too cute for words, but just close. The program will run on a green screen, but some text lines are lost without a color monitor. Some of the simulations are hard to make corrections to, and a lot of the "help" is not very helpful. Just the same, it's fun to play and play again—and learn from. It can do wonders for the ego of a computerphobe.

Micro Courseware Corp.
4444 Geary Blvd., Suite 300
San Francisco, CA 94118
(415) 751-5223

Publishes the *Blue Chip 1,* a disk-tutorial basic computer-literacy package using the IBM-PC. Covers four general computer applications: financial planning, business communication, project management, and database. Allows learners to enter and manipulate information and data.

The designers have included some fun games and learning exercises as well as good information. This is one of the "new breed" of tutorials that isn't simply a book on a disk. The timed basic computer definitions test, called dictionary dash, is almost worth the price of the program alone. More information, in some ways, than the Knoware program, but almost as much fun. Very good graphics. A tendency to overcorrect the trainee; specifically, the program won't let you make any mistakes, locks you out of wrong responses, and is a bit frustrating because of it.

Micro Power & Light Co.
12820 Hillcrest Road, #224
Dallas, TX 75230
(214) 239-6620

Publishes *Computer Literacy,* a 3-disk tutorial program covering basic microcomputer terminology, common applications, and programming. Runs on Apple II.

Micro Mentor, Inc.
4949 Morgan Avenue South
Minneapolis, MN 55409
(612) 922-0672

Publishes a line of interactive programs that use a computer video interactive format. The programs are designed to teach use of the IBM-PC using a combination of video-taped lectures and explanations and floppy disk tutorial as well. As with most interactive videos, you have to use the exact same hardware and software configuration the developer used. If you want a learning carrel–based CBT tutor, explore Micro Mentor. Six programs are available: *The Personal Consultant Series, Introduction to the PC, Using Programs, Disk Drives and DOS, WordStar,* and *dBase II.*

Personal Tutor Associates
(a Division of ExecSystems Corp.)
P.O. Box 246
Clinton, MD 20735
(301) 856-2280

Publishes diskette samplers (plus workbook and audio-cassette tape) for the following software packages and programming languages: EasyWriter II, dBase II, PFS: File/Report, Easy Filer, VisiFile, VisiCalc, TK! Solver, Multi-

Plan, Lotus 1-2-3, Easy Planner, VisiTrend/Plot, PASCAL, WordStar, AppleWriter, ScreenWriter, Supertext.

These programs are published for use on the following computer systems: Apple II, Apple IIe, Apple II+, IBM PC.

Also publishes an orientation tutorial for Commodore 64.

Reston Publishing Co., Inc.
11480 Sunset Hills Road
Reston, VA 22090
(800) 336-0338

Publishes *The Executive's Guide to the IBM Personal Computer: BASIC Programming and VisiCalc,* a disk/workbook tutorial that focuses on business applications of the IBM-PC, the concept of spreadsheet, plus extensive work on programming in BASIC. Also publishes *IBM-TEACH, BASIC TEACH,* and *TEACH PROGRAM FOR VISICALC.*

Software Training Co.
(a Division of American Training International)
3770 Highland Avenue, Suite 201C
Manhattan Beach, CA 90266
(213) 546-4725

Publishes skill-focused, disk-interactive tutorials with workbooks and job aids for the following commercial software packages, DOS, and programming languages: WordStar, EasyWriter II, Benchmark, MULTIPLAN, EasyPlanner, PeachCalc, BPI Gen. Acct., dBase II, Easy Filer, CP/M, PC-DOS, MS-DOS, BASIC.

The above tutorials are available for microcomputers using any of the following operating systems: PC-DOS, MS-DOS, CP/M, CP/M-86, Apple IIe DOS, Apple IIe 80 col., XENIX.

ATI turns out programs like popcorn. They aren't fancy and they aren't really CAI. They are pure software tutorial. No dancing mice or speaking chips, just software emulation and drill. Some people swear by the approach; others swear at it.

SOPHCO
663 West Aspen Way
Dept. W-4
Boulder, CO 80027
(303) 444-1542

DOS Tutorial is a menu-driven lesson in use of the MS-DOS operating system. A novel feature in the program identifies and corrects entry mistakes. The publisher has made an effort to keep access to command explanations very open so that the tutorial can also serve as a reference tool.

Texas Soft, Inc.
3415 Westminster Avenue
Suite 100
Dallas, TX 75205
(214) 369-0795

Publishes *Your Personal Computer Tutor,* a basic IBM-PC skills tutorial plus some games. Basic keyboard operations. Compatible with IBM-PC and "look-alikes" such as Compaq, Chameleon, etc.

VisiCorp
2895 Zanker Road
San Jose, CA 95134
(408) 946-9000

Publishes a series of disk-tutorial products for learning to use VisiCorp software products (VisiCalc, VisiFile, VisiTrend/Plot, etc.).

Advanced Systems, Inc. (ASI)
2340 Arlington Heights Road
Arlington Heights, IL 60005
(312) 981-4260

ASI commissioned ATI (are you following this?) to produce 24 tutorials that are sold under the MicroTutor label by ASI. All products use the split-screen device that is characteristic of ATI programs. The twist is that ASI has specified—or created—a very, very nice reference guide. Large print, stands on an easel next to your work/learning station. Why didn't the OEMs figure this one out? Tutorials range from *Intro to the IBM-PC* to *Peachtree A/P.* The *MultiMate* tutorial is very good.

APPENDIX D LISTENING TO LEARN: AUDIO-TUTORIAL OPTIONS

Consider the humble audio cassette. Once a medium of promise and preference, it has generally fallen on hard times. Replaced in the classroom by its pushy progeny, the video tape, and booted from the home computer world by yet another assertive cousin, the floppy disk, the audio cassette seems destined to a narrowly defined future as the medium of choice for people who like to take their rock 'n' roll when they drive, skate, or jog.

But hold your Walkman. There's still some instructional life left in that little plastic packet. It's true that no self-respecting 1984-vintage training technologist would ask a group of people to sit around a conference table listening to a taped lecturer drone on about selling and managing and whatnot, but that doesn't mean the game's over. In fact, a number of folks are finding the Plain Jane audio tape to be a rather elegant solution to a very pressing problem involving computer-literacy training.

Here's the problem: Once the computer-literacy lecture is over, once the troops have mastered the basic concepts of the microcomputer, and had some guided group practice, it's time to boot up and get on with it. Frequently, this is where all hell breaks loose, skills-training-wise. The accounting department people need to move into spreadsheet and accounts-receivable training. Two dozen secretaries and the whole PR group couldn't care less about accounting's needs and want word-processing particulars. The R&D group wants statistical analysis and project management. Marketing, of course, wants graphics and list management—by yesterday.

One way to meet the need—provided you have or can even hire the know-how—is one-to-one tutoring and very-small-group training. But if you have more than a couple dozen people to train, that rules the personal touch out. So does timing; the iron will grow cold, and you'll grow old before you get to everyone in need.

Another approach is the disk tutorial—computer-based training tailored to specific microcomputer hardware and software configurations and specific real-world applications. And there are a number of very fine computer-as-tutor packages around (see Appendix C). But not everyone believes that the disk tutorial is the best way to learn to use a microcomputer or an application-software package. And it certainly isn't appropriate for every learning style.

An alternative gaining significant favor in a number of quarters is the "audio tutorial": step-by-step instructions on audio tape. Though some versions are more complex, the basic audio tutorial is nothing more than a cassette tape. You stick the cassette in a player, put the player next to the computer, and turn on the player. A headset is useful—no, critical—if others are around the learning station.

Some audio-tutorial advocates go so far as to suggest that the audio-tape approach to learning to operate the microcomputer is not just an alternative, but a *superior* alternative. One such, Lee McFadden, president of FlipTrack Learning Systems of Glen Ellyn, Illinois, believes something very critical is missing from the disk-tutorial experience: the systems and software being learned. "Computer-aided instruction is very valid, very valuable. But in this application—learning to use specific hardware and software—it isn't as effective as audio," he says.

Though McFadden is admittedly biased (FlipTrack produces and markets sixteen audio-tutorial software learning packages), he levels a couple of interesting criticisms. "The CAI developer has to simulate the software in his program. That means the learner never experiences the software firsthand in the learning program. You really can't learn to use a software program that way. You can learn about the software, but you can't really learn to use it without using it." McFadden's idea of an ideal software learning situation is sitting down at the computer one-on-one with a very knowledgeable, skillful, and patient individual. "Failing the availability of that situation, the next best thing is an audio tutorial," he insists.

Others apparently agree. At least there are several other companies concentrating on the development and marketing of audio-tape-based micro-computer literacy programs.

MICRO Instructional, Inc., of Fort Lauderdale, Florida, publishes 110 different audio tutorials. Martin E. Hardee, manager of technical services for MICRO, agrees with McFadden's assessment that working with the actual hardware and software is important to both learning and trainee satisfaction. "People who are learning a new piece of software, for instance, want to do it right away. They want to experiment and discover what the software can do. In an audio format, you can help them with that. You can guide them through the procedural steps, point out things on the screen, and give them concept information at the same time."

Hardee also sees a special benefit of audio-tutorial training for the computer-reluctant novice and the new computer user suffering a bit of technophobia. "Everyone is a little fearful of a new piece of equipment of software," he says, adding, "But by letting the learners use the actual equipment and software, and by putting them through a program designed to give a lot of achievement and success early in the program, you can put that fear quickly to rest."

Edward Rutenberg of Electronic Protection Devices, Inc., in Waltham, Massachusetts, is product manager for Fastrain, an audio-tape-based learning device that incorporates features of both the audio-tutorial and disk-tutorial methods. Rutenberg believes the audio part of the Fastrain system is vital for effective learning of the computer concepts. "Having the nice, friendly human voice, combined with the hands-on practice and the visual stimulation of the controlled displays on the CRT, is a much more effective learning environment than any one of the three modalities alone. In tests we've found this trisensory mode to produce learning twenty to fifty percent more efficiently than when only one or two modes are involved in the learning," he reports.

WHAT TO LOOK FOR IN AUDIO TUTORIALS

Remember the sheep in Orwell's *Animal Farm*—the ones who ran about bleating, "all animals are created equal but some animals are more equal"? Well, translated to the case in point and de-double-speaked, not all audio tutorials are created equal. And as with any art form, some users are going to like and find useful just exactly the creation others can't stand. With due apologies to our ISD brethren, when the pencil hits the paper, style will be out; and style counts for much with the consumer. Nonetheless, there are a few general guidelines you can apply to evaluating any audio tutorial you are considering for your specific "Train 'em to press the right keys" situation.

1. *Is the narration easy and natural to listen to?* Words written to be heard are different from words written to be read. Pick the narration apart as you listen. Better yet, ask the producer for a copy of the script. Pay particular attention to these key points:

> *Complexity.* Is sentence structure simple? Are sentences short? Are key words placed so they will be heard? The more complex the writing, the less likely the learning.

> *Voice.* Is the narration written in an active voice? It should be.

> *Rhythm.* Do words and sounds flow smoothly, clearly, easily. They should.

2. *Are there examples and samples to work with? Is it actually tuto-*

rial? If the point of an audio tutorial is to bring a trainee into contact with live software and hardware, with guidance, then there had better be examples to work with. The trainee should be led through the material, not lectured to. FlipTrack's McFadden emphasizes that the purpose of practice is—in part, at least—"to give the learner experience at getting into and out of trouble. Making errors and solving problems—in a controlled way—is an important part of computer learning."

Note: Some producers put examples on the tapes. Some put them in auxiliary workbooks. Still others put them on a diskette. There is no research to support one approach over another. Ya pays yer money and ya takes yer choice.

As a rule of thumb, the program should present examples in a format most like the format of the information the trainees will deal with back on the job.

3. *Are unnecessary technical terms avoided and necessary ones "marked" in the narration.* Phrases like "Boot the system" are cool if you are a techie and need to show you are special. But isn't "Turn the computer on" sufficient for most users? Where jargon and "technicalese" cannot be avoided, are the words emphasized and defined? "The first step is to turn the computer on and load—or enter—the program into the computer. This is sometimes referred to as booting the system. Here's how you boot the system. First . . ."

4. *Is the narrator comfortable and easy to listen to? Is the pace a comfortable listening/learning pace?* A professional voice on a tape is a great idea, but if the narrator doesn't understand anything about the subject matter, it can show, especially in the way words are pronounced and pauses are used. These nuances *can* be written into an audio script, but normally, ignorance of the topic on the part of the narrator does show through.

MICRO Instructional's Hardee describes his solution: "We have found a knowledgeable narrator is priceless. We use an individual with a good speaking voice who also teaches computer courses. We think it makes a difference on the tapes. I've heard narrators who sound like used-car salesmen and narrators who sound like actors reading lines. I don't know how students understand either of them."

FlipTrack's senior editor, Patricia Menges, adds that "the narrator should have a friendly, confident voice. He needs to sound like he understands what he is talking about."

5. *Are there frequent pauses and suggestions to take a break?* On the one hand, the audio tutorial helps focus the trainees' attention on learning through the involvement of so many senses. The rest of the story, however, is that so much attending on the trainees' part leads quickly to satiation and, eventually, to fatigue. The tutorial that doesn't "break" the trainee frequently may not have been pilot-tested very thoroughly.

FlipTrack's Menges emphasizes that "if it is a good tape, you can't get a lot out of listening to it in your car. You have to stop, do things, try things out. You have to be in front of the computer interacting with the software to get anything important out of the program."

6. *Can you hear the narration in a thunderstorm?* Okay, so that's a bit of an exaggeration, but the audio tutorial that is going to be used on the job with people milling about and while the computer and printer—perhaps a multitude of computers and printers—are running has to have darn good sound quality. Test it with cheap playback recorders as well as your hotshot studio-quality equipment.

7. *Are there adequate visuals to back up the audio?* Publishers—and learning theorists—disagree here. Ronald H. Anderson, author of *Selecting and Developing Media for Instruction* (New York: Van Nostrand Reinhold, 1983), suggests visuals as a way of emphasizing the important points on an audio tape and as a way to help keep script clutter—especially minor detail—to a minimum. But some of the publishers of computer audio tutorials insist that the computer screen in action is itself visual display enough. Others provide job aids, checklists, and reminder cards.

If you opt for backup or hardcopy visuals, consider: Are the visuals clear and legible? Are they directly relevant to the narration? Are they simple and understandable at a glance? Are they physically easy to manipulate? If not, they should be.

8. *Is it technically correct?* Sometimes, in an effort to simplify ideas, terms, and procedures, scriptwriters simplify into inaccuracy. On the other hand, there are lots of shortcuts and time-savers that should be taught after the longhand, easy-to-understand procedure is learned. A subject-matter expert should check the tutorial out for these as well.

9. *Is the content specific enough?* The reason MICRO-Instructional has 110 audio tutorials and FlipTrack fewer than 20 has to do with a difference of opinion. The MICRO people believe that the best instruction deals with a specific piece of equipment and a specific piece of application software—though they do publish some generalized tapes as well. FlipTrack, on the other hand, tends to publish software—specific but machine generic programs. With a generic program, the need for visual support material, particularly organization/machine-specific visual support material, goes up, as does the need for in-house pilot-testing.

10. *Does it "fly" in your organization?* While all the publishers say that their materials are developmentally tested, none should take offense at the suggestion that to be perfectly safe, it might be prudent to run your own in-house pilot test.

MICRO-Instructional's Hardee suggests that, in addition to testing the program for learning, ease of use, and student acceptance, you also test the "fit" of audio tutorials to your whole training scheme.

Might the audio tutorial be better used as pre-classroom training to bring everyone up to speed? As post-class or post-course reinforcement? "Consider using an audio tutorial to orient people to the hardware and do the software teaching live," he suggests, adding, "Ask your pilot-test trainees for ideas about these things. They can be very helpful."

A final thought on getting exactly what you want in a keystroke audio tutorial: The producers and publishers of audio tutorials for learning to use the microcomputer are, by and large, used to working in a consumer, mail-order, onesie-twosie market. If you are in an organization that is a potential long-term, multiple-unit buyer, don't be afraid to ask for special service and even special volume prices. And definitely don't be afraid to call them up and ask them detailed questions about their products. The good ones are— justifiably— proud of their products, and more than willing to talk shop with another training pro.

AUDIO-TUTORIAL RESOURCES

There are two distinct types of audio tape-based computer-literacy learning programs: *computer-theory* programs and *micro-computer, keystroke-specific* programs. As the category labels suggest, the former are about computers in general, while the latter are of the "How to use the slinky XXI" and "using the WoopieStar Word-Processing Program on the Whoffer 90" variety. The computer-theory-type tapes are just that—all talk and concept. The keystroke-specific tapes are mostly skill-drill programs. Both have a possible place in your computer-literacy training program, and neither is sufficient, in and of itself, to make an individual computer literate.

COMPUTER-THEORY PROGRAMS These programs have been around, if not forever, at least as long as there has been corporate computing. I "took" (I'm never sure whether one takes an audio tape-based program or simply listens to it) my first in 1966 when I was trying to learn to do CAI on the PDP-8 (or 10, I forget which). The program consisted of six twenty-minute-to-a-side cassettes, and an eight- by 10-inch GBC bound book of line drawings. I think it was an American Management Association production, but I'm not sure.

I learned a lot about CPUs, batch processing, remote access, mag tape drives, and hard disks. I learned nothing about building CAI to run on the PDP-10 (or 8—I still can't remember which it was). I wasn't supposed to really; but twice through that 240 minutes of tape and I was ready to sling computer jargon with the best of 'em.

That, I think, was all the course authors really had in mind. Learning objectives and advertising aside, the all-about-computers audio-tape crash course is a marvelously quick way to learn the big-picture, broad-brush concepts that define computing. You can't usually *do* anything different—save talk funny—after taking one, but they give you invaluable practice at listening to, and not being awed by, computerese.

I've lost touch with this genre over the years, so I'm sure there are many more than the programs listed here. The following are, however, of generally good quality and do the deed as described by the builders.

MICROCOMPUTER LITERACY PROGRAM

CRM/McGraw-Hill Films
P.O. Box 641
674 Via Dela Valle
Del Mar, CA 92014
(619) 453-5000

1983, 6 audio cassettes, 60 minutes each, learner's print materials.
Purchase: $195.

Gives overview of microcomputing history, functions, and components. Explains how to select the personal computer and software to suit specific needs. Includes a short course in computer programming using BASIC. Intended for self-study.

American Management Association
AMACOM
135 West 50th Street
New York, NY 10020
(212) 586-8100

6 audio cassettes, 30 minutes each, print materials.
Purchase: $145.

The classic "computer knowledge for the non–computer expert" program. Designed to help the non-EDP manager learn to communicate knowledgeably with the EDP types. Focuses on how computers are used to solve management problems.

KEYSTROKE-SPECIFIC PROGRAMS

I told you just about everything I know about this breed earlier in the chapter. But it is bad form to introduce a major expository section with no exposition. So I'll tell a story to fill up the space.

Warning: If you don't like personal stories, do not read any further. Just skip the next paragraphs and go directly to the listings. Reading the remainder of this introduction has been adjudged a waste of time by some former friends of mine.

About six months after buying my shiny new IBM-PC, I had yet to master WordStar, that hard-to-learn, easy-to-use microcomputer word-processing software package with which every other word-processing package is invariably compared. Mind, now, I had already co-authored a book on the IBM operating system and even worked my way through two disk tutorials that described and explained WordStar to me. I was still reluctant to belly up to the keyboard, boot the Star, and go at it. Trying to make sense of the publisher's manuals only added to my frustration. The detail of the system—with its dozens of clever commands—both eluded and baffled me. Finally, determined that the product I had spent $300+ on would gather dust no more, I came up with a new strategy. Or, to be perfectly honest, a new strategy came upon me. "We need a computer story for April," my managing editor barked during one of our highly participative editorial planning meetings. "Audio tape," I blurted back. "Gesundheit," he retorted. "No!" I insisted. "I mean learning to use a computer from audio tape. How's that for a story with a twist?" I asked. (Okay, so Edgar Allan Poe I ain't. You try to put sex and violence into a training story twelve times a year and see how you like it!) "Can you put a resource center with it?" he asked. "Yeah, sure." "Sold. Give me fifteen hundred words!"

I wrote and phoned the major publishers of audio tutorials for review copies of their tapes, and within a couple of weeks I was ready to learn something and report on the effort. I sampled all the products I had at hand and settled on the FlipTrack product to make my big plunge into WordStar literacy. Why FlipTrack? Well, to tell the truth, I'm not 100 percent sure, but I think it has something to do with the green vinyl package and their print ads. Their print ads are everywhere—so are everybody else's—but the focal point of their ad is Lee McFadden, president of the company and narrator on the tapes. I figure if the guy has the guts to admit that not only does he own the company, but he did the tape and is proud enough of the whole thing to put his own smiling mug in the ads, well, this guy is going to get a tumble. Besides, if the program stinks, I know just whom to point the finger at. (I could see the sarcastic headline in my mind's eye: "Why is this man smiling? Because he just ripped me off for $69.95!")

What a disappointment! Within forty minutes of turning on the tape—with time out for wading through the MicroPro manual to figure out how to make a single working disk with operating system, spelling checker, and associated fodder all imbedded—I had typed and formatted a memo to a colleague, pounded out and edited a press release, and built a set of files for the chapters of this book.

On the other hand, I never completely finished listening to and working out the exercises on the tape. In fact, I eventually hired a tutor to spend a couple of hours looking over my shoulder correcting my mistakes and answering my nutty and frequently ill-formed questions about using WordStar to make and save lists and labels, write stories and book chapters, and write reports with both words and charts in them. The fact that I needed extra help to finish off the learning I wanted isn't the fault of the producers of the Cdex and ATI disks or McFadden and his FlipTrack tapes. "The fault, dear Brutus, lies not in our stars but in ourselves." The problem is the one we dealt with earlier—peculiar individual learning needs. And it makes sense. The microcomputer is meant to be individualized, flexible, and peculiarly personal. In the office setting, such personal peculiarities aren't as pronounced as they are when the subject at hand is me, the typical one-man band, chief cook *and* bottle washer independent consultant, but they nonetheless exist. And you, friend, are the one who is accountable to adapting your computer-literacy training to meet those individual *and* organizational needs. That's a lot to ask, but it is nothing less than the true price of doing *real* computer-literacy training in your organization.

SOME KEYSTROKE SPECIFIC AUDIO-TUTORIAL PROGRAMS TO LOOK AT

Electronic Protection Devices, Inc.
P.O. Box 673
Waltham, MA 02254

EPD, Inc., is the manufacturer of Fastrain, a device that combines features of both audio- and disk-tutorial modes. A unique feature of Fastrain is that the audio tape "cues" examples and displays from a simulation diskette. This limits the rewind/replay capability of the audio tape a bit—modules can be removed, but going back for a missed sentence or two could cobble the system. The trade-off gives more concise and exact samples and examples for trainees to work with. The device itself costs $498, which includes computer interface package and one learning package. Learning packages are available for:

WordStar

MultiPlan

dBase II

Lotus 1-2-3

BASIC

Introduction to the IBM-PC

FlipTrack Learning Systems
Division of Mosiac Media, Inc.
999 Main Street, Suite 200
Glen Ellyn, IL 60137

FlipTrack cassettes have what the publisher calls "a feature that allows a linear audiotape to be branching." Specifically, the A side of a FlipTrack cassette contains the basic instructions, while the B side has enrichment and special-topic information. If, for example, you want to know more about the WordStar menu feature than is explained on the A side of the tape, you can stop the tape, turn it over, and start right there to get the additional poop. A course has three to four tapes, depending. FlipTrack courses have the highest level of production values of the audio tutorials we reviewed. Seventeen FlipTrack tutorials are available. Among them are:

How to Operate the Apple II

How to Operate the Apple III

How to Operate the IBM-PC

How to Operate the IBM-XT

How to Operate the Franklin Ace 1000

How to Use VisiCalc

How to Use WordStar

How to Use WordStar plus MailMerge

How to Use MultiPlan

How to Use Lotus 1-2-3

MICRO Instructional, Inc.
3453 Northwest 55th Street
Fort Lauderdale, FL 33309

MICRO's courses are distinguished by their brevity—usually one cassette per course—and their specificity. Some courses come with example booklets. Xerox and KayPro give MICRO instructional tapes away to their customers. The MICRO Instructional courses are the most tightly structured of the audio tutorials we have reviewed. Among the MICRO courses are:

WordStar—General

WordStar—IBM-PC

WordStar—Advanced

dBase II

dBase II—Advanced

Lotus 1-2-3

Personal Tutor Associates
Division of Exec. Systems Corp.
11009 Brandywine Road
P.O. Box 246
Clinton, MD 20735

Of the audiotutorials we reviewed, these are the most lecturelike. Some courses, such as the VisiCalc course, come with a floppy diskette template. There are optimal disk-tutorial programs that can be purchased and used as follow-up for some programs. An interesting feature—or is it a peculiarity?— of the audio tapes is you can hear the narrator carrying out the commands and making the keystrokes he is talking about. All programs are three tapes long. Personal Tutor offers 28 programs. Among them are these:

The VisiCalc Audio Course

The Apple Writer II Audio Course

The PFS: File/Report Audio Course

The Lotus 1-2-3 Audio Course

The Commodore 64 Audio Course

The Vic 20 Audio Course

The Bank Street Writer Audio Course

APPENDIX E THE OLDEST LEARNING OPTION: BOOKS, MAGAZINES, AND MANUALS

The advent of the personal computer has been a boon to the publishing industry. By one estimate, there are over 5,000 personal-computer books on the market. There may be a thousand more under contract even as I write. *Books in Print,* the bible of what exists in the world of books, lists over 1,700 titles of books concerned with personal computers. One of these books simply lists all the computer books, *The Reader's Guide to Microcomputers* (Golden-Lee Books).

An acquaintance at B. Dalton Booksellers, the giant bookstore chain, tells me they have almost a thousand different computer books on their shelves, rivaling even diet and pop-psych books in bounty. Who buys all these books? Micromedia, a Los Angeles distributor of computer books, has calculated that "from three months before the purchase of a personal computer to nine months following purchase, on the average, there are ten books bought for every computer sold." If a sample of one—me—means anything, that is not an overestimate.

But books are only one part of the explosion of computer information in print. There are magazines for specific computers, magazines for specific users, magazines of software reviews, and magazines of computer-industry gossip. These aren't puny, struggling, eighty- and ninety-page magazines either. The September 1983 issue of *Byte* magazine ran to 688 pages; over 400 of those pages were advertisements. Issues of *PC* and *PC World,* magazines that treat the IBM-PC as the only computer your world will ever need, regularly run to 400-plus pages. And for every magazine there are a half-dozen newsletters.

Now, if you think you are going to turn to the listing and find stunning, comprehensive reviews of every one of these thousands of books and hundreds of magazines, you most assuredly have another thought coming. What we have here is much more modest. The books listed here are (a) beginner's books, books that you might want to have in your computer-literacy library and wouldn't shrink from recommending, should the chairman of the board be taken by a sudden urge to read up on personal computers and ask your advice; (b) books that I have read and been able to understand on my own; and (c) books that I have either read favorable reviews of or had recommended to me by others.

A word of caution: what we have here are good, readable, under-standable beginner's books. You won't find *The Complete Guide to MS-DOS Hidden Files* or *Building Word-Processing Software in Your Spare Time* here. These are the basics, man, just the basics.

BOOKS, BOOKS, BOOKS

My bias is very much in the direction of jargon-free, well-written books. I see no reason for most computer books to be written in the same embarrassing gibberish as computer manufacturers' manuals. But for some reason that seems to be the standard. I recall being told how wonderfully "user-friendly" the new *Orangutang II* manual was. Upon inspection, I found the new manual was really just the old manual printed in two colors, with some corny computer jokes tossed in for good measure. Yuck!

Leigh Goldstein, owner of Leigh's Computers in New York City, puts it well: "The manuals [that manufacturers ship with their equipment and software] are generally poorly written and confusing. You take a computer home, read the manual, and you still can't get the machine to work." No wonder the computer-book business is so healthy.

Remember that this listing of books is a mere smattering. I'm sure there are many, many more outstanding beginner (B) and intermediate (I) books and manuals available I haven't bumped into or heard of. There are a few advanced (A) books listed here, but be aware that—as the old story puts it—they tell you more about penguins than anyone but a member of the immediate family would want to know.

> *The Word Processing Book* (B)
> by Peter McWilliams
>
> *The Personal Computer Book* (B)
> by Peter McWilliams
>
> *The Personal Computer in Business Book* (B)
> by Peter McWilliams
>
> Prelude Press
> Los Angeles, CA
> $9.95 each

Peter McWilliams is a computer-book phenomenon. He has taken the traditionally dust-dry, Greek-grammar gray subject of personal computers and turned it into a first-class reading treat. He is living proof that the personal computer can enhance personal productivity—he wrote eight computer books in two years using one. Okay, so there is only a nickel's difference between four of them, so what? Each is tailored just enough to qualify as a new book.

These books are an almost perfect balm for computerphobia. Though he once experienced the shakes in the face of the machine, McWilliams has become expert at writing about personal computing using a minimum of computerese and a maximum of standard English. His books demystify computers in general and the small computer used as a word processor in particular.

Warning: McWilliams's books may not be for everyone. His writing bias is toward small business and the individual user. Also be warned that he is a storyteller who has crafted a *read* as opposed to a resource. His books are fun, funny, and a bit camp. For some, the McWilliams books are a bit *too* much fun. It takes all kinds, and McWilliams is one kind some people just aren't prepared for. Obviously I like him a lot.

A 60-Minute Guide to Microcomputers (B)
by Lew Hollerbach
Prentice-Hall, Inc.
Englewood Cliffs, NJ
$6.95

This is a fine little book. All the basics, none of the technobabble that makes introduction to computer books so infuriating to beginners. Well written and straightforward. Don't hesitate to recommend it to any beginning executive, manager, or professional who knows next to nothing about computers.

IBM's Personal Computer (I)
by Lew Hollerbach
Que Corporation
7960 Castleway Drive
Indianapolis, IN 46250
$15.95

This very popular book—make that well-selling; I can't prove the world loves it—is touted as a beginner's guide, but it really isn't. At least it isn't a guide for the square-one, "never done no CPU before, man" beginner. But for the advanced or tech-easy beginner, it is probably pretty good. Consider at least one copy for your corporate computer-literacy library.

The ABZ's of Word Processing (B)
by Robert M. Segal and Susan B. Kelley
Stranon Educational Press
New York, NY
$10.95

An overview of the word-processing function, but really a very nice computer-literacy primer. Good for those who have office automation to contend with.

The Random House Book of Computer Literacy (B)
by Ellen Richman
Vintage Books
New York, NY
$9.95

By and large, I can't handle those books that insist on starting with the water wheel to tell me how my personal computer works. Richman gets a "pass" on that pronouncement. This is a good little book. *Caution:* Before buying a dozen, be sure it fits your "corporate image" of background books. Lots of cartoons and "cute" here, so be sure it won't be viewed as a put-down to your beginners.

Computer Ease (B)
by Karl Albrecht
Shamrock Press
San Diego, CA
$12.95

A basic, basic primer on microcomputers; comes complete with review quizzes. The quizzes could give you some ideas for knowledge testing should you choose that strategy. On its own, this book is well worth considering.

Bits, Bytes, and Buzzwords (B)
by Mark Garetz
Dilithium Press
Beaverton, OR
$7.95

A very good basic primer on microcomputers. Not fancy or funny—if you're tired of cutesy computer books, this could be a blessing—but it is well written and easy to read. Its size and simplicity of style make it a reasonable "busy executive" book.

The ABC's of Microcomputers: A Computer Literacy Primer (I)
by Linda G. Christie and Jesse W. Curry, Jr.

Prentice-Hall
Englewood Cliffs, NJ
$7.95

Though called a basic primer, this is heavy enough to be called an intermediate book. It goes beyond the basics into the conceptual ether of some heavy stuff. Not a supertechie book by any means, but probably best for managers in a technical industry or used to dealing with technical material. Has some good checklists for buying hardware and software, evaluating documentation, and so forth.

The Beginner's Guide to Computers (B)
by Robin Bradbeer, Peter De Bono, Peter Laurie
Addison-Wesley Publishing Co.
Reading, MA
$9.95

A breezy book, based on the BBC's *Computer Literacy Project* television series. This book has already been a best-seller in England and isn't doing too badly in the U.S. either. Tons of metaphors and analogies, some a bit elaborate, but useful for a beginner course. British English is different from the North American version, but the differences don't interfere with understanding. Lots of visual material. A nice read.

Electronic Life: How To Think about Computers (B)
by Michael Crichton
Alfred A. Knopf
New York, NY
$13.95

This book has received some very mediocre reviews in the computer magazines. Just the same, it does have a place in the computer-literacy library. It is a good guide for the word literate who wants to start looking at computers.

Look, folks, some of our clients need a softer edge on this technology. For some people, being able to turn a light switch on and off is enough knowledge about electricity and electronics.

ProStar Training Guide (I)
by Jane Davis
Davis Rubin Associates
16 Inverness Court
Richboro, PA
$39.95

Okay, this *isn't* a computer-literacy "Hello, Mr. Chips" book. It is one of the hundreds, perhaps thousands, of books that try to explain the how-to that the computer manufacturers and software publishers mucked up in their original documentation (manuals). Funny thing. Most of the books that were supposed to be better than the manuals the OEMS provided were superior mostly in cover design and binding (who invented those overstuffed, junior-sized three-ring binders the computer manufacturers are so hot about?), paper quality, and type style. The gibberish level was often very nearly the same.

This manual by Jane Davis—she calls it a tutorial—is an exception. It is clear, concise, and, best of all, written for an average user interested in producing something with WordStar or one of the other ProStar programs, *not* for hobbyists. *All* documentation—hardware and software alike—should be so easy to read and learn from.

The Computer Glossary (I)
by Alan Freedman
The Computer Language Co.
New York, NY
$14.95

Yes, yes, I know what you're thinking. A dictionary? What did he do? Run out of things to fill up the pages with? Nope! Actually, the day after an ardent rep shoved a copy of this book in my hands and demanded I review it, I was ready to make a bonfire of it. But never being one to look a freebie in the binding, I put it on my shelf instead. Over the next few months I found it an invaluable resource. I still don't like demand, but this book overpowered my temperament because of its utility. Eleven hundred definitions, almost all in understandable, low-tech language. A blurb on the jacket says "de-mystifies the jargon and supplies the confidence everyone needs." A bit of overstatement. If you know a little about computers from some past life, this is a good tool for defanging the newspeak of micros, fourth-generation languages, etc.

OTHER USEFUL
COMPUTER-
LITERACY
BOOKS

Crash Course in Microcomputers (I)
by Louis E. Frenzel, Jr.
Howard W. Sams & Co.

Catching Up with the Computer Revolution (I)
Lynn M. Salerno, Ed.
John Wiley & Sons

Computer Literacy: A Hands-On Approach (I)
by Arthur Luehrmann and Herbert Peckham
McGraw-Hill Book Co.

An Introduction to Microcomputers: Volume O (I)
by Adam Osborne
Osborne/McGraw-Hill

MAGAZINES AND NEWSLETTERS

I won't try to tell you that I am intimately acquainted with all of the magazines in this listing. I have thumbed through most of them at the newsstands, but I've read and studied only a half-dozen or so. The real credit for this compilation goes to Michael Tchong, who publishes the *Micromedia Guide*. There is a check mark next to those I have familiarity with and think are pretty good for beginners and intermediate-level readers, computer literates.

Consider a few computer-magazine subscriptions for your computer-literacy library for two reasons: (1) to keep yourself current and (2) to circulate articles to your trainees after training, as a sort of subtle postgraduate refresher course. Most of these magazines are available on newsstands and in better bookstores. In fact, you should sample two or three issues before subscribing. Don't subscribe to anything on the basis of one issue.

GENERAL INTEREST

BYTE
McGraw-Hill
Peterborough, NH

This is one of the oldest, and techiest, of the computer magazines. It is for the real buffs. Okay for an engineering population or hi-tech audience. Not so hot for general-management types.

\ *Link-Up*
On-line Communications
Minneapolis, MN

Aimed exclusively at the computer user interested in telecommunication and local area networks. If you use The Source or any other link-up activity, it is pretty good.

Creative Computing
Ziff-Davis
New York, NY

Pretty sophisticated. Pretty good.

Info World
CW Communications
Palo Alto, CA

The weekly news magazine of the industry. Sort of a *U.S. News* of the computer world. Easy reading; interesting.

Dr. Dobb's Journal
People's Computer
Menlo Park, CA

A pretty technical journal, but suitable for hi-tech types just getting into the personal computer.

Personal Computing
Hayden Publishing
Rochelle Park, NY

The all-around personal computer magazine. Perfect for beginners. Has both technical and nontechnical articles, lots of reviews of hardware and software. Where they write about business, though, the tone is very "tinnie." They push the idea that hands-on trial-and-error is the best way to learn; treat corporate culture like shared yoghurt. Those two blind spots aside, really a well-balanced book.

Popular Computing
McGraw-Hill
Peterborough, NH

Another good beginner magazine. Less business-oriented than *even Personal Computing,* but still very good. Good reviews.

The Computer User
Computer User Publications
Minneapolis, MN

Started out as a personal-computer-user giveaway. Has matured to a wide-ranging newsprint magazine. Specializes in being readable. Focuses on small-business and individual user.

STRICTLY
BUSINESS

Computer Decisions
Hayden Publishing
Hasbrouch, NJ

This is a fairly technical magazine. The audience is MIS managers, but the writing is intelligible to general managers with a fair amount of computer savvy.

Datamation
Technical Publishing
New York, NY

This is *the* technical management report. Geared to the manager who knows a lot about computing already.

Desktop Computing
CW Communications
Peterborough, NH

Tries to cover topics of interest to new business personal-computer users. Uneven quality, but check out a couple of issues.

Business Computer Systems
Cahners Publications
Boston, MA

A very good combination of attention to computers and business concerns in one magazine. Not overly technical, but not superficial either.

ABOUT SOFTWARE

Softalk: IBM
Softalk
North Hollywood, CA

Specific to IBM-PC software and associated topics. "How to Find Lost Files" and "Undocumented Commands in Basic 2.0" are typical titles of articles. Pretty technical, but occasionally some general-interest articles do appear. Look a few copies over—*if* your organization is into IBM-PCs at a fairly sophisticated level.

LIST
Redgate
Vero Beach, FL

Actually a monthly catalogue of computer software, plus a few articles. The articles tend to be uneven but get better every issue. Worth looking at, if for no other reason than to get at the catalogue feature.

Software Supermarket
Amos Press
Sidney, OH

More of a consumer magazine than a business magazine, but the key is good writing and a concentration on comparing software in bunches. "Health and Wellness Software" and "Personal Money Management Software" are typical titles.

Softline
Softalk
North Hollywood, CA

A more technical approach to software evaluation. Good, comprehensive articles.

\ *InfoWorld Software Review*
CW Communications
Palo Alto, CA

A once-a-year service from InfoWorld, and a good one. Covers all the new and latest software on the market. InfoWorld software reviews carry a *lot* of weight in the industry.

COMPUTER-SPECIFIC MAGAZINES

APPLE   *A + for Apple microcomputing*
Ziff-Davis
New York, NY

Apple Orchard
International Apple Core
Santa Clara, CA

Call A.P.P.L.E.
A.P.P.L.E.
Seattle, WA

\ *InCider*
CW Communications
Peterborough, NH

The most businesslike of the Apple-specific magazines. With the advent of LISA and MACINTOSH, new life is bound to breathe in these pages.

Nibble
Micro-Spac
Lincoln, MA

Peelings II
Peelings II
Los Cruces, NM

DEC *Digital Review*
Ziff-Davis
New York, NY

Hardcopy
Seldin Publishing
Brea, CA

Personal & Professional
Personal Press
Ambler, PA

IBM *Business Computing*
PennWell
Littleton, MA

PC
Ziff-Davis
New York, NY

Good, solid magazine. Well-written articles. Ziff-Davis publishes a special *PC: Buyer's Guide* twice a year, featuring hardware and software for the PC.

PC Data
Autumn Revolution
Tulsa, OK

PC World
CW Communications
San Francisco, CA

Even better articles than *PC*. More creative, thoughtful reporting and writing. Less keystroke-specific information.

PC: Tech Journal
Ziff-Davis
New York, NY

Very technical magazine. Well done, but pretty tough going for beginners.

KAY PRO   *Pro-Files*
                 Non-Linear Systems
                 San Diego, CA

TANDY/RADIO SHACK   *80 Micro*
                           CW Communications
                           Peterborough, NH

                           Basic Computing
                           80 Northwest
                           Tacoma, WA

                           Computer User
                           McPheters, Wolfe
                           Cerritos, CA

                           PCM: Portable Computer Magazine
                           Falsoft, Inc.
                           Prospect, KY

                           The Rainbow
                           Falsoft, Inc.
                           Prospect, KY

FOR TRAINERS   These magazines and newsletters will appeal to trainers in the com-
ONLY   puter-literacy biz.

                 \ *Computers in Training*
                   Shamrock Press
                   San Diego, CA

A newsletter from the pen of Dr. Karl Albrecht. Covers current news and
views on the applicability of computers to training.

                 \ *Data Training*
                   Weingarten-Warren
                   Boston, MA

Tries to talk to data-processing *and* personal-computing trainers. Nice train-
erly focus.

                 \ *Electronic Learning*
                   Scholastic
                   New York, NY

Focuses on school and primarily primary grades at that. Also happens to spend quality space educating the reader. Much good information here even though *not* tailored to the training market.

> *T.H.E. Journal*
> Information Synergy
> Acton, MA

> *Teaching, Learning, Computing*
> Seldin
> Placentia, CA

> *Electronic Education*
> Electronic Communications
> Tallahassee, FL

APPENDIX F DOES THE HEAVY HAND DEFEAT ITSELF?*

David Kull, Management Issues Editor

An executive who has painstakingly developed his own programs and data for financial forecasting, when told of his company's plans to network personal computers, replies: "If anyone touches my machine, I'll kill him. . ."

A CEO, advised by data processing that a corporate inventory has uncovered a host of incompatible personal computers, decrees that the company shall buy only one model. . .

There is something about personal computing that stirs emotions among easygoing employees and pulls extreme reactions from otherwise reasonable business leaders. On one hand, using a computer to leverage the work of your mind is, as its name states, *personal.* Ideally, the individual employs the machine to translate ideas and information into intricate structures of intelligence, a process of thinking. On the other hand, a corporation may understandably fear that the power of personal computers and other personal computing tools, if not carefully controlled, will not fully support organizational goals.

The divergence of individual and organizational points of view over personal computing mirrors the classic division between laissez-faire and strict management philosophies. But while the issues specific to personal computing parallel the general argument (individual creativity carries special benefits; while technological and economic considerations call for some central controls), dissimilation of personal computers is a separate question. Other personal-computing options—mainframe-based microcomputer software, supercharged terminals—are not difficult to control. However, a company implementing personal computers must explore their unique implications for and requirements of the corporate culture. This approach will reveal the most effective implementation strategy as it illuminates the organization's basic management philosophy. Confusing the problem with the context, or

---

ignoring the background completely, usually leads to overly strict policies and lost opportunities.

"Corporate struggles over the introduction of personal computers may be an actual problem or a symptom of deeper troubles in the organization," asserts Ian Mitroff, professor of business policy at the University of Southern California, Los Angeles. "If a company has managed the question of freedom vs. control well in general, it shouldn't have any trouble managing personal computers."

The opposite is also true. A corporation's underlying troubles may be stirred up, and perhaps worsened, by the introduction of personal computing. In a troubled company, the corporate culture—the unwritten rules of conduct—may not easily accommodate aspects of the process.

For example, Mitroff says, "If one of the unwritten rules is, 'Don't share information; keep it close to the vest because it's power,' throwing in personal computers will only accentuate secrecy."

The organization should not count on technology alone to carry harmony and productivity into the workplace. The issues are primarily behavioral. A company adopting personal computers should decide how personal computing will promote characteristics it wants to foster and pare those that are undesirable. Executives, managers, and employees alike must perceive good reasons for acting in a particular manner. If the corporate culture does not provide incentive for creative, responsible computing, it won't happen.

"You can install electronic mail and put out all the memos you want asking employees to begin communicating", Mitroff argues. "But if they aren't used to sharing, they won't use the system; they won't magically become trusting."

A strategic campaign to alter organizational behavior is required in such instances. But it won't be an easy mission. Attempts to change long-established patterns must reverse a natural momentum and, sometimes, overcome entrenched interests. Data processing has traditionally been centrally controlled. Activities that shake this status quo, no matter how gently, will provoke defensive reactions.

Many companies over-react, says John J. Bray, president of Farm Corp., Boston, which has trained thousands of executives in computing. "Because data processing has always been centralized, management views any individual computing as a threat to authority," he says. "The brass over-reacts to the spread of personal computers by instituting very strict policies."

When directed against a perceived threat, strict policies—including restrictions on the models that can be purchased—can create the very resistance they're meant to counter. Employees are apt to feel that management is trammeling their rights to structure their own computing—that is, their thought processes. And they are apt to react too strongly.

Organizations that don't approach these conflicting interests with sensitivity risk losing many of the advantages of personal computing. In almost any business situation, the advantages generally become obvious at the local level only after some experimentation. The employees in charge of a promotional mailing list, for example, might discover that new names and addresses can be automatically gleaned from the company's own billing file.

Though organizations have legitimate reasons for centrally controlling personal computing, most management experts favor a relaxed attitude— particularly during the early stages of adoption, when individual creativity is likely to pay the greatest dividends. "When you want employees to think about new ways to use personal computing tools as competitive weapons, you should step back and let ideas flourish," says Michael Scott Morton, professor of behavioral and policy sciences at the Sloan School of Management at the Massachusetts Institute of Technology, Cambridge.

Though Morton advocates a trusting approach, he nevertheless believes that managers should be given responsibility for making their departments' business aims clear. Employees should know that their personal computing must be directed toward meeting tangible business needs. "There are so many tasks to be accomplished that no single executive can know exactly how they should all be done," says Morton. "You have a lot of very smart people in middle management; trust them to sort out the conflicts between personal and corporate goals."

In some corporations, employees accept fairly rigid policies from the start, often because the main applications are straightforward and amenable to mandated procedures. After personal computing has taken hold, controls can promote efficiency in any company. But Morton contends that, for most organizations in the early stages of adoption, "controls could act as a straight-jacket, not as a means for helpful coordination."

Morton relates attempts to dictate how employees would use personal computers and other tools to mistakes made in the early 1960s, when organizations were implementing centralized data processing. Many companies tried to transfer their manual procedures directly to mainframes, and lost many of the advantages of new technology in the process. Departments in the habit of updating files monthly, for example, often continued to do so— even when the computer allowed them to do it easily, and profitably, as often as they liked. Similarly, new and better ways of accomplishing tasks are possible through personal computing, but they can be discovered only through experimentation.

An organization's stance on personal computing can and should change as the technology is adopted by employees. Michael Treacy and John Henderson, also from MIT's Sloan School, have described four stages in the corporate adoption of personal computing, during which different management strategies take on increasing degrees of importance.

The stages begin with promotion, move through incorporation of day-to-day operations, and end with an economic-regulatory stance—the corporation institutes policies aimed at recouping its investment and controlling costs. The types of centralized involvement begin with organizational support, and progress through data management, development of a technical infrastructure, consolidation of operations, and ongoing evaluation.

The key in the early stages is to help individuals and departments with their own personal computing, Treacy says. As the number of users grows, the implementation stage begins, and the organization can move toward technical standards and data management. Treacy believes that mandated standards take on importance only during the later stages of adoption. Corporate-wide regulation of personal computing aimed specifically at controlling costs should begin only after it has become part of day-to-day operations throughout the organization.

The primary argument in favor of standards states that they are required to ensure compatibility of personal computers for communications. For most organizations today, Treacy says, this is not a legitimate concern. Few companies have enough personal computers to make compatibility a significant issue, he argues, and worries about future incompatibility are unreasonable. Further, because the equipment has only a three-to-four-year lifespan, a company loses little if it seeks interconnectability after acquiring a host of diverse machines. But by putting off a decision, or limiting itself to one brand of equipment, an organization may miss out on technological developments.

"Companies that standardized on the Apple II yesterday are standardizing on the IBM Personal Computer today," Treacy says. "This means they're missing out on the benefits of Apple's Lisa, which may be substantial for some employees. The technology is evolving faster than these corporations can react."

Not everyone is sanguine about the compatibility issue. William Gallagher, president of Computers Simplified (Oakland, CA), has helped many large corporations train executives in personal computing, and he contends that arguments in favor of putting off the interconnectability question are based on "a wish and a prayer." Organizations might hope that technological advances will make compatibility easier to achieve, allowing existing programs and machines to communicate, he says. But there's not much evidence that such a development will come about soon.

Even if an organization successfully connects incompatible machines, it may be adding to its training headaches. The time that employees need to learn a new technology represents a loss of productivity. "It usually takes me five to 10 hours to become proficient with a new piece of software—and I'm an expert," Gallagher says. "The typical employee might need a week."

Despite these concerns, Gallagher has seen large corporations vacillate over the kind of personal computers they will support. One large bank which had an Apple users group with hundreds of members, announced that in the future it would support only the IBM PC—it would buy only PC-compatible software and provide training exclusively on that machine. Although users were allowed to continue with applications already in place on their Apples, many were distressed by the new directive. In fact, several managers who had been instrumental in developing Apple applications left the company as a result of the edict.

Many corporations are standardizing on the IBM PC, even though it's not the best personal computer for all jobs and their reasons for choosing it are not always logical, says Gallagher. One questionable justification he's heard from several executives is the belief that they'll never get fired for buying IBM PCs. Returning to Ian Mitroff's point about the relationship between corporate culture and successful personal computing, a company that frowns on innovation among its middle managers is not likely to gain maximum advantage from the new technology.

Michael Treacy would leave the decision on whether or not to standardize to end users. Users should have the machines they want, he contends; if they want units that will communicate, they'll ask for interconnectibility. Intelligent support from MIS will help them see the advantages of communications and other advanced functions.

"MIS should provide leadership, not authority," Treacy says. "It should keep an eye toward the future, but not let the future dominate its thinking today."

The approach to personal computing taken at the Gillette Co. in Boston demonstrates how a corporation can weigh user autonomy against central controls—and shift that balance over time. According to John di Targiani, Gillette's vice president of information systems, influential users helped MIS draft a personal computing policy incorporating considerable flexibility. The company, through a committee made up of the directors of administration and project management, and plant and divisional controllers—among others—provides support for four kinds of personal computers, allowing exceptions to that limitation if users can make a good argument for them.

When the microcomputer policy was instituted in 1982, the committee enforcing it tended to accept even weak arguments. In one case, an executive claimed a need for portability, which was not a feature of any of the supported models. Although the committee felt it would be more efficient for the executive to acquire two machines from the approved list—one for the office, one for home—it granted his request. At that time, the group felt that fostering user acceptance of personal computing outweighed the need for strict adherence to standards.

The committee has since adjusted this view. Since personal computers are now firmly entrenched in the corporation, says di Targiani, "Lately, we've been taking a tougher stand on exceptions."

Personal computing raises autonomy-vs.-authority issues beyond the technical considerations of standards and compatibility. The new tools can alter long-established procedures to such an extent that organizations and managers may well feel they are losing track of their employees' activities. Is time spent at a personal computer really productive? Is the work produced with the machine really what the company has to have done? Most observers believe that these are nothing more than traditional personnel-management concerns. Good managers keep in touch with their employees, guiding those who stray from pursuit of the collective task back into the fold.

Still, managers must cope with several unique aspects of personal computing— some actual problems, some only perceived. In doing so, they'll be directing the vast changes personal computing is bringing to the workplace.

Some executives worry that employees will be so enticed by the computing segment of their jobs that they'll neglect other important tasks. They fear, for example, that the engineer who loves to make plots using graphics software will spend too much time making plots and not enough time engineering.

Consultant Tom Willmott of International Data Corp., Framingham, MA, sees potential for wasted time as individuals explore the capabilities of their personal-computing tools. "Executives won't be playing Pac Man at their desks," he says. "But they might spend too much time on tasks outside their job descriptions. Not everyone should spend 20 hours learning a spreadsheet program from the ground up."

Willmott points out that this is a traditional management problem. Coffee pots, telephones, and other office fixtures have long provided potential distractions. Managers should be aware of the potential for inefficient computer excursions, which may not be as obvious as other time-wasters like personal telephone calls. They should, however, be handled in the same fashion.

Many executives and other employees become enamored of personal computing. Do they face the danger of becoming part-time computer programmers and analysts when they're supposed to be managers, engineers, and secretaries? According to MIT's Morton, this is a minor problem.

"Not that many people are really entranced by the technology," he adds. "For those who are, after the first six months or so, reality sets in and the pressure of getting work done forces efficient use of the computer."

Michael Treacy, who worries little about holding beginning users to technological standards, also feels managers should guide individual computing toward collective goals. They should keep in touch with their departments' progress in adopting personal computing just as they would for any other major change or project. Employees who become used to going their own way with their machines might resist standards later, when the organization is ready to consolidate personal computer operations.

To provide effective guidance, managers need not be whizzes at the keyboard. They must know only enough to broadly understand what their employees are doing with their computers. William Gallagher tells of training a corporate vice president to use a spreadsheet program. After generating his first report in just a few moments, the executive said he'd recently asked a staffer for a similar document. "The employee said he could provide information in just a few hours using his personal computer," the vice president said, "I wonder what he was doing all that time."

While the executive's comment was made at least partly in jest, it illustrates a personal computing pitfall managers should avoid: They should recognize that individuals take to technology in very different ways, depending on their own outlooks and capabilities, the kind of work they do, the quality of the data they have on hand, and the machines and programs with which they begin. Also, the machines have limits, and managers shouldn't expect too much. Interactive, friendly programs can entice employees into attributing intelligence to the computers, which can lead to irrational expectations and decisions.

Some oversold executives who discover how ordinary the personal computer's contribution actually is tend to discount its usefulness. On the other hand, programs that display harsh messages or make it difficult for users to recover from mistakes reinforce the fears of those who approach a keyboard with trepidation. The variety of possible responses to computers argues in favor of organizations allowing individuals latitude in employing them, while it points up the need for informed support.

Policies governing personal computing should leave room for and even encourage, different work habits. But since information is clout, organizations may fear that the use of micro-computers and other personal-computing devices will cause unexpected shifts or concentrations of power. These concerns are usually exaggerated, most experts contend. The flow of information via personal computers usually conforms to established patterns.

Consultant Willmott calls the question of selfishly protected files a "non-issue." Managers might resist sharing micro-computer-developed information not out of proprietary feelings, he says, but because of the time, expense and inconvenience of passing it along. These issues can be dealt with through proper organizational support.

USC's Mitroff points out that a corporation with a tradition of open communications will have little difficulty accommodating and taking advantage of the individual's increased ability to process data. MIT's Morton notes that managers may well keep some files secret from their bosses. But he likens these documents to the personal notes and rough drafts that employees have always kept tucked away in their desk drawers. These idiosyncratic, private aids used to get work done ultimately contribute to the efficient operation of the organization, but the corporation serves no purpose by trying to gain access to them.

In a sense, attempting to strictly regulate personal computing is like trying to tell employees how to take notes, arrange their desks, decorate their offices, and think about the problems they're asked to solve. The personal computer holds out the promise of new, better solutions. But these solutions are the products of individuals, who, even as they contribute them to the corporate good, will feel the pride of creation. Companies operating in an increasingly complex world, faced with increasingly complicated tasks, must respect these feelings by acknowledging the contributions and granting their employees the freedom to produce them.

BIBLIOGRAPHY

ARTICLES

Albrecht, Karl. "Earth and Sky: A Meeting of Minds." *Training and Development Journal,* October 1983, pp. 70–75.

Barger, Robert Newton. "Computer Literacy: Toward a Clear Definition." *T.H.E. Journal,* October 1983, pp. 108–112.

————. "Training: A Built-in Market Worth Billions." *Business Week,* November 1, 1982, pp. 84–85.

Baxter, Ernest. "It's Your Decision." *Personal Computing,* August 1983, pp. 87–93.

Byrne, Richard B. "Computer Shock." *Portable Computing,* February 1983, pp. 38–43.

Colfin, Ronnie. "On Choosing Training Techniques." *Data Training,* December 1983, pp. 49–50.

Cushing, David. "How to Make It Big in the Computer-Literacy Training Biz." *Training,* August 1983.

Fuller, Doris. "Computerphobia: Modern Malady Spawns New Industry Offering a Cure." *Los Angeles Times,* March 20, 1983.

Hurley, Patricia. "Apple's Answer: The Worm Is Turning." *Training and Development Journal,* May 1983, pp. 16–18.

Inman, Virginia. "Learning How to Use Computers Is Frightening Experience for Many." *Wall Street Journal,* April 12, 1983, pp. 1, 49.

Jenks, James M. "Fear of Micros Is MicroFear." *Today's Office,* November 1983, p. 13.

Judd, Wilson A. "Individual Differences in Learned Controlled CAI." Paper presented at the Annual Meeting of the American Educational Research Association, March 1975.

Kellam, Paul. "The Future of Computing: Personal with a Capital P." *Personal Computing,* May 1983, pp. 211–215.

Knowles, Malcolm S. "Malcolm Knowles Finds a Worm in His Apples." *Training and Development Journal,* May 1983, pp. 12–16.

Kull, David. "Authority vs. Autonomy—Does the Heavy Hand Defeat Itself?" *Computer Decisions,* March 1984, p. 26.

Lasden, Martin. "Policies and Procedures—Working Out a Winning Strategy." *Computer Decisions,* March 1984, p. 52.

O'Connell, William. "Fear and Loathing at the CRT." *Desktop Computing,* November 1983, pp. 54–56.

Powers, William G. "The Effects of Prior Computer Exposure on Man-Machine Computer Anxiety." Paper presented at the International Communication Association Convention, April 1973.

Rohner, Daniel J., and Michael R. Simonson. "Development of an Index of Computer Anxiety." Paper presented at the Annual Convention of the Association for Educational Communications and Technology, April 1981.

Roman, David. "Computing in the Departments—Users: The New Corporate Heroes." *Computer Decisions,* March 1984, p. 84.

Rothfeder, Jeffrey. "Striking Back at Technological Terror." *Personal Computing,* February 1983, pp. 62–65.

Rubin, Charles. "Some People Should Be Afraid of Computers." *Personal Computing,* August 1983, pp. 55–163.

———. "Fear and Loathing in Computerland." *Executive Fitness Newsletter,* August 1982, pp. 1–2.

Spitzer, Dean. "Remember These Do's and Don'ts When Designing Your Next Questionnaire." *Training,* May 1979, p. 34.

Zemke, Ron. "Computer Literacy Crisis Creates Training Opportunity, Challenge." *Professional Trainer,* Spring 1983.

———. "Training and the Hi-Tech Revolution: More Than Meets the Eye . . . and Less." *Data Forum,* Spring 1983.

———. "Conducting the Computer Literacy Needs Assessment." *Training* (Minneapolis), September 1983.

———. "Using Computers to Learn Computing." *Training,* September 1983, pp. 33–36.

———. "Using the Computer to Teach Computing." *Training,* December 1983.

———. "Cognitive Style: Thinking about the Way People Think." *Training,* January 1984.

———. "The Information Center: Bringing Computing to the Masses." *Training,* February 1984.

BOOKS

Albrecht, Karl. *Mindex™ Your Thinking Style Profile.* San Diego: Karl Albrecht Associates, 1983.

Anderson, Ronald; D. Klassen; K. Krohn; and P. Cunnun. *Assessing Computer Literacy.* St. Paul: Minnesota Educational Computing Consortium, 1982.

Berner, Jeff. *Overcoming Computer Fear.* Berkeley: Sybex, 1984.

Bradbeer, Robin; Peter De Bono; and Peter Laurie. *The Beginner's Guide to Computers.* Reading, Mass.: Addison-Wesley Publishing Co., 1982.

Christie, Linda Gail, and Jesse W. Curry, Jr. *The ABC's of Microcomputers.* Englewood Cliffs, N.J.: Spectrum Books, Prentice-Hall, Inc., 1983.

Garetz, Mark. *Bits, Bytes and Buzzwords.* Beaverton, Oreg.: Dilithium Press, 1983.

Hanson, Joe B. *An Investigation of Cognitive Abilities, State Anxiety and Performance in a CAI Task under Conditions of No Feedback, Feedback and Learner Control,* Technical Report #16. Austin: Texas University CAI Lab, 1972.

Kirby, Patricia. *Cognitive Style, Learning Style, and Transfer Skill Acquisition.* Columbus, Ohio: National Center for Research in Vocational Education, 1979.

Long, Huey B. *Adult Learning.* New York: Cambridge: The Adult Learning Company, 1983.

Luehrmann, Arthur, and Herbert Peckham. *Computer Literacy: A Hands On Approach.* New York: McGraw-Hill, 1983.

Richardson, Frank C. *Development and Preliminary Evaluation of Automated Test Anxiety Reduction Program for a Computer Based Learning Situation.* Austin: Texas University CAI Lab, 1973.

Richman, Ellen. *The Random House Book of Computer Literacy.* New York: Random House, 1983.

Segal, Robert, and Susan Kelley. *The ABZ's of Word Processing for Executives.* New York: Stravon Press, 1983.

Sherman, Mark, and George Klare. *Attitudes of Adult Basic Education Students toward Computer-Aided Instruction.* Report No. TN-4. Cambridge: Harvard University Computing Center, 1970.

Smith, Robert M. *Learning How to Learn: Applied Theory for Adults.* New York: The Adult Learning Co., 1982.

Stevens, Phyllis. *Computer Programs to Reduce Math Anxiety.* Research Report 143. University of Virginia, May 1982.

Ulschak, Francis L. *Human Resource Development: Theory and Practice of Needs Assessment.* Reston, Va.: Reston Publishing, 1983.

Zemke, Ron, and Thomas Kramlinger. *Figuring Things Out: Trainer's Guide to Needs and Task Analysis.* Reading, Mass.: Addison-Wesley, 1982.

INDEX